# Getaway guide to
# Mozambique

Mike Copeland

SUNBIRD
PUBLISHERS

First published in 2006
Second edition 2009
Third edition 2011
Reprinted 2012

Sunbird Publishers (Pty) Ltd
An imprint of Jonathan Ball Publishers (Pty) Ltd
PO Box 6836, Roggebaai, Cape Town, 8012

**www.sunbirdpublishers.co.za**

Registration number: 1984/003543/07

Editor: Sean Fraser, Kathleen Sutton
Design and layout: Catherine Coetzer, Lauren Rycroft
Cartographer: John Hall
Editorial adviser: David Bristow

Reproduction by Resolution Colour, Cape Town
Printed by Star Standard Industries Ptd Ltd (Singapore)

ISBN 978-1-920289-29-4

PHOTOGRAPH CREDITS: (l = left; r = right; t = top; b = bottom)
All photographs by the author except for: Margy Beeves-Gibson: 48; Robyn Daly: 11, 21, 45, 60, 75, 82, 106,
200; Marcus Efler/Shutterstock: 73; Cameron Ewart-Smith: 1, 3, 15, 24, 26, 27, 36, 46, 61, 69, 176;
Alberto Loyo/Shutterstock: 180; Justin Fox: 13, 19, 29, 30, 32, 34, 52, 62, 79, 86, 89, 101, 109, 147, 169;
Ian Michler/Images of Africa: 67, 124, 140, 143, 175, 195; David Rogers: 18, 22r, 43, 77, 97, 117;
Patrick Wagner: 14, 91, 113, 134

In the research and writing of this guide, I
was assisted by so many kind and friendly
people: Janice at O Lar Do Ouro, the
Hotel Cardosa staff, Joao des Neves of The
Mozambique Advisor, Michelle at Casa Lisa,
Leo of Praia do Sol, Dries and Charles from
Paindane, Dave and Jill at Barra Lodge, the
Inhambane Tourism Association, Grant of
Pomene Lodge, Sabrina at Zombie Cucumber,
Carol from Vilankulo Beach Lodge, Marion
and Dave in Beira, James at Catapu, Russell
of the Blackfoot Bar, Genevieve in Pemba,
Laura on Ibo Island, Doogles in Blantyre,
Carrie in Maputo, Dave at Shoprite, Emilio
at Tiger Lodge, Cahora Bassa and Guy at
DaimlerChrysler for the loan of a super-
capable Jeep. Warm thanks to you all. I also
tip my cap to that early pioneer of tourism in
Mozambique, Senhor Alves.

Noticed on a menu at Sylvia Shoal:

*If God had not invented the Oceans,
The Portuguese would have.*

Mike Copeland
Paarl, October 2010

I dedicate this book to Pats, companion and
partner on all my visits to Mozambique.

# Contents

# Maps

## Map key

Note: Some maps are not to scale.

| | | |
|---|---|---|
| National route | Curios / craft shops | Place of worship |
| Main route | Diving centre / shop | Police station |
| Secondary route (4x4) | Garage, petrol /diesel | Post office |
| 4x4 route | GPS coordinates point | Resort / Beach |
| Accommodation | Information | Restaurant / Bar |
| Baker | Mechanic | Road, main route |
| Bank | Medical centre / hospital | Road |
| Bus terminus | Monument / statue | Shops |
| Camping | Parking | Telephone |
| Cinema | Place of interest | Train station |

# How to use this book

The first 10 chapters are filled with background information on Mozambique, its history, people and natural environment. Advice is offered on planning your trip, getting to your destination, staying healthy, and other practical aspects of travelling to and around Mozambique. Some of the advice and recommended equipment is applicable only for the less-developed parts of the country and should not be necessary if you are staying in and around the larger towns in the south.

Chapters 11 to 16 cover the southern half of the country – up the coast from the border with South Africa's KwaZulu-Natal province to the Save River, north of Vilankulo. Coastal resorts and islands make this the most visited section of Mozambique. The following section of six chapters describes the lesser-known but equally beautiful northern coastline – from Mozambique's second-largest city, Beira, up to the Ruvuma River and the border with Tanzania. Ilha de Moçambique, the World Heritage Site and jewel in a string of offshore islands, is the must-see destination in this section. The next chapter heads inland through the Niassa province and Malawi to Tete, and the book ends with some useful words and phrases in Portuguese.

This guide can be used to plan and travel the entire length of Mozam-bique, either with your own vehicle or using public transport. Bus routes and fares, road conditions and fuel availability, accommodation and food – it's all here. I start in the south and work my way north, so if you are travelling in the opposite direction – from north to south – you will just have to hold the book upside down!

It was difficult to decide which currency to quote in this book. By law all prices must be given in the local currency, the metical (MT, meticais is plural), but in practice, in the south, prices are often quoted in South African rands (R) because most visitors come from that country. Further north, the American dollar ($) is the preferred currency as visitors could come from anywhere. The rand and dollar, however, tend to fluctuate, whereas prices in meticais are remarkably stable (the average exchange rate during the research of this book was 4 MT to the rand, 30 MT to the dollar and 36 MT to the euro). As a result, I have decided to quote prices in meticais. The exception to this is that prices in South Africa are quoted in rands and for Zimbabwe and Malawi in American dollars.

Telephone numbers are listed as you would dial them in Mozam-bique (including the area code), and Malawian and South African telephone numbers are preceded by the international and regional dialling codes.

# Introduction

Mozambique is bouncing back. Holiday-makers are returning to the beautiful beaches and coral reefs, the restocked game parks and the legendary big-game fishing so popular in local waters. From five-star luxury in the south, to wild, no-star adventures up north, Mozambique has something for everyone. Investors, too, are returning and finding that there is profit to be made in the reconstruction and development of the country now that 40 years of strife have well and truly ended. Streets are being cleaned up and buildings renovated and painted, although bureaucracy and red tape may still make it difficult for Mozambicans to beautify their properties.

Those who remember 'the old days' will still recognise a lot in the new Mozambique. You are still likely to bump into a neighbour from Jo'burg in Maputo, or your neighbour from Harare in Beira. The beer is cold and refreshing and the prawns delicious, plentiful and cheap. The nightlife in Maputo is wild, and the tide still goes out so far that, to go for a swim, you need first to go for a jog.

Most of the tourism originates from South Africa – even non-African visitors usually enter via that country – which means that most tourists travel no further than Vilankulo and the Bazaruto Archipelago. It is a great pity (although some may consider it a blessing) that the wild-and-wonderful north is not visited by more tourists. In this guide, I have tried to cover all the regions as comprehensibly as possible and urge you to explore them all.

Mozambique is one of the fastest growing tourist destinations in Africa, if not the world. It is changing fast, especially prices, and guide books can't always keep up with the developments. So please feel free to let me know where this book needs updating or improving.

If you have ambitions to travel further afield in Africa (and I think everyone should), look out for my other books, *Getaway Guide – Cape to Cairo*, *Getaway Guide to Namibia* and *Getaway Guide to Botswana*. And if you want to drop me a line, my address is mcopeland@telkomsa.net.

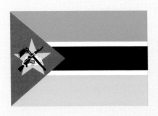

## Mozambique's flag
The flag is made up of three horizontal bands, from top: green, white-edged black and yellow. In the middle band they have managed to fit a red triangle, yellow star, open white book and a crossed rifle and hoe in black!

# Ten things not to miss

Mozambique is the ultimate holiday destination, with something to suit all tastes. Here are my top recommendations of places to visit.

### 1. Ilha de Moçambique (p. 151)

Once the island base from where the Portuguese ruled the east coast of Africa, Ilha now casts a charming spell over visitors with her beautiful old architecture, history and culture. A worthy World Heritage Site, boasting a fortress, palace and quaint, narrow streets, this island also offers comfortable accommodation and delicious local cuisine.

### 2. Maputo (p. 77)

No visit to Mozambique would be complete without dropping in to her capital city. Maputo is cosmopolitan and vibrant with good music, great food and pulsating nightlife. Here, most visitors will experience their first taste of grilled prawns, fresh Portuguese rolls and cold 2M (Dois Em) beer.

### 3. Gorongosa National Park (p. 136)

Mozambique's premier game reserve is making a comeback. Its once-teeming game herds and predators are returning and the main camp, Chitengo, has been refurbished. Nature lovers can revel in the bush experience and bird-watchers might even catch a glimpse of the endemic green-headed oriole.

### 4. Inhambane Coast (p. 97)

The tropical beaches that stretch from Paindane in the south to Praia da Barra and across the bay to Linga Linga in the north attract more holiday-makers than any other part of Mozambique. And with good reason – they offer all the sun, sand and sea that you could wish for.

## 5. Limpopo National Park (p. 26)

Transfrontier parks are the future of global nature conservation and Mozambique has committed the Limpopo National Park to an ambitious project that includes Kruger National Park in South Africa and Gonarezhou National Park in Zimbabwe. Saddle up your 4×4 and explore this wilderness before it is commercialised.

## 6. Vilankulo and the Bazaruto Archipelago (p. 113)

Sail away by dhow to this perennial favourite of divers, fishermen, beach-combers, sunseekers and all holiday-makers. Visit the islands to play castaway in a luxury lodge or stay in Vilankulo, a fast-developing town with good ameni-ties and a wide selection of restaurants and accommodation.

## 7. The Quirimbas Archipelago (p. 171)

Just off Pemba and high up Mozam-bique's north coast, this cluster of small islands is the ideal getaway destination, and best explored by sailing dhow. The main island, Ibo, was once an important outpost of Portuguese maritime power and still offers an old fort and crum-bling colonial buildings.

## 8. Niassa Reserve (p. 28)

This vast and pristine wilderness area of 42 000 square kilometres in the far north of Mozambique is home to the coun-try's largest concentrations of game and is earmarked for possible inclusion in a future transfrontier park. Difficult to reach and with minimal tourist infra-structure, this is a destination for the well-equipped adventurer.

## 9. Ponta do Ouro (p. 71)

This coastal stretch south of Maputo is really in South Africa's backyard and is very popular during that country's school holidays. It buzzes with visitors who enjoy water sports in the warm water and the laid-back atmosphere, but bring your 4x4 to negotiate the area's sandy tracks.

## 10. The last choice is yours

Get out there, explore this fascinat-ing and rapidly expanding country and decide for yourself what should be included in this list of favourite places to visit. My choice? Beira, slumbering in splendour and just waiting for a Prince Charming to wake it with a kiss and welcome it into the 21st century.

# Facts, figures and highlights

Mozambique is a long, narrow and predominantly tropical country on the eastern seaboard of southern Africa. Its coastline is washed by the warm waters of the Indian Ocean, while inland it is bordered by six countries – Malawi, Zambia, Zimbabwe, Swaziland, Tanzania and South Africa.

The Indian Ocean stretches along Mozambique's entire eastern boundary, and plays an important role in the local economy.

## Size

With the exception of the Tete and Niassa provinces, most of Mozambique lies within 300 kilometres of its 2 500-kilometre coastline. At 801 600 square kilometres, it is about the size of the UK and France combined and, compared to its neighbours, it is more than twice the size of Zimbabwe and a little over two-thirds the size of South Africa.

## Topography

Most of Mozambique comprises a low-lying coastal plain that lies at less than 350 metres above sea level, rising to mountains and plateaus along the Malawi and Zimbabwe borders. Two of southern Africa's major rivers, the Limpopo and Zambezi, flow through the country, as well as the Save, Lurio and Rovuma. There is also over 200 kilometres of Lake Malawi coastline in the extreme northwest.

One of the fine tiled murals in the Predio Infante de Sagres in Beira.

## Climate

Mozambique lies mostly within the tropics and has a mild, humid climate with southern summer rainfall (October to March). The average maximum January temperature for Beira is 32 °C with a minimum of 24 °C, while for July it is 25 °C and 16 °C respectively. The south, towards Maputo, is slightly cooler, and heading north, a little warmer. For a five-day forecast of weather almost anywhere in the world, go to www.yr.no.

## Cities and towns

Maputo is the capital, but it is fairly isolated down south. Other main towns are: Beira, Nampula, Pemba, Inhambane, Xai-Xai, Tete, Quelimane and Nacala. There are 11 provinces: Maputo Province, Maputo City, Gaza, Inhambane, Sofala, Manhiça, Zambezia, Nampula, Cabo Delgado, Niassa and Tete.

## Language

The official language is Portuguese (see Chapter 24 – Portuguese words and phrases). Makonde and Swahili are spoken in the north, while pidgin Fanagalo (learnt by workers on the South African mines) is still spoken and understood in the south. There are also a number of vernacular Bantu languages, and English is becoming more understood as tourism grows.

## Population

The population is estimated to be 22 million (resulting in a fairly low population density of about 27 people per square kilometre), with the densest habitation around Maputo. There are 16

The fantastically shaped mountains around Cuamba dominate the scenery in the northern parts of Mozambique.

main ethnic groups, including Makua, largely in the north and the largest; Makonde, also from the north and famous for their carvings; Sena from the central provinces; and Shangaan, dominant in the south. The infant mortality rate (110 deaths per 1 000 live births) is said to to be the highest in the world, and the average life expectancy is a very pessimistic 41!

## Currency

The metical (MT) is the official currency. The plural is meticais (pronounced *meticaysh*). At the time of researching this book, the rate of exchange was 4 MT to the South African rand, and 30 MT to the US$. Although the MT has been fairly stable, inflation and the fluctuating rand and dollar mean that you should check the latest exchange rates prior to departure. Whenever possible, change your money at a *cambios* money exchange office. They are private, secure, efficiently run and offer good rates. Banks also offer good rates, but can be frustratingly slow. If stuck, change at your hotel, a shop or garage. But avoid street hustlers – you could easily be ripped off. For an easy-to-use currency converter, check out www.xe.com.

## Time

Time in Mozambique is Universal Time plus 2 – the same as all of its neighbours (except Tanzania, which is one hour earlier). In the far north of Mozambique, you may come into contact with Swahili Time. This is a confusing way of counting 12 hours of actual daytime as a day and 12 hours of night-time as the night. In other words, whereas our day officially starts at midnight (while it is, in fact, still dark), the day in Swahili Time starts at sunrise, our 6 am. As a result,

Mozambique is holiday country and families swim, fish and sail along its seaboard.

10 am for the Swahili is 4 pm for us (16 hours after the start of our day, but only 10 hours after the start of the Swahili day), and 4 am is 10 pm for us – told you it was confusing!

## Visa requirements

All visitors, except citizens of South Africa, Swaziland, Zimbabwe, Zambia, Malawi and Tanzania, require visas. Visas can be obtained either in advance at a Mozambican embassy, high commission or consulate, or on arrival at an airport, if arriving by air. Visas purchased at the border cost US$25 or R170, at the time of going to press. These are valid for 30 days and can be extended for a further 30 days.

Visas issued by Mozambican embassies can be for single or multiple entry, and are issued for a stay of one–three months in the case of single entry, and one–twelve months for multiple entry.

Single-entry visas issued at embassies cannot be extended within the country. Note also that the period of validity and the period of stay are not the same – visas can be valid for a 30-day stay in the country within a 60-day window of opportunity for entry into the country. Therefore you must always check the terms of your visa carefully, overstaying is considered a crime and the fines are 1 000 MT a day.

If you are going to be entering Mozambique through one of the less-used land borders, you should ensure that you purchase a visa before you leave. Entering the country without a valid visa is a crime, fines are high and you can be subject to deportation. A proper visa is a green barcoded form stuck into the passport. There should be no restrictions on the use of such a visa, though reportedly those issued at Ponta do Ouro and other small border posts can only be used to exit from that border post again.

Visas issued by Mozambican embassies vary in price depending on the type of visa applied for and the speed with which you need it to be issued. In general visas valid for longer periods, issued in a hurry, are the most expensive. Visa fees vary depending on the country where the application is made. You should check with the relevant Mozambican embassy, but as a guide for applications lodged in South Africa, same-day visas cost $13 (R85), next-day visas $10 (R65), and if you are prepared to wait a week the cost is only $5 (R35). However, applications lodged at the Mozambican Embassy in London cost £40 for single entry and £70 for multiple entry using normal service, which takes three working days; and for a same-day service single entry costs £60 and multiple entry £110.

When you apply for a visa at an embassy or border, your passport must be valid for at least six months and have at least two clean pages in it.

Check for the latest visa information at www.the-gsa.co.za.

## Government

Mozambique is a multiparty democracy, with 250 elected representatives in a national assembly. There are two main parties, Frelimo and Renamo, and about a dozen minor ones. Renamo enjoys support in the centre of the country, while Frelimo is strong in the south and north. Elections were last held on 28 October 2009. They were generally considered to be peaceful, free and fair, giving Frelimo 74% of the vote and 191 seats, and Renamo 17% and 51 seats. President Armando Guebuza (Frelimo) succeeded Joaquim Chissano as Head of State in 2004.

## Tourist highlights

The most impressive destination must be Ilha de Moçambique, a World Heritage Site that was the country's original island capital. The solid old fortress of São Sebastião (St Sebastian), Governor's Palace, quaint streets and old houses make this the unpolished gem of the African east coast. Other interesting islands are Ibo, in the Quirimbas, Bengueru off Vilankulo and Inhaca off Maputo. Although both the history and architecture are fascinating, most visitors come for the fishing, diving and swimming – the Quirimbas and Bazaruto archipelagos, Pemba, Vilankulo, the Inhambane area and Ponta do Ouro are world famous for their reefs, channels and golden beaches. And don't forget the music and nightlife of Maputo!

The firm white sand and warm water are ideal for walking.

# History and economy

The tragedy of African history is that a lot of the really interesting stuff has been lost. Impermanent documentation, or none at all, makes it difficult to trace what actually happened prior to the arrival of the European powers. Fortunately, though, the east coast of Africa was well connected to the Indian Ocean trading routes and is mentioned in early travel writing.

The grand entrance to the old dockyard on Ilha de Moçambique.

As early as the 1st century AD, a Greek-Egyptian captain wrote of the trade between Red Sea ports, Arabia, East Africa and India. Rome was linked to China along this network of inter-mediaries. By the 9th and 10th centuries, the unifying effect Islam was having on Arabia helped trade in the Indian Ocean region to flourish, and by the 13th century, the entire East African seaboard was linked by a string of thriving ports and city-states – Mogadishu, Brava, Malindi, Pemba, Zanzibar, Mombasa, Mafia, Kilwa and Sofala, the port for Monomatapa's gold in the far south. No one bothered going further south, as trade there was regarded as being of no value. Iron implements, cloth, glass and beads were brought south to exchange for ivory, gold and slaves. Populated by skilled traders who decorated their substantial dwellings with carpets from Isfahan and porcelain ware of Sung China, a unique culture developed – Swahili, a blend of Arab and African. The famous early traveller, Ibn Battuta, who visited Mombasa in 1330, found a peaceful, well-organised and flourishing city.

## Enter the Portuguese

The ancient system of trade was rudely interrupted in the late 15th century when Europe decided to break the stranglehold the Ottoman Turks had on the Red Sea route to the East. It was the Portuguese, the greatest seafaring nation at the time, who first sailed around Africa and pioneered a new route. First Bartolomeu Dias and then Vasco da Gama clawed their way around the Cape and on to the riches of India.

With their superior ships and trained soldiers, the Portuguese destroyed the

Visitors shop for the colourful fabric worn as *capulanas* by local women.

Subsistence fishing is an important activity in hungry Mozambique.

established African coastal trade. Da Gama ravaged Mombasa, D'Almeida burned Kilwa and Da Cunha ruined Brava and Zeila. With the precious metals of Monomatapa their main interest, the Portuguese set up forts at Sofala (1505) and the island of Moçambique (1507). Then, using the mighty Zambezi River as a highway into the interior, they established a fort at Tete and traders ventured up the Mazoe River to attend the gold fairs at what is now Mount Darwin in Zimbabwe.

The southern point of Portuguese influence was Bahia de Lagoa (Delagoa Bay, and later to become the city of Lourenço Marques, now Maputo), with the offshore island of Inhaca serving as a fortified outpost. Feeling safe on islands, they set up a fort on Ibo in the Quirimbas Archipelago and, in 1558, built the São Sebastião fortress on Ilha de Moçambique, from where they ran their southern African sphere of influence.

Portugal continued to dominate trade between India and Europe despite strong competition from the Dutch, English and French. The São Sebastião fort withstood a number of sieges by the Dutch at the beginning of the 17th century, the first battles fought between European powers on southern African soil. (In fact, had the Dutch been successful, they would not have needed the Cape of Good Hope as a stopover en route and so changed the course of African history.)

But the Portuguese rule on the East African coast was greedy and corrupt. Influential positions were bought and sold, and governors and captains traded for their own profit. Powerful traders built up large estates with private armies, and skirmished with each other as well as with indigenous peoples. Around the middle of the 17th century, the slave trade in Mozambique picked up, with the bulk of this human cargo going to Brazil, another Portuguese colony. In 1696, the fall of the mighty Fort Jesus in Mombasa to Arab Omani

The doors of this small shop may have closed a long time ago, but business continues.

forces signalled the end of Portuguese influence north of the Rovuma River, and trade was concentrated in the south. The slave trade continued to grow during the 17th century, as did the trade with Monomatapa. Gold, copper, tin, iron and lead were carried off as tribal wars were instigated and puppet chiefs gained support.

## Portuguese East Africa

The 19th century was a time of consolidation and stabilisation for the fledgling country as borders were set during the frantic Scramble for Africa. Treaties were signed with Oom Paul Kruger of the Zuid-Afrikaansche Republiek, which allowed him a railway line and access to the port of Lourenço Marques (made the official capital of Mozambique in 1898), and similar concessions were granted to the British in Nyasaland (now Malawi) for the use of Beira. Boundries were drawn with Britain in the south and west, and with German East Africa in the north, and the country of Mozambique (then known as Portuguese East Africa) took on its modern shape. Huge foreign charter companies were granted rights to trade and the territory began to prosper.

During the first half of the 20th century, thousands of settler *colonatos* poured into the colony from the motherland, and Mozambique boomed under the iron fist of the Portuguese dictator, Salazar. Modern towns with red-roofed buildings, boulevards and bandstands sprung up. The *assimilado* system granted Portuguese citizenship to an African if he could meet certain strict requirements. Labour, however, was still regarded as a resource to be exploited, and most able-bodied local men ended up working on the South African mines, to the benefit of the South African and Portuguese governments.

## Winds of change

In 1951 Mozambique was made an overseas province of Portugal, but the winds of change were blowing through

Africa and resistance to colonial rule was growing.

In 1962, Frelimo, the Mozambique Liberation Front led by Eduardo Mondlane, launched its first military campaigns. By 1966, the north of the country was largely under their control, but the war dragged on until the overthrow of Antonio de Oliveira Salazar in Portugal in 1974. Portugal's new socialist government swiftly granted its colonies independence and Mozambique became a People's Republic in 1975 under the leadership of Samora Machel.

The country was in a bad shape after the civil war, a situation aggravated by the wholesale exodus of Portuguese skills and capital after Independence. Mozambique supported the Zimbabwe African National Union (ZANU) in their struggle to liberate Rhodesia, and the African National Congress (ANC) in their attempts to do the same in South Africa. The governments of these two countries, in turn, did their utmost to destabilise their new neighbour and supported, trained and equipped the Mozambique National Resistance (Renamo).

This was a sad time for southern Africa, and matters only improved in the early 1990s when South Africa restricted Renamo's support and Mozambique switched from Marxism to a market economy. A peace agreement was signed between Renamo and Frelimo in 1992, and this was followed by full elections in 1994. A comfortable win for Frelimo confirmed Joaquim Chissano as president. The most recent elections, regarded by observers as peaceful, free and fair, were held on

## What's in a name?

It is said that the name Mozambique is derived from Musa Mbiki, the name of the Sultan of Ilha de Moçambique when the Portuguese arrived there in the 15th century. It makes one wonder if South Africa's ex-President Mbeki could not possibly have East African island roots!

28 October 2009, giving Frelimo 74% and Renamo 17% of the vote. President Armando Guebuza succeeded Joaquim Chissano as Head of State in 2004.

## Rebuilding Mozambique

Since 1994, the country has made great strides and what was once the 'poorest country in the world' is now regarded as the 'fastest growing economy in the world'. The inflation rate is down and Mozambique is attracting more foreign investment than any other sub-Saharan country. Sasol (South Africa's massive oil-from-coal project) has invested $1 billion in the Pande gas fields near Vilankulo, while some Zimbabweans who lost their farms to land reform in that country have resettled in Mozambique and set up tobacco plants and other enterprises.

Tourism is flourishing and the badly damaged infrastructure is being rebuilt. All of this creates sorely needed employment to complement the subsistence fishing and dry-land agriculture that currently dominates – cashew nuts, manioc (cassava), maize, mangoes, peanuts and coconuts being the most common crops cultivated here.

# 3

# People and culture

It is an unfortunate fact of life that those who are poor and repressed are usually good, honest and decent people, and it is the rich and powerful nations, who have all the means and rights that a strong democracy guarantees, that become arrogant, greedy and aloof. Mozambicans have suffered a long struggle for independence, a bitter civil war and a strict Marxist government, and they are good, honest and decent people. They are also happy and relieved just to be allowed to lead normal lives and work hard to get ahead. Respect plays an important part in the social fabric of Mozambican life and age is revered. It's an old-fashioned system that demands that you, the visitor, show respect in order to gain respect.

With the hostilities of war behind them, Mozambicans – particularly the children – have learnt to smile again.

A Makua woman (left) on Ibo Island wears the white cosmetic face mask so common in the region. Men gather around for a game of *Bao* (right).

With a population of 22 million, Mozambique is not too densely populated. There are 16 main ethnic groups speaking a variety of languages and dialects, with Portuguese the official language. The education system is improving. Under Portuguese rule, the Roman Catholic Church was closely linked to the state and was thus blamed for colonial abuses. After independence, a backlash against the Church saw the destruction and expropriation of many churches and their holdings and a subsequent drop in the practice of Christianity. With Islam strong in the north, the current estimate is that 40% of Mozambicans are Christian, 20% Muslim and the rest animist. The new government is strictly secular.

## Arts and crafts

Woodcarvings are the most visual of the crafts practised by local craftsmen, sandalwood being the preferred medium in the south and African blackwood (aka ebony) in the north (test for fakes by smelling for shoe polish or rubbing a damp finger over the wood for dye). The Makonde tribe in the northern Cabo Delgado province is famous for its carved masks. Clay pots, grass mats and batik prints are all finely crafted and make excellent souvenirs, as do the colourful cloths, called *capulanas*, worn by women around their waists. Just about any tailor at the local market will be able to make up any sort of garment you want from a piece of this brightly printed cloth.

## On the menu

Mozambican food is usually quite spicy with chilli pepper (piri-piri) being the main culprit. The most basic dish is maize meal served with a stew of fish, meat or beans. Usually for sale in markets and at bus stops, it is very cheap.

Snack bars will serve coffee, cold drinks and beer with your omelette, burger or prego (thin steak) roll. Chicken grilled flat, basted with a piri-piri sauce and served with chips is available anywhere anytime. Good, fresh and reasonably priced seafood is a feature of most restaurants, with prawns and calamari the most popular. Genuine local specialities such as Cozido a Portuguesa (meat, dumplings, cabbage and rice) and Galinha a Zambeziana (chicken with lime, garlic and piri-piri) are hard to find, but well worth looking for.

Mineral water and the ubiquitous Coke and orange cold drinks are available all over, as are the excellent Mozambican beers: 2M (Dois Em), Manhica and Laurentina. The Portuguese wine sold locally is not very good, but better South Africa wine is often available.

Postscript: I do not advocate handing out used clothing, sweets (especially the practice of throwing them out the car window to kids as you drive by) and other gifts to local people along the way. It re-inforces a culture of begging and living off handouts, while at the same time creates an expectation that all travellers will do the same. Of course, should you befriend someone, or would like to show your appreciation for a special favour, then by all means be generous. But I have always found that local people best appreciate just being treated in an honest, friendly and non-condescending way. This nurtures a more natural and equal friendship between local and visitor.

Northern Mozambique's Makonde tribe are best known for their fine carvings.

# 4

# The natural world

Mozambique is effectively split in half by the mighty Zambezi River (although some may argue that the divide is further south at the Save). Infrastructure, development and tourism blossom in the south, while the north remains less developed, gloriously off the beaten track and unspoiled. Coastal dunes line the entire length of the country, giving way to tropical forests, miombo woodland and savanna inland. Coral reefs teem with fish just offshore, supporting a local fishing industry that relies on beach-built dhows (although far too many foreign trawlers carry off the biggest catches).

While Mozambique boasts an extraordinary natural heritage, it is the country's vast and diverse sea life that is the most impressive.

## In the wild

There are seven proclaimed national parks, five game reserves and three transfrontier parks in Mozambique. Though the once abundant wildlife has been severely depleted by years of civil war, subsistence hunting, logging and poaching, there is hope on the horizon, with the establishment of Transfrontier Conservation Areas (TFCAs). Facilitated by The Peace Parks Foundation, which boasts as its patron Nelson Mandela, and inspired by the late Anton Rupert, TFCAs link existing game reserves to form huge mega-parks. The game from well-stocked (and in the case of Kruger's elephants, overstocked) reserves will be allowed to migrate into poorly stocked areas. Annual migrations to make use of the best grazing will again be possible. Tourists will be able to travel freely between countries, and local communities will benefit from employment and the sustainable harvesting of natural resources. Sounds like an unobtainable dream? Well, it's working in the Kgalagadi, so why not here? Check out the websites www.peaceparks.org and www.dolimpopo.com.

While the Morromeu Buffalo Reserve on the Zambezi delta is well known for its outstanding birdlife, and draws ornithologists from around the world, the Reserva do Gili, between Quelimane and Nampula, survives really in name only. Many of the parks and reserves

## National parks

* Parque Nacional de Banhine – Gaza (7 000 km²)

* Parque Nacional do Bazaruto – Inhambane (1 430 km²)

* Parque Nacional da Gorongosa – Sofala (4 000 km²)

* Parque Nacional do Limpopo – Gaza (11 223 km²)

* Parque Nacional das Quirimbas – Cabo Delgado (7 500 km²)

* Parque Nacional de Zinave – Inhambane (4 000 km²)

* Parque Nacional de Chimanimani – Manica (1 000 km²)

## Reserves

* Reserva Nacional do Gilé – Zambezia (2 100 km²)

* Reserva Especial de Maputo – Maputo (780 km²)

* Reserva Nacional de Marromeu – Sofala (1 500 km²)

* Reserva Nacional do Niassa – Niassa (42 200 km²)

* Reserva Nacional de Pomene – Inhambane (200 km²)

## Transfrontier parks

* Great Limpopo Transfrontier Park – peace park that consists of the Limpopo National Park (Mozambique), Kruger National Park (South Africa) and Gonarezhou National Park (Zimbabwe)

* Lubombo Transfrontier Conservation Area – peace park that consists of Maputo Elephant Reserve and Futi Corridor (Mozambique), Tembe Elephant Park (South Africa) and the Lubombo Conservancy (Swaziland).

* Chimanimani Transfrontier Park – in the Chimanimani mountains along the Zimbabwe/Mozambique border

Following severe degradation during the war, the wildlife is slowly recovering.

are protected only by their isolation, but at least they do still exist and might rise again sometime in the future.

## Maputo Elephant Reserve

The Maputo Elephant Reserve (see page 62), on the coast south of the capital, is struggling to make a comeback. Roads have already been improved, game rangers have been appointed and about 300 elephants call the reserve home, but the reserve still needs to be properly fenced as the elephants tend to roam and clash with local villagers. The plan is to link this reserve with others in South Africa and Swaziland to create a TFCA.

## Limpopo National Park

The Parque Nacional de Banhine, north of Maputo, will also be linked to the Greater Limpopo National Park to form a TFCA. The land between the Limpopo and Elephants rivers and the north shore of the Massingir Dam was declared Mozambique's newest national park, the Parque Nacional de Limpopo, in 2001 and together with South Africa's Kruger National Park and Gonarezhou

National Park in Zimbabwe it forms the Great Limpopo Transfrontier Park (see page 62).

This will allow the migration of game and alleviate elephant overcrowding in Kruger. Some boundary fences have come down and game is being translocated. Already a new border gate called Giriyondo has been built and opened near Letaba Camp on the South African side in the Kruger National Park. Together with the border gate at Pafuri in northern Kruger, these two routes offer interesting alternatives for adventurous visitors to Mozambique. (See Chapter 9 for Pafuri details.)

It is 70 km from the main entrance of Parque Nacional do Limpopo to the Giriyondo border post, about two hours' drive at the maximum speed limit of 40 kph. The park is open 06h00–18h00 while the border opens at 09h00 and closes at 15h00 in the winter months and 16h00 in the summer months.

There are several possibilities for accommodation in the park (see www. ppf.org.za). The park administration operates two campsites. The Albufeira campsite is located just past the main entrance and has 8 simple but comfortable double chalets with good views of the Massingir Dam. Each chalet has its own bathroom and kitchen with basic equipment and a braai. There is also camping available. Similar facilities are available at the Águia Pesqueira (Fish Eagle) camp, one hour's drive into the park. The view from these chalets over the dam is excellent. Each chalet in both camps costs 1 200 MT per night. Along the 4×4 trail that meanders through the park there are some basic campsites with hot showers and fireplaces and firewood is available. A private operator runs the Machampane tented camp with 4 tents overlooking the river and good possibilities of game viewing.

## Zinave

The national park of Zinave, on the southern bank of the Save River northwest of Vilankulo, has no infrastructure and very little game, but because it is so isolated and sparsely populated it will probably survive well enough until the new super transfrontier park, of which it will also be a part, is created. To find out more about the activities of the Peace Parks Foundation, visit their website at www.peaceparks.org.

## Gorongosa

Gorongosa National Park (see pages 62 and 136), northwest of Beira, is another wildlife area in Mozambique that deserves a positive report. Dating back to the early 1920s, when it started as a small 1 000-square-kilometre reserve, it was not until 1951 that the first tourist accommodation was built at Chitengo. Declared a national park in 1961, it was increased in size to 5 300 square kilometres. Over the next couple of decades, it became world famous for its abundance of big game, but the civil war and poaching of the 1980s wiped out almost all the animals and destroyed the park's infrastructure. The headquarters of Renamo were located here. In 1995, with the help of the European Union, an emergency programme was drawn up to rehabilitate this African jewel. Since then, the headquarters at Chitengo have been restored and, importantly, game rangers are being trained and are out combating the once-wholesale poaching. The park reopened for visitors in 1998 with efficient, dedicated staff. The numbers of game are on the increase and one can easily see warthog, waterbuck, impala, duiker and a variety of birds. The Carr Foundation of the USA has become involved and animal relocation is taking place, as is the upgrading of Chitengo

Mozambique is a bird-watcher's paradise.

campsite with new ablutions and the building of more bungalows. It is nice to see a game park coming back from the brink of annihilation. (See Chapter 18.) Check out www.gorongosa.net.

## Niassa

The vast Niassa Reserve, a wilderness area of 42 000 square kilometres, covers parts of Cabo Delgado province and is set along the southern bank of the Rovuma River. It contains the largest concentration of game in Mozambique, including Cape buffalos, 200 endangered Cape hunting dogs, lions, leopards, a variety of antelope, including Lichtenstein's hartebeest, eland, around 9 000 sables, zebras and as many as 12 000 elephants! Three species, Niassa wildebeest, Boehm's zebra and Johnston's impala, are endemic to the Niassa area.

Poaching, and proposals to begin surveys for mining in the reserve, remain major threats but a dedicated group of private investors, working in partnership with the Mozambican government, has done considerable work there. Research and investment are ongoing, with the results being documented by the National Geographic Society.

The Reserve is now protected by a buffer zone in which hunting is permitted, and where investors are obliged to focus on community development as well as commercial activities. There is also a possibility of stringing together a transfrontier park that could include conservation areas in Tanzania and Malawi.

Driving to the park's headquarters on the eastern boundary at Mecula is difficult and there are few internal roads. The park's headquarters are for staff only and do not host visitors, but Lugenda Wilderness Camp offers tourists a unique opportunity to explore this pristine wilderness. Visit www.lugenda.com for further details.

## Bazaruto

The most popular marine park in Mozambique is the Bazaruto Archipelago National Park (see page 119), which includes myriad reefs, several islets and five islands: Santa Carolina and Bazaruto off Inhassoro, and Benguerra, Magaruque and Bangue opposite Vilankulo. The park ends in the south at the spectacular Cabo São Sebastião. Protected since 1971, the islands are home to duikers, bushbuck, freshwater crocodiles and over 180 bird species. The bays and beaches nurture dugongs, whales, dolphins and turtles, while the reef habitats harbour or attract over 2 000 fish species.

## The birdlife of Mozambique

This has faired better than the mammals and is still excellent, although – as is the case almost worldwide – habitat degradation remains a problem. A combination of coastal, grassland, forest, riverine, wetland and mountain areas harbour over 900 documented species, including many endemics such as the green-headed oriole and Gunning's akalat. The Mozambique Bird Atlas Project has an interesting website: www.aviandemographyunit.org.

# 5

# On the road

The best time to visit Mozambique is during the cooler, less-humid winter months from May to October – the threat of malaria is lower then, also. But, whatever time of the year you visit, try to avoid the overcrowding and higher prices during the South African school holidays. Most visitors to Mozambique come from neighbouring South Africa or Zimbabwe. They visit the southern half of the country and spend their time enjoying the beaches, islands, water sports and fishing. A fortunate few will travel the full length of Mozambique, either as part of a trans-African trek or southern African round trip.

Many roads leading down to the coast are quite rough and undeveloped.

## From South Africa

From KwaZulu-Natal, in the south, it is possible to enter Mozambique along the coast, via Ponta do Ouro, or through Swaziland. From Gauteng, in the west, it's a comfortable run down to Maputo via the border at Komatipoort. Either way, your destination will be Maputo. With its bustling markets, vibrant nightlife and easy access to the offshore island of Inhaca, the capital should keep you busy for a good few days.

For the first-time visitor with a week or two at his or her disposal, a meander up the coast as far as Vilankulo would be the best introduction to Mozambique. The coastal towns of Xai-Xai and Inhambane have the basic necessities and infra-structure to visit the beach resorts that dot the coast here, and Vilankulo offers the opportunity to cross to the islands of the Bazaruto Archipelago. (See also Chapter 16.)

Having your own transport gives you travelling freedom.

## From Zimbabwe

Visitors from landlocked Zimbabwe will travel via Mutare and probably head for Mozambique's second-largest city, Beira. This route also provides easy access to the slowly recovering Gorongosa National Park to the north, and the offshore islands of Bazaruto to the south.

However, for the complete Mozambican experience, you should also visit the far north, and the ulti-mate is to travel the entire length of the country from Ponto do Ouro in the south to the Rovuma River in the north. This route hugs the coast as far as Inhassoro, then heads inland to cross the Save River, past Gorongosa National

Park and across the Zambezi, back to the coast at Ilha de Moçambique, Pemba and finally completely off the beaten track to the Rovuma River with Tanzania beyond. You could keep heading north until you hit Cairo, or you could turn around and swing through Malawi and back south via Zambia and Zimbabwe. What a great trip that would be! (See also Chapter 23.)

## Travelling around

You don't have to drive your own vehicle in Mozambique, and sometimes it's better not to. The advantages of having your own wheels are obvious – speed, comfort, security and, of course, convenience. The advantages of using public transport (hitching or free rides are not really an option in Moz) are less obvious, but also important. You will get to see and experience Mozambique and its people in a most wonderful way. Living at the level of the locals, you will not be considered a threat, nor will they be jealous of you and your possessions. You will be shown courtesy and kindness and learn more about the people, their customs, traditions and language. You will feel a part of the rhythm of Africa. (See also Chapter 3.)

## Road travel

The roads down south are fairly good, although sometimes potholed, and if you stick to the tar, two-wheel drive is sufficient to get you around. Many of the sandy tracks down to the coast, however, are strictly for 4×4s. The further north you go, the rougher conditions become, and the tougher

## Vehicle spares and tools

You cut back on this list if you are not straying too far off the beaten track.

♦ The workshop manual for your vehicle

♦ Full set of socket, ring and open spanners (compatible with your vehicle)

♦ Selection of screwdrivers (large and small, Phillips and flat)

♦ Selection of nuts, bolts, washers and self-tapping screws

♦ Pliers and vice grip

♦ Set of Allen keys (compatible with your vehicle)

♦ Shifting spanner and monkey wrench

♦ Hammer

♦ Spade

♦ Axe or saw

♦ Hacksaw

♦ File

♦ Wheel spanner

♦ 2 jacks (one high-lift)

♦ Tyre levers (long and strong)

♦ Puncture-repair kit (including patches, gaiters, plugs and solution)

♦ Tyre pump or on-board compressor

♦ Pressure gauge, valves and valve tool

♦ 2 spare tyres and tubes

♦ Battery jumper cables

♦ Fanbelts (one universal)

♦ Engine oil, gearbox oil and brake fluid

♦ Q20 spray and grease

♦ Gasket silicon and contact adhesive

♦ Towrope

♦ Jerry cans (if no on-board auxiliary tank)

♦ Siphon pump or funnel for water or fuel

♦ Assortment of rope, string and wire

♦ A selection of plastic cable ties

♦ Electric wire, fuses, connectors and light bulbs

♦ Set of spark plugs and spanner), points and condenser (petrol only)

♦ Set of fuel, air and oil filters

♦ Spare radiator and fuel hoses with clamps

♦ Insulation, masking and filament tape

♦ Pair of warning/hazard triangles (legal requirement)

♦ Yellow reflective vest (legal requirement)

♦ Fire extinguisher (a good one, no toys!)

♦ Spare set of keys (do not keep these inside the vehicle)

♦ And if you know your vehicle has a particular weakness, make sure you carry the appropriate replacement parts.

North of Vilankulo you reach the enormous Save River Bridge.

your vehicle should be. Avoid travelling after dark. Compared to so many other African countries, Mozambique's roads are uncrowded, the drivers quite courteous, and their vehicles in fairly good condition. The only drawback to driving here is dealing with the traffic police, the *transitos* (recognisable by their navy and white uniforms). They are, however, being curbed by a government that wants to encourage tourism, so if you have not committed an offence, stand up for your rights and argue. Try not to hand over any documents or licences to a *transito*, or you could well be his hostage until he returns them. The Ministry of the Interior in association with the national tourism association has established a hotline to assist tourists in this regard. The number is 84-800-22-22 or 800-22-22-22.

Travel light – don't be tempted to take the kitchen sink, and try to avoid a roofrack or trailer. Remember that the more you take, the more effort you have to expend in carrying, maintaining and protecting your possessions.

Spare parts are not easily available, particularly for new exotic models. The cities of Maputo and Beira have agencies for most of the better-known marques, but out in the country you are more likely to find parts for old-model Land Rovers and Toyotas. Service and check your vehicle and all equipment before you go. New, untried and untested gear could let you down. Fortunately, Mozambican mechanics are great 'fixers' and their ability to get you going again will always surprise.

Fuel is quite freely available in the south, but as you venture further north it becomes harder to find and it is advisable to carry spare fuel in jerry cans or an extra fuel tank. Diesel is slightly easier to obtain than petrol (and cheaper) and unleaded petrol is not always available. (If the nozzle of a leaded fuel pump will not fit your non-leaded tank, poke a long screwdriver or thin iron rod down your tank's filler pipe to open the obstruct-

ing flap.) The average price of fuel per litre in Mozambique is 31 MT for diesel and 37 MT for petrol (leaded and unleaded). Emergency fuel (sometimes contaminated) is often sold in 20-litre yellow plastic drums at the roadside along stretches where there are no garages for kilometres.

Remember, the Portuguese word for petrol is *gasolina*, diesel is *gasoleo* and

## Off to Mozambique

### Fly-in packages
Air Holidays, tel: +27-(0)11-803-8223, fax: +27-(0)11-803-8076, e-mail: reservations@airholidays.co.za, website: www.airholidays.co.za
Go Africa Tours, tel: +27-(0)11-447-0815, fax: +27-(0)11-447-0823, e-mail: info@goafricatours.com, website: www.goafricatours.com

### Yacht charters
Barra Yacht Charters, tel: +27-(0)11-314-3355, fax: +27-(0)11-314-3239, e-mail: reservations@barralodge.co.za, website: www.barralodge.co.za
Island Quest, tel: +27-(0)12-329-2917; e-mail: info@islandquest.co.za, website: www.islandquest.co.za

### Overland bus tours
Unusual Destinations, tel: +27-(0)11-706-1991, fax: +27-(0)11-463-1469; e-mail: info@unusualdestinations.com, website: www.unusualdestinations.com

Sunway Safaris, tel/fax: +27-(0)11-803-7400, e-mail: sunway@icon.co.za, website: www.sunway-safaris.com

### Booking agents and travel advisers
Mozambique Adviser, tel: 82-000-0005, e-mail: mozambique@adviser.co.mz, website: www.adviser.co.mz

Mozambique Connection, tel: +27-(0)11-803-4185, fax: +27-(0)11-803-3861, e-mail: res@mozcon.com, website: www.mozcon.com

Dana Tours, tel: 21-497-483, fax: 21-497-428, e-mail: info@danatours.net, website: www.danatours.net

Africa Stay, tel: +27-(0)11-791-0519, e-mail: info@africastay.com, website: www.africastay.com

Mozambique Tourism, tel: +27-(0)11-803-9296 or +27-(0)11-234-0599, e-mail: travel@mozambiquetourism.co.za, website: www.mozambique tourism.co.za

Mozambique Tours, tel: +27-(0)31-207-3370, e-mail: mit@iafrica.com, website: www.mozambiquetravel.co.za

A 4×4 vehicle is essential on Mozambique's rural roads after heavy rains.

don't ask for *petroleo* unless you particularly want paraffin...

Don't venture into Mozambique without good tyres. The best all-round tyres for load, speed and reliability on bad roads are truck tyres – radial or cross-ply. A high-ply rating is also important, especially for the sidewalls. And rather choose a high-profile than a low-profile tyre, as the best footprint for sand is long rather than wide. The higher profile will also give you better ground clearance.

What about taking your motorbike? Sure. If it's a good strong off-roader, you can have a lot of fun in Mozambique. But take care, there's a lot of sand, and anything can happen on an African road. When you're on a bike, you're not protected by the vehicle's bodywork!

## Safety in numbers?

One choice you will have to make way upfront is whether to travel alone, with a companion, in a group or in convoy with others.

This is a very personal decision. Most purist travellers love to immerse themselves in the culture of a foreign country, and if you're travelling alone on public transport, nothing will dilute this experience or come between you and the locals. On the other hand, more gregarious travellers like the companionship, fun and security of groups or convoys.

Make up your own mind, but don't be afraid to try something new. Oh, and pick your travelling companions carefully – the success of your trip will depend on it.

# If driving in Mozambique

**Ensure that you have:**

* A valid driver's licence

* Third-party insurance cover valid for Mozambique (this may be purchased at the border)

* Your original vehicle registration papers or a letter from the bank (if leased or on hire-purchase)

* 2 warning triangles

* A blue and yellow triangle displayed on the front of your vehicle if you are towing any type of trailer or caravan

* A yellow fluorescent vest, which must be worn when exiting the vehicle in the case of an accident or breakdown

* Temporary import papers, which are obtained at the border

## ON THE ROAD

* Obey all traffic signs and driving regulations.

* The speed limit in urban areas is 50km/h unless otherwise indicated.

* On avenues that have a service road on the side, ensure that left turns are made only from the service road on the extreme left.

* No U-turns are allowed at traffic lights. Be aware of all illegal manoeuvres.

## POLICE

There are different types of police officials. All should have their ID badge displayed. In the event of a police check or if you are stopped for an alleged offence, the different type of police will treat you as follows:

**Transit police**

* These are traffic police (*transitos*). They are identified by their white shirts and caps and navy blue trousers.

* In the event of a traffic offence they can issue you with a spot fine, payable immediately. Insist on a receipt.

**Civil police**

* They are dressed in grey uniforms and caps.

* In the event of an offence they may also fine you on the spot provided they issue you with a receipt. Alternatively they may accompany you to the nearest police station where you can pay the fine.

If you do not understand what infraction of the law you have committed, call the Green Line, tel: 84-800-22-22 or 800-22-22-22, where someone will be able to assist you with an English/Portuguese translation.

PLEASE NOTE: Although you are a foreigner, the police have authority to confiscate your documents and/or driver's licence and/or your vehicle for certain offences. These include (but are not limited to) driving under the influence of alcohol; if your car documents do not match those of the vehicle itself; or if you are involved in an accident.

Call 112 in the case of an emergency.

## ACCIDENTS

* In the case of an accident, do not move your car.

* Put on your yellow vest and call the police on 112.

* Keep your belongings safe.

* Take photos of the scene, if possible.

* Contact your embassy or consulate in the event of a death.

* Obtain full details of independent witnesses and your passengers.

# 6

# What to pack

Take only what you know you will need, and not what you *think* you might need. Take only the necessities, and remember, the only thing you can never take enough of is money. If you're backpacking and using public transport on your travels, then obviously you have to be even more brutal in cutting down to the bare minimum.

A good storage system makes packing easy.

## Documents

These are the most important items in your luggage. Without documents you can't cross borders, and you'll need them for both yourself and your vehicle.

Your **passport** should be valid for at least six months after you expect to use it, and it should have at least two pages for each country you intend to visit – one for the visa and one for the entry and exit stamps. There seems to be a direct correlation between the importance of the country and the size of its rubber stamps – the less significant the country, the larger the stamps (and the bigger the tantrum of the border official when there is no clean page to use it on).

Everyone, citizen or foreigner, is required to carry some form of photo ID on their person in Mozambique, and police or immigration officials can stop you and request to see your ID. Carry your original passport on you at all times. A photocopy is not acceptable, though for safety reasons do keep a copy of your passport somewhere safe – it makes replacing it easier if something goes wrong.

At the time of writing, **visas** were required by all visitors to Mozambique, except citizens of South Africa, Swaziland, Zimbabwe, Zambia, Malawi and Tanzania. Obtain one in your home country before arriving in Moz – visas are available at airports, but it's better to get one before you start your trip. In South Africa you can apply at any one of the following places:

Mozambique Consulate-General, 131 Oxford Road, Rosebank, Johannesburg, tel: +27-(0)11-327-5704

Mozambique Consulate, 11th Floor, Pinnacle Building, 8 Burg Street, Cape Town, tel: +27-(0)21-426-2944, fax +27-(0)21-426-2946

Mozambique Consulate, 320 West Street, Durban, tel: +27-(0)31-304-0200, fax: +27-(0)31-304-0774

Mozambique Consulate, 64 Bester Street, Nelspruit, tel: +27-(0)13-752-7396, fax: +27-(0)13-755-1207

The following institutions are also able to assist with visas:

Mozambique Accommodation Solutions, tel: +27-(0)11-794-5614, fax: +27-(0)86-689-7335, e-mail: info@mozambique-accom.com, website: www.mozam-biqueaccom.com

Mozambique Connection, 1st Floor, Hing Yip, Cnr 9th & Wessels, Rivonia, tel: +27-(0)11-803-4185, fax: +27-(0)11-803-3861, e-mail: mozcon@pixie.co.za

The Visa Shop, 6th Floor, Thibault House, Thibault Square, Cape Town, tel: +27-(0)21-421-1059, fax: +27-(0)21-421-1065, e-mail: visashopcpt@worldspan.co.za

The Visa Shop (above) also has branches in Durban and Johannesburg. Further afield, Mozambique has representation in the following countries:

France: 82 Rue Lougier, F-75017, Paris, tel: 1-476-49132, fax: 1-426-73828

Germany: Adenauerallee 46, D 53113, Bonn, tel: 228-224-024, fax: 228-213-920

Malawi: Commercial Bank Building, Lilongwe, tel: 265-784-100 (Same-day transit visas are available for travel through the Tete Corridor to Zim.)

Tanzania: 25 Garden Avenue, Dar es Salaam, tel: +255-22-51-67843

United Kingdom: 21 Fitzroy Square, London, W1P 5HJ, tel: (0)171-383-3800

United States: 1990 M Street, NW 570, Washington, tel: 202-293-7146, fax: 202-835-0245

Zambia: Villa 46, Mulungushi Village, Lusaka, tel: 1-250-468

Zimbabwe: Herbert Chitepo Ave, Harare, tel: 4-790-837

Normal processing time for visas is seven working days, but they can be issued quicker on payment of a premium. Single-entry tourist visas are valid for entry within 60 days, and allow you to stay in the country for 30 days. For the latest information on visas visit www.the-gsa.co.za.

Never travel without a **yellow fever certificate** – you're not always asked to show it, but that's better than being delayed and having to endure an inoculation on the border.

When it comes to **vehicle documentation**, a South African driver with a South African vehicle only needs the registration papers (and, very important, a letter of authorisation on an offi-cial letterhead if the vehicle is not being driven by the registered owner).

Visitors driving vehicles from non-neighbouring countries will need a **Carnet de Passage**. This internationally recognised document (issued by your local automobile association) facilitates customs formalities when crossing borders with a vehicle, and guarantees the payment of duties and taxes in the event of the vehicle not leaving the country again. The motoring organisation that issues it will then have to pay the duties, and demand reimbursment from you, the owner of the vehicle – so make sure that your vehicle leaves Mozambique when you do! If you are South African and need a carnet for countries further north, contact:

Automobile Association (AA) of South Africa, tel: +27-(0)861-11-1994, e-mail: aasa@aasa.co.za, website: www.aa.co.za

One page, in triplicate, is required for each country. One section is stamped and retained at the border on entry, the second is stamped on exit and the third is your proof of entry and exit. Please note that this does not free you from paying the local road taxes and third-party insurance. The AA in South Africa will also help foreigners, but with more stringent financial requirements.

**Third-party insurance** covers damage, injury or death to another person or property in Mozambique, and must be carried by all visiting vehicles. This is available at the border (690 MT, $23 or R175; trailers 360 MT, $12 or R90). Cover is limited to R1 000 000 – with an excess of R1 000.

While **vehicle insurance**, covering theft of the vehicle, is recommended, it is not a necessity. Most South African motor-insurance policies include Mozambique in their territorial limits, but check yours to be sure.

**Drivers' licences** issued in neighbouring countries are recognised, but it might be a good idea to bring an international driver's licence issued by your local automobile association.

Keep every scrap of paper accumulated at the border post safely in a file, as you will be asked to show your documentation if stopped by an official (and chances are extremely good that you will be!).

## Customs

You are entitled to bring in items of personal use to the value of 5 000 MT. In addition you may bring 2,25 litres of wine and 1 litre of spirits, 200 cigarettes or 100 cigarillos or 50 cigars or 250 g of tobacco, 50 ml bottle of perfume or 250 ml bottle of eau de toilette and a reasonable amount of medicines. Customs duties will be payable on goods exceeding these limits.

You should declare large amounts of cash in any currency, enabling you to expatriate unused funds on leaving Mozambique.

Upon leaving Mozambique note that a license is required for exporting over 2 kg of seafood. You are allowed to take out a reasonable number of handicrafts, but licenses are usually required to take out blackwood and other large timber items. Ivory, sea shells and tortoiseshell may not be exported from Mozambique.

## Maps and guidebooks

If you're reading this, then you already have the best guidebook available. (Sorry, I had to squeeze that in!) Also check out the Bradt *Guide to Mozambique* by Philip Briggs or Lonely Planet's *Mozambique*.

For maps, I recommend the National Geographic *African Adventure Atlas*. The only problem with this magnificent encyclopaedia-like book is that it's thick and heavy and therefore not ideal if you're travelling light. Get a copy of Map Studio's *Illustrated Atlas of South, Central and East Africa* to travel with. Michelin's *Map Number 955* on central and southern Africa is also very good.

## GPS and navigation

A GPS is not generally necessary for coastal holidays in southern Mozambique. And you could even get by without one in the north, but I have listed GPS coordinates for those not-so-easy-to-find places. A small handheld GPS will give your position anywhere on earth to within 10 metres. Clever people can plot courses and create waypoints, but for dummies like me it's just reassuring to know where I am, and that I'm taking the right turn-off. Mount it on the dashboard of the vehicle and connect it to a powerpoint with an adaptor. An external antenna will improve the instrument's accuracy.

## Photography

There is as great a variety of subjects to photograph in Mozambique as anywhere in the world, so be sure to take plenty of film or memory sticks. Unless you're a professional, don't take too

Intricately carved kists on offer at the woodcarvers' market in Quelimane.

much equipment. Travel light and be ready for anything, anytime.

Try to take your photographs in the early morning and late afternoon – the strong African sun washes out colour in the middle of the day and could give you very bland photographs. If at all possible, try to take your time. Get in close – the subjects of so many shots are simply too small and too far way otherwise, and are lost as a result. Stand so that the light source is behind you and selectively expose and focus for your main subject. Don't be shy to use your flash as fill-in if the subject is not well lit, even during the day. Then compose your shot.

Always make sure that people are comfortable with you photographing them. Try to engage them in conversation first, then motion with the camera that you want to take a shot of them and gauge their reaction. Usually, if you have just bought something from them in a market, or if they are showing off something of which they are proud, you will have no problem.

Although you might want to give sweets or pens to the people you photograph, you will probably also be asked for money. Try to resist the temptation as it creates the impression that travellers are an easy source of income. And don't promise to send them a copy of the photograph unless you honestly intend to.

Never photograph anything that might be considered of military or strategic importance, and show sensitivity at religious sites. Develop an eye for colourful detail – the intricate jewellery worn by women or unusual items for sale at a market often make better photographs than the overall shot.

For good close-ups of animals or birds, you will need a powerful telephoto lens. Get as close as possible to the subject with your vehicle, without leaving the road or disturbing the animal; switch off the engine so as not to cause camera vibrations and sit patiently waiting for something interesting to happen. Photos taken on a beach or over water are prone to glare and overexposure.

If you are hoping to sell your photographs, some publications still accept slides. Otherwise, digital or print film is fine. Rather wait until you are home to have your film developed.

So, basically all you will need is a camera (a 28–90mm or similar lens is ideal on a 35mm camera), memory sticks or film (100 ASA is good for all-round work) and spare batteries.

## Communication

Some people just have to stay in touch with everything they are trying to get away from. Family, friends and business back home can survive without you – relax! But, if you really must hook up with your 'past life', then a **cellular phone** is probably best.

Mozambique uses the GSM900 network (same as in South Africa) and if your cellphone is linked to international roaming you will be fully connected (pay-as-you-go phones are restricted to international SMS roaming only). It is also possible, and more economical, to purchase a local Mozambician sim card (about 120 MT). The local network is operated by Vodacom and mCell and is surprisingly widespread. Airtime, known as *giro* for mCel and *bazza-bazza* for Vodacom is cheap, and available everywhere.

Another communications option you might want to use is **e-mail**, in which case you will need look out for Internet cafés (listed, where available, under towns). For a list of internet cafés in most major cities around the world – and their physical addresses – click on www.cybercafes.com.

If you are to be cut off from these means of communication, consider **two-way radios**. These are available as inexpensive, portable 'walkie-talkies', which are usually restricted to line-of-sight reception. Vehicle-based radios are reasonably inexpensive, work well up to 10 kilometres and are ideal for keeping a convoy connected. But, the ultimate form of communication is a **satellite phone** – improving all the time, and still very expensive, it will connect you from anywhere to anywhere.

## Clothing and personal gear

The beauty of travelling in Mozambique, and most of Africa, is that the weather is mild and you don't need to pack for extreme temperatures.

Choose comfortable clothing that will not show dirt, and will wash and dry easily. Clothing should not offend local customs and religions.

A useful tip to make the chore of laundry a little easier (if travelling in your own vehicle) is to seal your dirty clothes with water and soap powder in a bucket with a secure lid. Stashing this anywhere aboard a bouncing vehicle all day will have the contents as clean as the proverbial whistle and they will just need a good rinse before you hang them out to dry.

## Travel wardrobe

Here is a suggested clothing list:

* 2 pairs trousers or skirts: light cotton is comfortable and washable and trousers with zip-off legs can double as shorts. Zips on the pockets make life a little more difficult for pickpockets. Denim jeans aren't ideal as they're bulky, difficult to wash and even more difficult to dry quickly

* 4 shirts: I prefer collared shirts to T-shirts – they're smarter, cooler and have pockets (best with buttons)

* 2 pairs shorts: it gets hot in Moz and you can also swim in them

* Socks and underwear: they're light and easy to pack, so take at least 4 sets

* Sweater: take a lightweight sweater for the evenings, or a light rainproof jacket if visiting during the rainy season

* Shoes: a pair of light boots or walking shoes, as well as a pair of sandals or thongs

* Cap or hat

* Towel and bathing costume

### TOILETRIES

* Soap and shampoo
* Toothbrush and toothpaste
* Hairbrush and nail clippers
* Toilet paper
* Sanitary towels and/or condoms
* Shaving kit

* Sunblock
* Mosquito repellent

### EXTRAS

* Backpack: If you are using public transport, take a good strong internal-framed one with a zipped flap to turn it into a carry bag; otherwise a small daypack will do for excursions to the beach or market

* Multipurpose tool or Swiss Army knife (remember not to stow this in your hand luggage if flying)

* Torch and spare batteries
* Matches or lighter
* Notebook and pen
* Travel guidebooks and maps
* Watch with built-in alarm

* Reading material (bird and mammal reference books, and some recreational reading)

* Plugs and adaptors to run or recharge electrical gear

* Pocket calculator
* Sunglasses and reading glasses

* Contact-lens cleaner and spare spectacles

* Binoculars

* Diving or snorkelling gear (or any other sporting equipment)

* Photographic gear (see page 39)

* Mosquito net

# 7

# Eating and sleeping

It is tempting to try to be self-sufficient. Camping and cooking for yourself is comfortable, pleasurable and predictable. But, it's also good to experience the lifestyles and flavours of the country and its people in the hotels, pensãos, restaurants and cafés – they are the pulse of Mozambique.

Accommodation may be rustic, but the setting is usually idyllic.

It is a misconception that Mozambique's tourist industry is slowly recovering to its previous levels – it's actually recovering very fast, and already way ahead of what it ever was in its 'heyday'. World-class hotels such as the Polana in Maputo and the Pemba Beach Hotel in Pemba will satisfy the fussiest multimillionaire tourist, while the many backpacker lodges dotted around the country are just what the budget traveller looks for. In even the 'lowest' of establishments, the staff are knowledgeable and courteous, the rooms are almost always neat, with fresh bedding, and the bathrooms clean and tiled. Unfortunately, the water and electricity supply is occasionally interrupted, so check this when booking into a place (the more expensive hotels have stored water and standby generators). Also check whether the air-con and fans work and how noisy they are. One aspect of Mozambique's buildings that does leave a lot to be desired is the state of the electrical installations – some can be quite dangerous, so take care. The newer hotels and camps are usually the best because they are generally in good nick. However, maintenance is not a high priority, so even these (and especially the reed-and-palm-frond huts) can reach their 'sell-by date' quite quickly, and can become quite dilapidated within a year or two. Remember, too, that quoted prices may be negotiable, particularly if you travel out of season. Breakfast is often included in the room rate, so check when booking in. There are many privately owned and unlicensed lodges offering accommodation in Mozambique. When advertised, promoted and usually paid for outside of the country, it means that local people do not benefit and legitimate operators lose business. If they are not properly registered and licensed, then I have not listed them. Other establishments only operate during the high season and close up out of season – these places might also not be listed.

## Going camping

Camping gear and equipment are hard to find in Moz, so bring what you need. Don't be tempted to 'free-camp', no matter how attractive and isolated the spot looks. You will probably be gawked

## Camping checklist

The following is some of the equipment you might need, but because comfort is such a personal thing, try not to be too influenced by my suggestions on choice of gear:

◆ Tent with a built-in mosquito net (vehicle roof-top tents are easy and safe)

◆ Camp stretcher and/or foam mattress

◆ Sleeping bag and inner sheet

◆ Pillow

◆ Light, folding camp chairs and table

◆ Lamp (first choice should be a fluorescent type that works off your vehicle's battery)

◆ Clothesline and pegs

◆ Washbasin and soap

*Note: some campsites have electrical points.*

## Outdoor cooking checklist

- Cooker and fuel
- Ice-box or small fridge (the compressor type is best)
- Barbecue grid in a bag
- Sack of wood or charcoal
- Firelighters and matches
- Mugs and/or glasses
- Plates and bowls

- Pot (a traditional black, cast-iron pot is ideal for cooking over a fire)
- Frying pan and kettle
- Chopping board and a sharp knife
- Cutlery and can opener
- Washing-up bowl, soap and cloth
- Paper towels and refuse bags
- Water supply in containers

at, possibly robbed and definitely fined if caught by an official, because it is illegal. Stay over at properly run sites with adequate security for yourself and your vehicle. You will also sleep much better if you choose a spot high on a ridge. The breeze up there will not only keep you cool, but also might keep the mosquitoes at bay. Rumours have claimed that camping has been banned in Mozambique. This is not true, and there are many legal campsites all over the country. The authorities have, how-ever, closed some sites where the owners have licences to operate a hotel or lodge, but not a campsite as well. Some of these operators have now circumvented this problem by renting you a small reed hut or shaded area – putting up a tent next to it is then perfectly acceptable!

## On the menu

Restaurant menus are remarkably similar in selection and price in Mozambique. This is simply because all menus must

The comforts may be basic, but welcome after a day on foot.

Camping is generally a good and inexpensive option throughout Mozambique.

## Grub's up!

You may want to consider taking along some of the following cooking ingredients:

**Durables**

✦ A selection of canned meats, fish and vegetables (just a few for emergencies – they're heavy)

✦ A selection of dehydrated foodstuffs (taste first – some are disgusting!)

✦ Breakfast cereal or muesli mix

✦ Sugar

✦ Powdered milk

✦ Tea and/or coffee

✦ Powdered isotonic drink

✦ Crisp bread or crackers

✦ Biscuits or rusks

✦ Salt, pepper, herbs and spices

✦ Stock cubes and garlic

✦ Dried fruit and nuts

✦ Rice and pasta

✦ Cooking and salad oil

✦ Peanut butter and/ or Bovril

✦ Bottled water, cold drinks and beer

✦ Honey or jam

**Semi-durables**

✦ Bread

✦ Potatoes, onions, cabbage and carrots

✦ Apples and oranges

✦ Cheese and margarine

✦ Bacon and salami

**Perishables**

✦ Meat

✦ Eggs

✦ Salad

✦ Tomatoes

✦ Soft fruit

## Counting the cost

Some prices charged at Shoprite supermarkets in Mozambique:

- Loaf white bread — 22 MT
- Mineral water (1 litre) — 18 MT
- Can of beer — 30 MT
- Bottle Coke (500 ml) — 18 MT
- Longlife milk (1 litre) — 60 MT
- Washing powder (1 kg) — 120 MT
- Lettuce — 20 MT
- Potatoes (1 kg) — 50 MT
- Onions (1 kg) — 52 MT
- Frozen chicken (1 kg) — 110 MT
- Boerewors (1 kg) — 280 MT
- Beef mince (1 kg) — 290 MT
- Eggs (1 doz) — 65 MT
- Bully beef (300 g) — 60 MT
- Cooking oil (750 ml) — 60 MT
- Tea (100 bags) — 115 MT
- Instant coffee (250 g) — 100 MT
- Sugar (1 kg) — 32 MT
- Rice (1 kg) — 35 MT

be passed and registered with the local authorities, and it's a hassle to have them changed. If you get tired of chicken and fish, ask your waiter whether there are specials on offer. Prices in the cheaper restaurants – where the locals might eat – range from 100 MT to 150 MT for a plate of chicken and chips or fish and rice, for example. In the more tourist-oriented establishments the same food could cost double, but be better presented. The selection could be bigger, too, with prawns for around 400 MT and pizza at 250 MT. If you will be cooking for yourself, fresh fruit, vegetables, beer, fish and even meat are available. There are some well-stocked supermarkets, and local produce is generally cheap and usually of a high standard. So, don't bring too much – you would be denying yourself the adventure of local food. Restaurant food up north is a spicy mix of Middle Eastern, Indian and Portuguese cuisine, but down south, where tourist tastes are catered for, the menus are all alike – flat chicken, steak and seafood. All along the coast, good and fresh seafood is always available, and the bread and rolls baked across the country are some of the best in Africa. Fresh fruit, vegetables and cashew nuts are sold everywhere, as are cold drinks, mineral water and excellent local beer. Basics are available at village stores (called *bancas*), and with Woolworths in Maputo and Shoprite in Maputo, Beira, Chimoio and Nampula there is just about nothing you can't buy.

## Packing your food

How do you fit it all in? The most basic packing system is a set of plastic ammo boxes. They are strong and seal quite well, but they have their drawbacks. They can't lock, may not be strong enough and are always under a pile of other equipment when you need something. Steel trunks overcome some of these problems, but are still heavy and bulky. The answer is a custom-made packing system that fits into the back of your vehicle and consists of a series of drawers that pull out without disturbing your other equipment – but be warned, they aren't cheap.

# 8

# Health and safety

Mozambique can be a minefield of diseases, germs and nasty bugs, but don't let worrying about them spoil your trip. With a little preparation and care, you should be able to avoid most of them. Of course, Mozambique has real minefields too and a number of nasty bugs of the human kind, but these are also easily avoided.

The danger of malaria increases in the wet season, when mosquitoes breed both quickly and rampantly.

## Consult the professionals

If you plan an extended, off-the-beaten-track trip, see your doctor or travel clinic for advice and shots at least six weeks before you leave. You may need to have a dental check-up, and organise a supply of any special medication you require. If you wear glasses or contact lenses, take spares and sufficient cleansing solution.

Doctors in Mozambique are resourceful and have a sound knowledge of local diseases, even though they often lack effective drugs and equipment. If you are diving, or there is a dive shop nearby, ask them for help or advice as they will have had specific medical training. Your hotel manager should also be able to refer you to the best local facilities.

However, medical facilities tend to be better in South Africa, so if possible, seek treatment there. And remember to inform your doctor where you have been and what you have done; this will help his or her diagnosis. If you can't get to a doctor, go to www.health24.com, where you can access wide-ranging medical information and advice.

## Immunisation

A yellow-fever vaccination is essential and is valid for 10 years (carry your certificate with you). Tetanus is a serious wound infection, so its vaccination is a must too. Also discuss cholera, hepatitis, typhoid, polio, tuberculosis, meningitis and rabies with your doctor before you depart. The list may be scary and you will probably not encounter any of these, but let your doctor guide you in what you need.

## Medical insurance

Don't visit Mozambique without adequate medical insurance, the type that evacuates you if necessary. Your medical aid might already cover you and some vehicle insurance policies also include this cover. If not, consult a travel agent or contact the companies listed below.

**Netcare 911, Cape Town, tel: +27-(0)10-209-8911, fax: +27-(0)10-209-8405, e-mail: customer.care@netcare.co.za, website: www.netcare.co.za**

**Europ Assist, tel: +27-(0)11-991-8000, fax: +27-(0)11-991-9000, e-mail: info@europassistance.co.za, website: www.europassistance.co.za**

## Along the way

Sensible eating, drinking and personal hygiene will help determine your general well-being throughout your trip. You should be in tune with your body and know how far you can push it, and how much dirt and infection it can fight off. Travellers from within Africa tend to have a stronger immunity against local germs, and can usually eat and drink almost anything. Visitors from outside the continent, however, should take greater care with what they eat and drink and might have to stick to bottled water and well-cooked food.

Tap water in some towns and

## Watch what you eat

Travellers with even a slightly sensitive constitution would do well to remember the wisdom of 'peel it, boil it or leave it'.

resorts is okay to drink, but check first. Otherwise, drink bottled water or even soft drinks (or beer!).

## Tummy trouble

Hopefully, you will suffer from nothing more serious than diarrhoea during your visit to Mozambique. Most of us drink or eat something that does not agree with us at some time or another. The best thing to do is to rest up somewhere comfortable and safe, stop eating, avoid alcohol and drink plenty of clean fluids.

If you have it bad, you will need an oral rehydration fluid. This sounds very impressive, but is really just sugar, salt and water – so a flat Coke with some salt added, or a Bovril drink with sugar should do the trick.

Only use blockers such as Imodium or Lomotil as a last resort; they simply stop the body from excreting the bacteria that is causing your discomfort and so prolong the agony.

## Malaria

This disease is endemic in Mozambique, so it's best to take precautions wherever you are going to be. Your first defence against malaria is to avoid being bitten by mosquitoes. You don't need to know which type (the *Anopheles*), or sex (female) carries the infection, or what strain of malaria is most deadly (*Plasmodium falciparum*) – all mosquitoes look and sound the same, and you should treat all strains as potentially hazardous to your health.

Mozzies are most active between dusk and dawn, so it makes sense to wear long pants, long-sleeved shirts

> ## Homemade rehydration solution
> * ½ teaspoon salt
> * ½ teaspoon baking soda
> * 8 teaspoons sugar
> * 1 litre clean water

and socks, and use insect repellent in the evenings, especially if you are spending time outdoors. And when you go to bed, sleep under a net or an overhead fan.

With malaria, prevention is definitely better than cure so consider a course of prophylactic drugs – your doctor will be able to recommend which type is best.

Symptoms of malaria often include fever, sweating and shivering, but can also include extreme aching of joints, headaches, upset stomach, vomiting, coughing and other symptoms not typically assumed to be malaria. If you feel ill and there is no obvious cause (such as something you ate), have a malaria test as soon as possible. Time is of the essence with this disease and it's better to have a test than to wait.

The test is simple: a small pinprick in the finger and the resulting drop of blood is wiped onto a microscope slide for inspection. The instrument used to draw the blood should be shown to you in its packaging before being opened in front of you for use.

Fortunately, most rural doctors and clinics can recognise and treat malaria. Treatments may vary depending on what is available, with quinine being the least pleasant, and Coartem the least unpleasant. Never self-diagnose or self-medicate, malaria is a potentially fatal disease, and the medicines used to treat it are similarly no joke and should not be taken without being prescribed.

If you are taking malaria medication, be sure to drink plenty of fluids and no alcohol for several weeks after the treatment, to give your liver time to recover. Your doctor may also advise you to take an antibiotic along with or after the malaria treatment. Don't forget to have a second test a couple of weeks after finishing treatment, to be sure that the disease is completely out of your system.

Malaria is a serious matter and it's best to consult a knowledgeable doctor or travel clinic for the latest recommendations before you go. Also see www.malaria.com for more about malaria.

## Bilharzia

Just visible to the naked eye, the bilharzia worm infects freshwater snails in lakes and rivers. If you enter the water or wash in it, the worm could decide that you are a better host than the snail and bore into your skin – and then multiply there!

Running water is safest, but still be sure to dry yourself well after bathing. Symptoms begin slowly with lethargy and only after several months result in a high fever and blood in the urine. Bilharzia sounds scary, but your doctor can prescribe a quick and effective cure.

## HIV/AIDS

While the list of bugs and diseases common to Mozambique shouldn't spoil your trip (few will ever be encountered), there is one that needs special mention – HIV/AIDS. If you're not careful in Mozambique, you are likely to contract it and it will indeed kill you. So, no unprotected sex, no dodgy blood transfusions, and no using non-sterile needles.

# 9

# Getting there and getting around

Surrounded by so many countries, Mozambique is accessible from virtually every corner. Southern Mozambique is normally entered from South Africa through Komatipoort, while the north is reached from Zimbabwe via Mutare. But with Swaziland, Malawi, Tanzania and even Zambia sharing borders with Mozambique, there are many other options.

You will always find some mode of transport – even if it's only a bicycle.

# Getting there by road

**From South Africa** Most overland traffic enters from South Africa at Komatipoort through the Lebombo/Ressano Garcia border post (open 24 hours). The other popular entry point from South Africa is up the coast from KwaZulu-Natal via Ponto do Ouro (08h00–17h00). Adventurous overlanders sometimes cross through Pafuri (08h00–16h00) in the north of the Kruger National Park, but have the problem of crossing the sometimes very deep drift across the Limpopo River lower down at Mapai in Mozambique. The other border posts in the south are from Swaziland via Goba or Namaacha (07h00–17h00). There are daily bus links between Johannesburg and Maputo at around R250 single and R500 return. Look out for Translux and Intercape.

**From Zimbabwe** Zimbabweans have to enter either through Mutare on their way down to Beira, or via Nyamapanda to Tete. There is no direct bus service between Zimbabwe and Mozambique – mini-buses operate on both sides, but you will be required to walk across the border.

**From Malawi** Travellers can choose between Zobué and on to Tete, via Milanje and down to Quelimane, Nayuchi to Cuamba, or Mandimba to Cuamba and on to Nampula and Ilha de Moçambique. All these borders are open 06h00–18h00.

**From Zambia** You can enter via Cassacatiza and on to Tete, though public transport through this border is sporadic at best (06h00–17h00).

**From Tanzania** Tanzania has a couple of small bush border posts, the most important two for overlanders being the Negomane border post across the Rovuma River at the new Friendship Bridge, and the Namiranga post (no vehicular crossing here) at the mouth of the Rovuma (both open 06h00–17h00).

## Overland routes

**From South Africa** Working clockwise from the south, the first overland route is from KwaZulu-Natal in South Africa via the coast to enter Mozambique at Ponta do Ouro. Get onto the N2 from Johannesburg/Ermelo in the north or from Durban in the south, turn off to Jozini and travel north to Kosi Bay. Once you have crossed the border, you will need a 4×4 to negotiate the dunes to the resort of Ponta do Ouro, and the road is also pretty rough via Bela Vista on to Maputo.

An interesting alternative overland route for 4×4 drivers entering via South Africa is through the northeastern corner of the Kruger National Park at Pafuri. Once you have crossed into

Beautiful, tropical Pangane Beach in the north of Mozambique.

# The Maputo Corridor Logistics Initiative

In an effort to improve the operational efficiency at borders and promote corruption-free border crossings, the Maputo Corridor Logistics Initiative (MCLI) has issued a pamphlet to assist travellers using the Lebombo/Ressano Garcia border post. First, they advise that you obtain your visa (if needed) from a Mozambican consular office before making your way to the border (although visas are obtainable at Ressano Garcia) and that you buy insurance and change money legally at the Border Country Inn Complex just before Lebombo (these services are also available at the border). The following is a list of the procedures you must follow to cross into Mozambique:

**In South Africa**

1. Collect your gate pass on which both the vehicle registration number and the number of people in the vehicle will be recorded.
2. Park in the designated area, whereafter all passengers disembark and proceed to the frontier office.
3. The driver of the vehicle reports to the Vehicle Registration Desk and presents the original vehicle registration document (or official copy). An authorising letter (on an official letterhead) is also required if you are not the owner of the vehicle.
4. The driver completes form DA 341 and hands it, together with the gate pass, to the official at the Vehicle Registration Desk, who then stamps both documents.
5. All passengers proceed with their passports and the gate pass to the South African Immigration Desk where the passports are stamped.
6. Drive to the exit gate, hand in your gate pass, and proceed to the Mozambican frontier gate.

**In Mozambique**

1. Collect your gate pass on which both the car registration number and the number of people in your vehicle will be recorded.
2. Park in the designated area, whereafter all disembark and proceed to the frontier office.
3. If you did not obtain Mozambican

Mozambique, a scenic dirt road runs south along the Limpopo River to the deepwater drift at Mapai. You then have the choice of travelling east all the way through the bush to Vilankulo, or continuing south to join the Mozambican EN1 at Macia.

**From Swaziland** There are two routes into Mozambique from Swaziland. The southern one, via the border at Goba, is little used now and joins the Namaacha route. The main border crossing is in the north of Swaziland at Namaacha and follows a reasonable tar road down to Boane and on to Maputo via Matola.

The Lebombo/Ressano Garcia border post through Komatipoort is by far the most popular overland route between South Africa (and Swaziland) and Mozambique. The road from Johannesburg or Pretoria goes through Witbank and down the N4 through the lush forests and pretty scenery of Mpumalanga (toll costs are R200). Nelspruit is the last large town before vehicle insurance beforehand, purchase this at one of the insurance offices on site for 500 MT or R150 (valid for 30 days).

**4.** If you do not have a visa, report to the Migracao Desk and apply for one. It costs 350 MT (R171) and takes 10 minutes (if not crowded).

**5.** If you do have a visa, report to the Migracao Desk with your passport/visa and 40 MT (R12).

**6.** Each person will be required to fill in the Mozambican entry form you will receive from the official.

**7.** The passport is stamped, but make sure you receive a receipt for the 40 MT (R12).

**8.** The driver of the vehicle reports to the Vehicle Registration Desk with the original vehicle registration document (or official copy). An authorising letter (on an official letterhead) is required if you are not the owner of the vehicle.

**9.** Present the DA 341 (from the South African side) and gate pass (from the Mozambican side) and have both stamped.

**10.** Pay 27 MT (only MTs are acceptable). The stamped form is your receipt.

**11.** Return to your car and request an officer (usually dressed in a blue uniform with orange pull-over vest) to inspect your vehicle and its contents, after which he will stamp your gate pass.

**12.** Proceed in your vehicle to the gate, hand over the gate pass, and drive through.

*Note: If you are carrying anything that requires customs declaration and documentation (such as expensive camera equipment, laptops and the like), present yourself to both the South African and Mozambican customs desks when passing through the border. And should you experience any bribery or corruption, phone the MCLI in South Africa, tel: +27-(0)80-000-1190 or in Mozambique, tel: 21-307-437. The website of the MCLI is www.mcli.co.za.* Other anti-corruption contact numbers are:
Maputo: 21-307-324
Beira: 23-323-293
Northern Region: 26-526-834

skirting the Kruger National Park to Komatipoort. The busy Lebombo border post is reasonably hassle-free, and then it's a quick, effortless ride down the new toll road to Maputo (a toll of 130 MT is payable about halfway down and another 25 MT near Maputo).

**From Zimbabwe** Zimbabwe's main access into Mozambique is via Mutare. There is a good tarred road down from Harare via Marondera to Mutare. The border post at Machipanda is seldom busy and you should have no problems.

Heading east to Beira on Mozambique's EN6, you have the options of turning north to Tete, or getting onto the EN1 to either move south to Vilankulo and on to Maputo, or north to Gorongosa, Nampula and beyond.

**From Zambia** Zambia's short border with Mozambique has only one small, little-used border crossing at Cassacatiza, which links the South Luangwa region with Tete. The road from Tete to Cassacatiza is, however, very scenic and forested, and the road is, at the time of writing, in good condition and well worth the effort for the more adventurous traveller.

**From Malawi** Malawi's busiest link with Mozambique is the Zobué/Mwanza border post between Tete and Blantyre. Another route runs from Blantyre, through the Milanje border post and down to the coast around Quelimane. Other alternatives are via Liwonde to the Nayuchi border post, or from Mangochi to Mandimba. Both these routes will take you through Cuamba and on to Nampula in northern Mozambique. For backpackers with no vehicles, there is one more adventurous way of entering Mozambique from Malawi – across Lake Malawi on the ferry to Likoma Island followed by a short boat ride to Cóbué in Mozambique. You would then make your way down via Lichinga, Mandimba and Cuamba to Nampula to eventually relax on Ilha de Moçambique.

**From Tanzania** The Rovuma River forms a formidable border between Tanzania and Mozambique. At Mwambo – the mouth of the Rovuma – there is a passenger ferry. This is one of Africa's wilder border crossings, not because it is dangerous, but because it is so off the beaten track. But the vehicular option is across the new bridge that has been constructed over the Rovuma at Negomane. From Mocimboa da Praia a tar road runs to Mueda and then deteriorates into bad gravel via Nazombe up to the new bridge. Across in Tanzania a newly constructed road takes you from Masuguru all the way to Lindi on the coast – a new and exciting route into Tanzania!

## Public transport

Most of the above-mentioned borders are serviced by public transport of some sort. Fast, international bus routes run between Johannesburg and Maputo or through the Tete corridor between Zimbabwe and Malawi.

**Johannesburg–Maputo** Intercape Mainliner: tel: +27-(0)861-28-7287, e-mail: info@intercape.co.za, website: www.intercape.co.za; Translux: tel: +27-(0)11-774-3333, fax: +27-(0)11-774-3318, website: www.translux.co.za; Panthera Azul: tel: +27-(0)11-337-7438, e-mail: pantazul @netactive.co.za.

**Harare–Beira** There is no direct, non-stop bus between these two destinations. Take local transport to Mutare and then from the border to Beira.

**Tete Corridor** Intercape and Translux have temporarily suspended their services on this route.

Some international overland safari companies visit Mozambique:

Drifters: tel: +27-(0)11-888-1160, fax: +27-(0)11-888-1020, e-mail: drifters@drifters.co.za, website: www.drifters.co.za

## Getting there by air

Scheduled air links with Mozambique are offered by South African Airways (SAA), Linhas Aéreas de Moçambique (LAM), SA Airlink, TTA Airlink and Pelican Air. SAA flies between Durban or Johannesburg and Maputo, SA Airlink has regular services from Johannesburg to Beira or Pemba and TTA Airlink flies daily between Maputo and Johannesburg. LAM flies from

Johannesburg to Maputo, Inhambane and Beira, from Luanda and Dar es Salaam to Maputo, and provides internal links to all major Mozambican cities. It also has code-sharing agreements with Kenyan Airways linking to Nairobi, and with TAP linking to Portugal. Pelican Air links Johannesburg with Vilankulo.

At the time of writing, airport tax is included in the price of some air tickets, but this is subject to change, as are the airline's routes and schedules, so check out websites (www.flysaa.com, www.lam.co.mz or www.pelicanair.co.za) or check with your travel agent.

Several private charter flight companies fly in and out of Mozambique from South Africa:

Charlan Air Charter, tel: +27-(0)11-701-3920, fax: +27-(0)11-701-3921, e-mail: charters@charlan.co.za
King Air Charter, tel: +27-(0)11-701-3250, fax: +27-(0)11-701-3288, e-mail: king.air@mweb.co.za
National Airways Corporation, tel: +27-(0)11-267-5100, fax: +27-(0)11-701-3646; website: www.nac.co.za
Nelair Charters, tel: +27-(0)13-741-2012, fax: +27-(0)13-741-2013, e-mail: coret@nelair.co.za, website: www.nelair.co.za

## Getting there by sea
Although Mozambique has a long coastline and many ports, there is no regular coastal passenger service.

Several shipping companies do, however, offer cruises to Mozambique from South African ports. As attractive and enjoyable as these excursions are, they cannot really be regarded as options to get into the country, as it's not possible to break your journey for a stayover in Mozambique. These cruise companies change from year to year, but one of the established ones is:

Starlight Cruises, tel: +27-(0)11-807-5111

Another option – if you really must arrive by sea – is to hang around the yacht club in Durban or Richards Bay until you find a yacht that is heading north and needs crew.

Alternatively, an exciting ocean option is between the southern Tanzanian port of Mtwara and the northern Mozambican port of Mocimboa da Praia. Local trading dhows sail these waters and, although I've never heard of anyone who's ever done it, you could always be the first! Let me know if you do…

## Getting there by rail
It is also possible – but only just – to enter Mozambique by train. The South African main line, on Spoornet's Shosholoza Meyl, runs between Johannesburg and Komatipoort daily, and costs between R150 and R500. A shuttle bus then makes the connection between Komatipoort and Maputo. This service has, however, proven quite dangerous, with the likelihood of theft.

For the adventurous traveller who wants to try one of the wildest train border crossings in Africa (and possibly the world!), head for Liwonde in Malawi. This little-known rail route from Liwonde through the border at Nayuchi goes to Cuamba and down to Nampula in northern Mozambique (see Chapter 23).

## Crossing borders

The following are just a few personal suggestions on the protocol to follow when crossing the border.

♦ Approach the border slowly and sedately – make no commotion or disturbance.

♦ Park sensibly in the correct areas without blocking others.

♦ Dress properly – at least sandals, shorts and shirt – and don't wear a hat, cap or sunglasses.

♦ Wait your turn – unless it's a complete free-for-all.

♦ Greet and smile at all officials – act politely and never make snide, whispered comments, or laugh.

♦ Expect polite treatment, but don't make an international incident out of official rudeness – it is only you who will suffer.

♦ Have all documents ready, but you don't have to be super-organised – this only seems to challenge officials into asking for something you don't have!

♦ Make sure you have been to both immigration and customs and have all the stamps and documentation (including insurance) you will need to show at the next roadblock.

♦ Don't smuggle anything – you may be searched and will have to bear the consequences.

♦ Avoid all bribery or 'fixers' – even if strongly hinted at. You have a right to be treated fairly.

♦ Don't take photographs.

♦ Once formalities have been completed, don't rush off, and be ready to stop if asked.

## Chancing it

Of necessity, I've listed some pretty dodgy border posts and entry routes here and, if you're feeling adventurous, then give them a go. But, take local advice first, because anything can happen – and usually does!

## Getting around by road

Although Mozambique's roads are improving all the time, there are still a number of bad potholes, sandy tracks and muddy wallows. Roads are used not only by cars, but by cyclists, pedestrians and animals, so drive carefully, and unless it's absolutely essential don't drive after dark. Don't be afraid to hoot to warn other road users of your presence, and be particularly careful if driving closely behind other vehicles as pedestrians and cyclists have a nasty habit of moving back into the road after the first vehicle has passed. Also be aware that if there's a branch in the road it may not be because it's just fallen off a tree – this is often used to warn other drivers that there is a broken-down vehicle just ahead. One can only hope that the legal requirement to carry warning triangles in all vehicles will reduce this less conventional, and less obvious, method of giving warning.

The traffic police, *transitos* (who wear navy-and-white uniforms), are only allowed to stop you for traffic violations and will also ask to see your papers. Stick to the speed limit (especially in towns), don't cross a solid white line, and follow all road signs.

Civil police (who wear grey uniforms) may also stop you to inspect your documents, so always carry your passport, driver's licence, vehicle registration documents, temporary import permit and third-party insurance. Make sure that you wear your seat belt (passengers, too), carry two warning triangles and wear shoes and a shirt when driving.

If threatened with a fine, it is okay to argue politely, especially if the fine is not warranted. Say, 'Sorry, *non comprendo*,' plead poverty and offer an ice-cold Coke with a smile. Fines start at 1000 MT (R350) and, if you do need to pay one, demand an official receipt.

Towns are quite well signposted with street names and numbers, but this is not true of the countryside. You can probably average 600 kilometres a day on tar and half that on reasonable dirt. Driving in Mozambique is on the left.

## Public transport

The main intercity bus routes are between Maputo and Beira, Beira and Tete, and Beira and Nampula. The largest Mozambican bus companies are TCO and TSL. Express buses are fast and direct, while the non-express ones stop at small towns along the way. There are no designated bus stations – Mozambique's buses leave from the company's office or depot (see listings in towns).

Off these main routes, and for shorter hauls between small towns, local buses ply the roads. Where conditions become too rough for these smaller buses (which are sometimes no more than benches in the back of a truck), light pick-ups and trucks run. Mini-buses and light pick-ups are known collectively as *chapas* (pronounced 'shappas') in Mozambique and run almost anywhere, in towns and out in the countryside. Remember, this is Africa – people are on the move, and if a vehicle has wheels, someone will take you where you want to go (for a fee, of course).

## Getting around by boat

Ferry boats from Maputo take you across the bay to Catembe or out to Inhaca Island. It is also possible to take a short ferry ride between Inhambane and Maxixe, and various kinds of boats will get you to the islands of the Bazaruto Archipelago from Vilankulo and to the islands of the Quirimbas Archipelago, north of Pemba.

## Getting around by air

The Mozambican airline, LAM, runs scheduled flights between all major cities. Fares are relatively expensive, unless you find a special offer – visit www.lam.co.mz for more details. Some charter companies operate from outside Mozambique (see listings on page 57), but a few that are local include:

San Air, Quelimane, tel/fax: 24-21-3085
STA, Nampula, tel: 26-21-4653
Unique Air Charters, Maputo, tel: 21-46-5592, fax: 21-46-5525
Air Viatur, Pemba, tel: 72-221-4310

### Dealing with accidents
You will have to present your third-party insurance, driver's licence and vehicle papers. You will need to inform the insurance company immediately and will be required to make a statement at the nearest police station.

# 10

# Practical information

One's first visit to Mozambique can be a bit of a culture shock. It is so different from other southern African countries and even unlike its Central and East African neighbours. But, relax, Mozambicans are friendly and laid-back. The following information should ease your way into and around the country.

Mozambique's waters are famous for their game fishing.

For easy reference, the following categories are listed alphabetically.

## Activities

**Birding** Unlike Mozambique's wild animals, which were decimated during the civil war, birdlife survived reasonably intact. The country's wide variety of habitats and climatic conditions support a large number of species. From the mangrove swamps and offshore islands to the montane forests of Namuli, endemics abound. Unfortunately, there is a big gap in scientific knowledge and literature on Mozambique's birds, a shortcoming the Mozambique Bird Atlas Project is attempting to rectify. The project also publishes two field guides, *Birds of the Maputo Special Reserve* and *Birds of the Niassa Reserve*. Find out more on the website www.aviandemographyunit.org. Other interesting websites are: www.sabirding.co.za, www.fatbirder.com, www.birding-africa.com and www.camacdonald.com/birding/africa-mozambique. Mozambique Bird Club is based at the Natural History Museum in Maputo (bento@natural.uem.mz).

**Diving** Warm, clear water, near-pristine coral reefs and an abundance of sea life make Mozambique a divers' paradise. Snorkelling, scuba diving and spearfishing are all catered for. Some of the best sites are at Ponta do Ouro, Inhaca Island, Zavora, Paindane, Jangamo, Tofo, Barra, Morrungulo, Pomene, the Bazaruto Archipelago, Nacula, Pemba and the Quirimbas Archipelago. With smaller, colourful reef fish such as fusiliers, coachmen, snapper and goldies, and game

fish such as kingfish, barracuda and brindlebass, as well as turtles, mantas, dolphins, dugongs and whales, I wasn't lying when I said it was paradise! Bring your own gear, hire on the spot or – if you've never dived before – take a dive course and enter a whole new world. There are a few rules and regulations of which you should be aware: divers' tax is applicable, spearfishing is not allowed with scuba gear, shellfish season is from 1 July to 31 December, and the lobster and crab season is from 1 November to 28 February.

**Fishing** The Mozambique coastline is famous for its game fishing. The clear, blue waters teem with king mackerel, dorado, wahoo, kingfish, bonito and yellowfin tuna. Boats can be launched or chartered from fishing resorts almost anywhere along the coast – Ponta do Ouro, the Inhambane coast, Pomene, Bazaruto Archipelago, Inhassoro, Beira and Pemba are

Diving is one of the most popular drawcards to the Mozambican coastline.

Too many shells means that far too much fishing has been taking place here.

particularly good. The sailfish season peaks from June to August, but summer is the best time if it's marlin you're after. Angling from the shore can also be productive, saltwater fly-fishing is increasing in popularity and catch-and-release is encouraged. Driving on the beaches is banned (the fine is a hefty 5 000 MT), except at strictly controlled boat-launch sites. A marine tax of 600 MT is payable to the local marine officer before you can launch your boat (jetskis 300 MT) and there may be a slipway fee of around 50 MT.

**Game-viewing** At the moment, the chances of seeing great herds of game and the Big Five are pretty slim, but things are looking up. **Gorongosa National Park** has reopened. Chitengo camp has been cleaned up, and it is possible to camp there or stay over in bungalows. The park's roads are passable (sometimes only by 4×4) and there is now a team of dedicated rangers. It's

amazing how wild animals survive by hiding out in pockets of bush all around the country and, with protection and grazing in the park, the animals will start returning. There is also a plan to reintroduce game and upgrade the camp.

**Maputo Elephant Reserve** is reasonably accessible and still has elephants and game rangers, so all is not lost there.

The **Niassa Reserve** up on the Tanzanian border probably has the most game as it slumbers in peaceful isolation, but getting there can be something of an expedition.

The recently declared **Great Limpopo Transfrontier Park**, linking South Africa's Kruger National Park with others in Mozambique and Zimbabwe, has an optimistic future. (See page 25 for more details.)

**Hiking and mountain climbing** Although opportunities for these two activities do exist, they are not well catered for in Mozambique. But knowing the hiking and climbing fraternity, this is just the sort of challenge they welcome. The granite domes, inselbergs and sheer rock faces that occur between Cuamba and Nampula will make any true rock climber drool, while the hills around Gurue offer great hiking opportunities. (There are, however, still a few landmines around and even fewer facilities, so beware.) It is also possible to hike along the beach between the resorts of Jangamo, Tofo and Barra, or between Morrungulo and Pomene.

**Off-road driving and quadbiking** While off-road opportunities may be hard to find in your home country – or you have to pay exorbitant fees just to drive on a commercial 4×4 track – you don't have to look far in Mozambique. In fact, it is sometimes quite difficult to avoid a good **4×4** challenge here. The sandy tracks down to the beach resorts in the south and the muddy trails in the north are true challenges, but remember, if something breaks you can't just phone the local garage to come and tow you in, so you will need to be relatively self-sufficient in this regard.

**Quadbikes** are a completely different ballgame, however, and I can only condone them if used sensibly. In Mozambique you see too many irresponsible riders (sometimes unlicensed youngsters, but many adults too) tearing up the enviroment and disturbing others. Many holiday-makers tow quadbikes down and they are also for hire at a few resorts. Please use them with care and consideration. Note: Riding on beaches is illegal.

**Surfing** Let's be honest, there're a lot of hungry sharks off Mozambique. But if you really must surf, the best breaks are 'Backdoor' and 'Monument' at Tofinho, just south of Tofo in the Inhambane province. Spoken of with awe in surfing circles around the world, the steep take-off over a shallow reef ledge will get the adrenalin pumping as you rush in at the rocky headland. Most beaches and points have something to surf, but there are not too many boards around, so bring your own.

**Water sports** Windsurfing, sailing, water-skiing and jet-skiing are all popular. Equipment can be hired at most of the larger resorts. Renting a local dhow with captain and crew is a great way to access and explore the islands off the coast.

## Car hire

If you need to hire a vehicle to tour around Mozambique, do so in South Africa if you can. South African operators offer 4×4 vehicles and campers, and complete all the documentation necessary to cross the border. Check the advertisers in *Getaway* magazine (see the website www.getawaytoafrica.com/magazine/allfeatureindex/ or contact:

Britz 4×4 Rentals, tel: +27-(0)11-396-1860, e-mail: info@britz.co.za, website: www.britz.co.za
Kea Campers, tel: +27-(0)11-230-5200, fax: +27-(0)11-230-5166, e-mail: info@keacampers.co.za, website: //sa.keacampers.com
Bushlore Africa, tel: +27-(0)11-792-5300, e-mail: info@bushlore.com, website: www.bushlore.com

AJC 4×4 Hire, tel: +27-(0)82-909-0225, e-mail: andre@ajc4x4sa.co.za, website: www.ajc4x4sa.co.za

In Mozambique, car-hire firms tend to operate mostly from the large cities and towns such as Maputo, Beira and Pemba. See the individual listings under those towns. You are unlikely to find them in smaller towns.

## Credit cards

The acceptance of debit and credit cards is gaining ground in Mozambique and many hotels, garages, restaurants and shops accept them, particularly in major towns and popular tourist destinations.

Most banks present in Mozambique, including Barclays, FNB, BCI, Standard Bank and Banco Internacional de Moçambique (BIM), have ATMs that accept both Visa and MasterCard.

## Customs regulations

You may import, free of duty and tax, the following items:

◆ 1 litre spirits
◆ 2.5 litres wine
◆ 400 cigarettes
◆ other goods (such as groceries) to the value of $200/5 000 MT.

The import of firearms is controlled and only permissible for hunting purposes through a recognised hunting operator registered in the country. If you have items such as a laptop or expensive camera equipment, it is advisable to declare them.

## Electricity

Electricity is 220V and uses the two-

or three-pinned round plugs (same as South Africa). Surges, 'brownouts' (when voltage drops quite drastically, with possible dire consequences for electricity-driven equipment) and blackouts (complete power cuts) are common, so protect sensitive electrical appliances. Some resorts that are not hooked up to mains electricity generate their own, but then frown on guests using their own appliances.

## Public holidays

1 January – New Year's Day
3 February – Heroes' Day
7 April – Women's Day
1 May – Workers' Day
25 June – Independence Day
7 September – Victory Day
25 September – Armed Forces Day
4 October – Day of Peace
25 December – Christmas Day

## E-mail and internet

Most large towns have internet cafés, and hotels and lodges sometimes offer internet access for their guests. There is also a TDM (national telephone company) office in every town, sometimes with internet access.

For tourist and other information on Mozambique, browse the following useful websites:

www.mozcon.com
www.mozambiquetourism.co.za
www.moztour.com
www.clubofmozambique.com
www.mozambiquetravelservice.com
www.ofroadandsea.com
www.mozguide.com

www.cia.gov
www.fco.gov.uk
www.acismoz.com

## Embassies

The following countries have embassies in Mozambique (all of which are based in Maputo):

**Australia:** 1st floor, 33 Story Building, corner Zedequias Manganhela and Vladimir Lenine, tel: 21-42-2780
**Canada:** 1128 Av Julius Nyerere, tel: 21-49-2623
**France:** 2361 Av Julius Nyerere, tel: 21-49-1603
**Germany:** 506 Rua Damiao de Gois, tel: 21-49-2714
**Malawi:** 75 Av Kenneth Kaunda, tel: 21-49-2676
**Netherlands:** 285 Rua de Mukunbura, tel: 21-49-0031
**Portugal:** 720 Av Julius Nyerere, tel: 21-49-0316
**South Africa:** 41 Av Eduardo Mondlane, tel: 21-49-0059
**Swaziland:** Av Kwame Nkrumah, tel: 21-49-2451
**Tanzania:** 852 Av Martires de Machava, tel: 21-49-0110
**United Kingdom:** 310 Av Vladimir Lenine, tel: 21-42-0111
**USA:** 193 Av Kenneth Kaunda, tel: 21-49-2797
**Zambia:** 1286 Av Kenneth Kaunda, tel: 21-49-2452

## Maps

I like to use the *Road Atlas to Southern and East Africa* (scale 1:1 500 000) published by MapStudio, tel: +27-(0) 11-807-2292, fax: +27-(0)11-807-0409,

e-mail: research@mapstudio.co.za, website: www.mapstudio.co.za.
Another good map is *Michelin Map No. 955* of Africa south of the equator (scale 1:4 000 000).
Sunbird Publishing has also produced a number of good maps and atlases of southern Africa, tel: +27-(0)11-622-2900, website: www.sunbirdpublishers.co.za.

## Office hours

**Banks** are open 08h00–15h00, Mondays to Fridays, and some are open on Saturday mornings in larger towns. Changes to standard government working hours, making **government offices** open across the traditional 'siesta' period have been followed by many offices, but most **shops** continue to open 08h00–12h00 and 14h30–18h00 on weekdays, and 08h00–12h00 on Saturdays.

## Post, parcels and couriers

The postal system is probably too slow to be of much use to travellers making their way around Mozambique, but EMS offers a reliable delivery service within the country and DHL, FedEx and SkyNet are all represented. LAM, the national airline, also offers a small package courier service known as 'Portador Diário', which delivers items between airports serviced by LAM.

## Radio and TV

The local radio stations play some good African music, but television is pretty poor. Satellite TV is shown in many tourist bars, restaurants and hotels – great for keeping up to date with international news and sport.

## Shopping

Every city, town and village has at least one market where you should find the basic necessities. In smaller towns, there are generally very few shops, but in the cities (Maputo, Beira, Nampula and Chimoio), there are branches of Shoprite, the South African chain of supermarkets, where you can stock up with anything your heart desires. For souvenirs and mementos of Mozambique look out for woodcarvings and masks by the Makonde tribe in the north, intricate silver jewellery from Ibo Island and baskets and pottery from around Inhambane. *Capulanas*, the colourful cloth worn by women around their waists, can be bought at almost any market and make an easily transportable memento that can be used as a tablecloth, wrap or wall hanging. And that old Mozambican standby, cashew nuts, still makes a good gift for the guy who's been looking after your dog back home. A special plea to all visitors to Mozambique – don't buy shells, coral, ivory or turtle products. Not only is it illegal, but it will only encourage the harvesting of the 'commodities' and continue to do the country and the environment irreparable harm.

## Telephones

Your best option in Mozambique is a cellular phone. You could have your existing cellphone linked to 'international roaming', which has the advantage of retaining your original phone number, but is not available to pay-as-you-go clients (except SMS). A better option is to buy a local starter pack and sim card when you enter the country (about 120 MT and avail-

## Tipping and bargaining

Tipping is not usually expected in the cheaper bars and restaurants, but between 5% and 10% is customary in up-market establishments (unless a service charge has already been added to the bill). Too much tipping spoils the delicate relationship between tipper and tippee, so rather show extra appreciation by personally thanking staff for good service. Bargaining is a necessary evil if you don't want to be ripped off. The further off the beaten track you go, the less you need to bargain; it's the smooth operators in the big towns that see a tourist coming and hike the price. The prices of curios and handicrafts (in fact, anything that a tourist may buy) are usually inflated – it's even acceptable to bargain down the price of accommodation. But don't be too mean – the service provider usually needs the money more than you do. And don't bargain just for the fun of it; only enter into negotiations if you truly are interested in buying.

able everywhere, even at border posts). Airtime can be purchased anywhere. Operated by Vodacom and mCel, the network is amazingly widespread and still expanding. The service is not expensive, and SMSs are almost for nothing. Even some out-of-the-way lodges have obtained reception by erecting high antennas – ask them to hook up your phone if you must make

A fishing dhow in the waters off Ilha de Moçambique.

a call. Please note that a Mozambican sim card and number is cancelled and becomes invalid if not used for 45 consecutive days.

The local fixed-line telephone service in Mozambique is reasonable and there are public pay phones that operate on either of the mobile networks or the fixed-line network in many places. Look out for cellphone staff manning a table with a phone on it near a market or shop, or locate TDM's green and white offices in all major towns. Sometimes this is only a converted shipping container, but there will always be a line and a public phone from which you will be able to make calls, including international ones. TDM offices also sometimes have an internet connection and fax facilities.

The international dialling code for Mozambique is 258. The local area codes are used every time you dial a number, even when you are calling from within that area. Cellphone numbers begin with 82 (mCel) or 84 (Vodacom), with no zero in front of them whether dialling locally or internationally.

## Tourist information
The **National Tourist Organisation** (ENT) has an office at 1179 Av 25 de Setembro, Maputo, tel: 21-42-1794, fax: 21-42-1795.

## Visa extensions
If you are nearing the end of your visa, it can sometimes be extended at an immigration office (*serviços de migração*), depending on where the visa was issued. Obviously *serviços de migração* can be found at borders, but also at some ports

## Dialling codes
To make an international call from Mozambique, dial 00 before the international code for the country you require. For, example to dial South Africa, dial 00-27 and then the number.

**Local area codes are as follows:**

| | |
|---|---|
| ◆ Beira | 23 |
| ◆ Chimoio | 251 |
| ◆ Chokwe | 281 |
| ◆ Inhambane | 293 |
| ◆ Maputo | 21 |
| ◆ Nacala and Nampula | 26 |
| ◆ Pemba | 272 |
| ◆ Quelimane | 24 |
| ◆ Songo and Tete | 252 |
| ◆ Vilankulo | 293 |
| ◆ Xai-Xai | 282 |

and in all provincial capitals. But be warned – do not let your visa expire, or you will be in for a hefty fine. If in doubt about renewal, check well before the expiry date. As a general rule, only visas issued at Mozambique's borders can be renewed within the country.

## Phone numbers
Various changes have been made recently to the dialling codes, fixed line and mobile phone numbers. This book reflects the latest information at time of going to press, but more changes are rumoured to be in the pipeline, so be sure to check before dialling.

# South of Maputo

Your long journey through Mozambique begins by approaching the Ponta do Ouro border post (open 08h00–17h00) from Kosi Bay in the extreme north of KwaZulu-Natal in South Africa. Coming off the N2 from either Durban or Johannesburg, the road passes through Jozini and then Kangwanase (turn left where the road forks after the Spar supermarket) before reaching the border. Hopefully, you have a smooth passage through the formalities (see Chapter 5 for tips on crossing borders) and you find yourselves on Mozambican soil (S26° 51.841 E32° 49.761).

The bountiful coral reefs around Inhaca Island reward divers with extraordinary sights of colour.

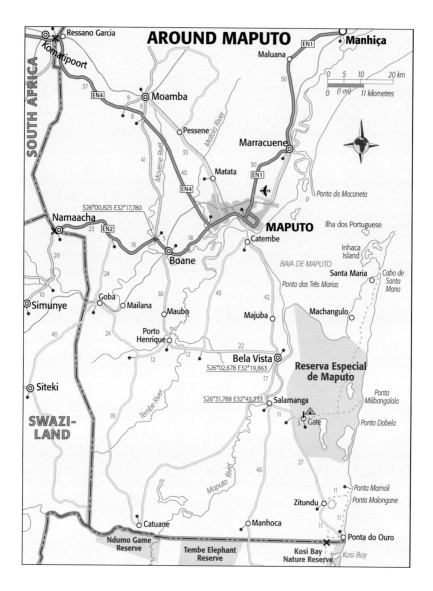

AROUND MAPUTO

Ressano Garcia

EN1

Manhiça

Maluana

SOUTH AFRICA

Komatipoort

37

EN4

9

Moamba

6

8

0   5   10        20 km

0   (1 cm)   11 kilometres

Pessene

Marracuene

41

33

40

Matata

EN1

EN4

S26°00,825 E32°17,780

Namaacha

23   EN2

5

18

Catembe

MAPUTO

Ponta da Macaneta

Ilha dos Portuguese

20

18

Boane

Inhaca
Island

BAIA DE MAPUTO

24

Santa Maria

Cabo de
Santa
Maria

Ponta das Três Marias

10

Goba

30

43

42

Simunye

Mailana

Maubo

Majuba

Machangulo

40

24

Porto
Henriqué

22

12

12

Bela Vista

S26°02,678 E32°19,863

17

Reserva Especial
de Maputo

Siteki

S26°31,788 E32°43,233

Salamanga

11

Ponta
Milibangalala

SWAZI-
LAND

70

Gate

3

Ponta Dobela

27

Maputo River

40

11

Ponta Mamoli

Zitundu

Ponta Malongane

11

Catuane

Manhoca

11

Ndumo Game
Reserve

Tembe Elephant
Reserve

Kosi Bay
Nature Reserve

Ponta do Ouro

Kosi Bay

Please note that reportedly visas bought here can only be used in the southern area and you may not exit through any other border post. Swing left and head north to take the sandy track to Bela Vista and on to Maputo (14 kilometres to Zitundu), or keep right and east along the border fence towards the coast and Ponta do Ouro. Tracks to Ponta veer off in all directions, but hold your heading and after 8.5 kilometres of sandy 4×4 tracks over the dunes you will reach the little marketplace in the centre of town (S26°50.385 E32°52.994).

## Introducing Ponta do Ouro

Ponta do Ouro (meaning 'Point of Gold') saw its first small wave of adventurous visitors in 1995, when the border opened, and it's been increasing ever since. Mains electricity arrived in 2002 and by 2003 all landmines had been cleared. Houses are being renovated and wealthy Maputans visit over the weekends. But, other than the small stretch of tar near the market, the roads in town are all as sandy and churned up as they are on the way from the border – especially during the South African school-holiday season. This is also the time when quadbikes, jetskis and the South African rand dominate, English is widely understood, and you can't even get a decent hot piri-piri chicken in the crowded restaurants. But the holiday-makers don't come to have their palates burned, they're here for the great golden beach, good surf, diving, fishing and other water sports, such as kite surfing. A headland to the south forms a large protected bay, ideal for launching boats, and the packed dive-school boats attest to the fact that Ponta has been rated one of the top 10 dive sites in the world.

Over the hill and down towards the beach is the nucleus of a little town centre. Clustered around a parking area are a few shops, bars, restaurants, a petrol station and public access to the beach. Just above the beach is the beautifully positioned Florestinha do Indico restaurant and bar, ideal for sundowners, and where you can feel the sand between your toes. Behind it, on the square, is Babalaza, another laid-back eatery with a local flavour and wide veranda that serves good espresso. Next door, above the shops, is the spacious Fishmongers Baracas, serving tasty surf-and-turf specials, and popular with holiday-makers. Next door again is the Bula-Bula restaurant with indoor, patio or garden tables. Café del Mar overlooks all of this from the highest dune across the road and serves up the best view, cold draft beer and loud music. All menus in Ponta offer very similar options of omelettes, steak rolls, grilled chicken and a good selection of seafood, dominated by prawns. Prices range from 150 MT for light meals to 600 MT for a big plate of prawns.

On this same square are a couple of little grocery shops – don't expect too much, but at least you can buy ice, bread and booze – and over on the northern side is the Petromoc service station selling petrol and diesel (although, how they drag the tankers in here over the dunes remains a mystery to me). South of the square, at the entrance to the campsite, is the bakery, Scandals, which sells delicious bread, rolls, pies and muffins, as well as light meals and good filter coffee. Back at the market, where we came in, is the neatly tiled Peixeria e Talho Tembo, selling fresh fish, cheese, eggs, chicken, bacon and vacuum-packed meat and sausage from South Africa – all at prices only slightly more than those across the border. The Peixeria can also organise game-fishing expeditions.

## Accommodation in Ponta

As can be expected, there is a good selection of accommodation in Ponta, but you must book in advance if you are planning to visit during the South African school holidays or long weekends. The large **Beach Resort**, on the beach just south of the square, is the official campsite. The ablution blocks are adequate, the sites well shaded and partially grassed, and accommodation costs 340 MT per person per day midweek and 400 MT over weekends and holidays. They also have well-used two-bed chalets at 1 300 MT per chalet per night midweek and 1 540 MT on weekends and holidays. Two-roomed, four-bed chalets are 3 000 MT and 3 720 MT and six beds will cost you 5 000 MT and 6 000 MT. All chalets have a gas hotplate, cutlery and crockery. For bookings, tel: 21-40-3217 or 21-40-9617. Lifeguards are on duty during the busy holiday periods (although the beach is quite safe for swimming) and the resort is also home to a couple of dive operations, a dolphin research centre, small shop, bar and restaurant.

This is a very popular and busy place, and not for someone looking for a quiet, restful holiday.

The other large accommodation complex is the **Motel do Mar**, on a quieter section of the beach. They rent out double-storeyed apartments, which are serviced and kitted out for four people, with fridge, hotplate, cutlery and crockery. A complicated pricing structure ranges between 2 000 MT, midweek out-of-season non-sea-facing and 4 750 MT for a sea-facing apartment during high season. They also have a small bar and restaurant. For bookings and info, tel/fax: 21-65-0000.

Away from the busy beach is the compact, quiet and well-run **O Lar do Ouro Guest Lodge**. Neat-as-a-pin double or twin en-suite rooms (with mozzie nets and screens) are set in a small garden with pool and patio. Dinner, bed and breakfast per person per day costs 2 000 MT to 2 500 MT

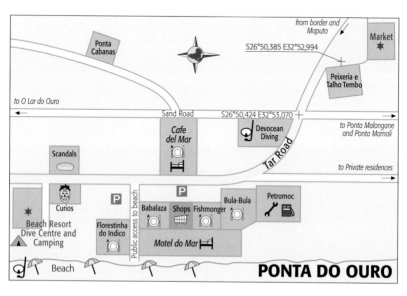

**PONTA DO OURO**

A scuba diver gets a closer look at a giant stingray.

(off-peak to peak). Theresa is an excellent cook, and Janice makes sure everything runs smoothly. Contact them, tel/fax: 21-65-0038, local cell: 82-776-1280, South African cell: +27-(0)82-574-0213, e-mail: info@pontadoouro.com, website: www.pontadoouro.com.

Other accommodation options in Ponta are the reed huts with shared ablutions behind the **Café del Mar** – a great position, but noisy due to the late-night bar. Dinner, bed and breakfast here costs 1800 MT. Contact DC on tel: 21-65-0048, fax: 21-65-0049, e-mail: cafedelmarponta@tropical.co.moz. There is also **Ponta Cabanas**, three streets back from the beach: they offer self-catering cabanas that sleep four for 2600 MT to 2800 MT per night (off-peak to peak). Contact pontacabanas@mozbookings.com.

For peaceful and affordable accommodation nestled in a tropical garden, try **Ntsuty Lodge** at S26°50.790 E32°53.320. The wooden chalets sleep four and share a swimming pool and kitchen. Rates per person are 1100 MT to 1380 MT. Book through www.pontadoouro.co.za.

## Diving off Ponta

Because of the accessible tropical reefs (Pinnacles, Doodles and Bass City), variety of fish, lack of current and excellent visability (up to 30 metres), diving is hugely popular in Ponta. The best diving conditions are from November to May, but it gets very crowded during the South African school holidays. There are a couple of dive operations based at the campsite, with their own reed huts or tented accommodation. **Simply Scuba** is based in South Africa, tel: +27-(0)11-678-0972, fax: +27-(0)11-678-0970, e-mail: dive@simplyscuba.co.za, website: www.simplyscuba.co.za. The other operation, **Scuba Adventures**, also has South African contacts, tel: +27-(0)11-648-9648, fax: +27-(0)11-487-2605, e-mail: info@africascuba.travel. Set back from the beach, with very comfortable accommodation in a beautiful and restful garden setting, is **Devocean Diving**. Speak to Kerry or Damien on the South African cell: +27-(0)82-332-9029, Moz cell: 84-811-4626, website: www.devoceandiving.com. All the above-mentioned operations offer gear hire, individual dives, a range of courses and accommodation packages.

Another exciting dive option available at Ponta do Ouro is snorkelling with the dolphins. **The Dolphin Centre**, based at the campsite, is involved in research and the conservation of the approximately 200 bottlenose dolphins in the area. They offer four-day packages (10 500 MT all inclusive) or individual dives (1 300 MT), which take you into the realm of these mammals, with the bonus of possibly encountering humpback whales. Contact in South Africa, tel: +27-(0)11-462-8103, or on cell: +27-(0)82-920-8952, e-mail: info@dolphin-encountours.co.za, website: www.dolphin-encountours.co.za.

## Out and about in Ponta

There is no bank in Ponta do Ouro, but also no need to change money, as the locals will accept almost any currency, especially South African rands. For medical emergencies, first speak to your lodge owner or dive master, as there is no hospital or pharmacy in town. They will be able to assist or advise you whether to use the little local clinic (opposite the big radio tower down the Ponta Mamoli road) or evacuate down to the Manguzi hospital in KwaZulu-Natal.

For public transport, there are *chapas* (see page 59), which leave for Maputo daily from the border or Ponta; from Maputo, they depart from the Catembe Ferry. The town is quite safe, with very little crime or harrassment. There are public phones around town (the number for the one at the camp entrance is 21-65-0006), good Mozambique cellphone reception and, if you get up onto the highest hill in town, you can even get reception for a South African cellphone number. There is a well-stocked craft market down near the campsite and the police station is just off the main intersection in town. Finally, if you don't have a 4×4, you can still visit Ponta by driving to the nearby border and organising a transfer through the place where you are staying – your car will be safe and under guard till you return.

## Beyond Ponta

Leaving Ponta do Ouro, you can head inland to join the 'main road' by leaving town the way you came in. But, instead of heading for the border, keep slightly north and follow the power lines to meet up with the road leading up from the border (all sandy, 4×4 driving). This passes through Zitundu and eventually Bela Vista on its way to Maputo. A more interesting alternative is the coastal track up past Ponta Malongane and Ponta Mamoli. Start at the main signposted intersection in Ponta do Ouro (S26°50.424 E32°53.070) and head north out of town through the residential part, passing the medical clinic on your left. After approximately 8 kilometres of sandy track, you will reach the **Ponta Malongane Holiday Resort**. Like a self-contained village, it offers all you need for a holiday by the sea: horse riding, fishing charters, diving, snorkelling, shop, bar and restaurant – and all are very conservation conscious (they ban quadbikes). Well-shaded camping is 320 MT to 520 MT per person (out-of-season midweek to in-season weekend), while four-bed rondavels with en-suite bathrooms cost 3000 MT to 3600 MT per night. The dive centre and fishing charter seem to operate only during the busier times of the year, so be sure to check with them first. Contact Malongane in South Africa, tel: +27-(0)13-741-1975, fax: +27-(0)13- 741-3730, e-mail: reservations@malongane. co.za, website: www.malongane.co.za.

The narrow, sandy track winds north through the coastal forest, skirting small lakes where busy pied kingfishers work the waters (the area offers a selection of pristine birding habitats).

After 11 kilometres, you will reach an old, potholed tar road. Turn left and travel a further 3.5 kilometres to the **Ponta Mamoli Resort** (another 8 kilometres brings you to Zitundu and the 'main road' to Maputo). This resort offers a bar, restaurant, pool and air-conditioned conference facilities, and also suggests that you celebrate your wedding there. Accommodation is in modern timber chalets built amid the dunes on raised decks and linked by wooden walkways. With en-suite hot showers, overhead fans, mosquito

The southern resort of Ponta Mamoli offers many activities, including horseriding.

nets and daily servicing, they cost between 3500 MT and 7760 MT per person per night, inclusive of dinner and breakfast. The resort boasts a water sport centre that offers turtle expeditions as well as the usual diving and fishing. For bookings contact the resort on tel: +27-(0)35-592-8100, website: www.pontamamoli.com.

Head back to Zitundu via the incongruous old tar road and rejoin the sand road north to Salamanga. This road has some deep wallows that fill with water during the rainy season, but are quite easy to negotiate as the sand hardens when wet. After 27 kilometres, you will reach the turn-off to the **Reserva Especial de Maputo**, also known as **Maputo Elephant Reserve** (S26°31.788 E32°43.233), and 3 kilometres down this road is the gate and main camp. Entry fees are 275 MT per person and 275 MT per vehicle. A daily fee of 140 MT is levied for camping, which is the only accommodation available. The main route is down to Ponta Milibangalala (what a great name!) on the coast, where there are also camping facilities. Halfway down this road is a signposted road north to Cabo de Santa Maria. Outside the reserve (so no camping fees) and at the northern tip of a peninsula, it is just a stone's throw away from the southern tip of Inhaca Island. There are reported to be at least 300 elephants in the reserve, but not much else other than similar flora and fauna to that on the road coming up. We saw fresh elephant dung and footprints, but the forest is dense and the ellies very skittish, so don't expect to see much.

Continuing north, the road improves a little after the reserve turn-off, and **Salamanga** town, with its bridge (watch out for the vicious speed bumps!) across the Maputo River, is reached after another 11 kilometres. It is here that the decent tar road starts, and buses run up and down from Maputo (actually from Catembe, across the bay by ferry). About 17 kilometres up the road is the short turn-off to the pretty little town of **Bela Vista**. There is no reason to turn in here, but if you do, you can eat and sleep at the neat little **Complexo Quinta Mila**, down an avenue of old flamboyant trees and overlooking the wide Maputo River. Prices are very reasonable: 900 MT for a double room and 1 250 MT for en-suite. A basic meat, fish and chicken menu with a selection of cold drinks makes it a pity that there's no real reason for stopping over here. Contact Emelia, tel: 21-62-0027, cell: 82-320-4500.

If you are heading for the Ressano Garcia border and South Africa, you could turn west to Boane just north of Bela Vista (S26°19.612 E32°39.646). Then it is 64 kilometres of sand and dirt (passable with a two-wheel-drive) to the tarred road at Boane (S26°02.678 E32°19.863). A right turn here would take you down to Maputo via Matola, but turn left to continue your drive to the South African border. About 5 kilometres up the road is the turn-off left (S26°00.825 E32°17.780) to the Swazi border at Namaacha, and another 41 kilometres will bring you to the main EN4 toll highway between Maputo and the Ressano Garcia border post into South Africa.

But from Bela Vista, you're on your way to Maputo, so head straight for 42 kilometres on a good gravel road until you reach **Catembe**. With its position across the bay from Maputo, Catembe offers an impressive view of the capital city's skyline. The ferry costs a mere 20 MT per person and an expensive 400 MT per vehicle. Smaller, cheaper, but way more dodgy passenger-only ferries ply this route more frequently, but check them out first.

Driving onto the ferry is pretty painless – to the end of a long jetty and then down a ramp – but you have to wait until there are at least eight vehicles on board before she will depart. If the ferry is still across on the Maputo side, the wait can be much longer, so be prepared. You will dock at the jetty the Inhaca Island ferry used in times gone by, opposite the Ministry of Finance, and there you are – you've arrived in downtown Maputo.

# Maputo

Maputo is developing so fast that it is difficult to give it an accurate and up-to-date description. Visit it today and you will find a 33-storey building, shopping malls selling international fashion brands, new state-of-the-art hotels with bluetooth internet connections and lovingly restored old buildings. Residents are painting and improving their homes and street crime has diminished. Business and industry is booming and it's becoming easier to get things done. And a whole new generation of residents and tourists has grown up not knowing who or what Lourenço Marques was. Yes, Maputo is striding ahead – but I wish they would fix the holes in their roads and sidewalks!

The rusty old ferry runs from Maputo across the bay to Catembe.

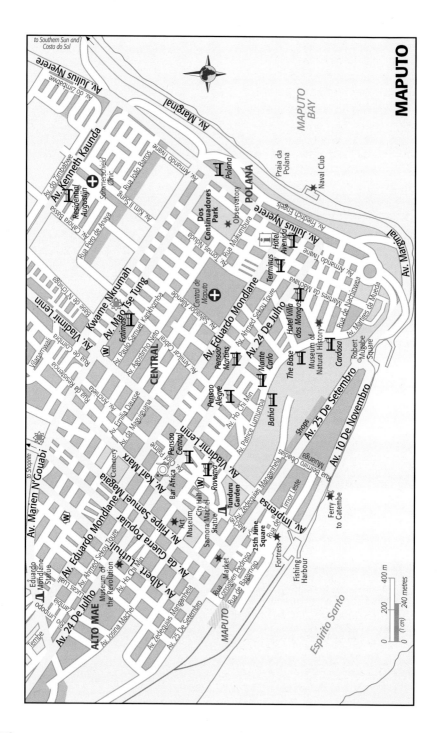

MAPUTO

MAPUTO BAY

to Southern Sun and
Costa do Sol

POLANA

CENTRAL

ALTO MAE

MAPUTO

Espirito Santo

Praia da
Polana

Naval Club

Dos
Continuadores
Park

Observatory

Hotel
Avenida

Terminus

Hotel Villa
das Mangas

Monte
Carlo

The Base

Museum of
Natural History

Cardosa

Robert
Mugabe
Square

Central de
Maputo

Pensao
Martins

Pensao
Alegre

Bahia

Shops

Residencial
Augustin

Sommerschield
Clinic

Pensao
Central

Pensao
Rovuma

Bar Africa

City Hall

Samora Machel
Statue

Tunduru
Garden

Art
Museum

Eduardo
Mondlane
Statue

Museum of
the Revolution

Rua Market

25th June
Square

Fortress

Ferry
to Catembe

Fishing
Harbour

Av. Julius Nyerere
Av. do Zimbabwe

Av. Marginal

Av. Armando Tivane

Av. do Zimbabwe

Av. Kenneth Kaunda

Rua da Resistência

Rua Pero de Anaya

Rua João Barros

Av. Kim Il Sung

Av. Tomas Nduda

Rua Mukumbura

Av. Julius Nyerere

Av. Friedrich Engels

Av. Armando Tivane

Martires da Machava

Rua de Nachingwea

Rua Martires da Mueda

Av. Marginal

Kwame Nkrumah

Av. Mao Tse Tung

Av. Vladimir Lenin

Vilankulo

Rua de Coimbra

Rua Antónia

Av. Emilia Dausse

Av. da Marquana

Av. Eugénia

Av. Paulo Samuel Kankhomba

Av. Agostinho Neto

Av. Salvador Allende

Av. Amilcar Cabral

Av. Fatima B...

Av. Eduardo Mondlane

Av. Ahmed Sekou Toure

Av. 24 De Julho

Av. Ho Chi Min

Av. Patrice Lumumba

Av. 25 De Setembro

Av. 10 De Novembro

Av. Marien N'Gouabi

to Shoprite

Cemetery

Av. Karl Marx

Av. Filipe Samuel Magaia

Av. Eduardo Mondlane

Av. da Guerra Popular

Av. Albert Luthuli

Av. Ahmed Sekou Toure

Av. Ho Chi Min

Lucas Luali

Rio Limpopo

Zambia

Tembe

Av. 24 De Julho

Av. Josina Machel

Av. Zedequias Manganhela

Av. 25 De Setembro

Av. Vladimir Lenin

Av. Zedequias Manganhela

Medici

Rua Consiglieri Pedroso

Rua de Bagamoio

Rua Belmiro Obadias Muianga

Rua de Timor Leste

Av. Imprensa

0    200    400 m
0  (1 cm)  240 metres

Maputo has style – leafy avenues lined with jacaranda and flame trees, an accessible and popular seafront, an interesting variety of buildings and architecture, and seafood and sidewalk cafés. The people have style, too. They appreciate the good life – good food, good music, nice clothes and regular siestas. It's difficult not to fall under the city's spell.

## The old city

But it hasn't always gone well for Maputo. The Portuguese navigator, Lourenço Marques, came ashore in 1545 to find a protected bay with potential for trade. Later Inhaca Island, just off-shore, was chosen by the Portuguese as a safe base for a small settlement. The Dutch and British tried to estab-lish trading posts in the 17th and 18th centuries, but there was little profit to be made in this quiet outpost – it was simply too far outside the sphere of East Coast Swahili influence. What changed Lourenço Marques' (as Maputo was then known) fortunes was the

discovery of diamonds and gold in what was then the Transvaal Republic. The Witwatersrand developed, a railway line was built in 1894 and Lourenço Marques (or simply LM) and its port began to prosper. By the mid-20th cen-tury, the city had also become the play-ground of hordes of Transvaal holiday-makers. But independence, politics and civil war put an end to all that and it is only now that the city, with a new name and new attitude, is rising again.

## Getting around Maputo

Maputo has a very easy-to-follow, rectangular shape with its streets laid out in a grid pattern. The old hub of the city was above the port and ranged up Av Samora Machel towards the botanical gardens and cathedral. But lack of renovation and restoration in this area (which has great potential) has meant that the main shopping, eating, drinking, staying and general strolling-around area has shifted to Av Julius Nyerere in the Polana district. These two areas are linked by the city's

Inhaca Island is blessed with some of the most pristine beaches in Mozambique.

## Swimming in Maputo

Use your hotel's pool, if it has one. The beaches are tidal and shallow, and the water is murky from pollution and river inflow.

main thoroughfare, Av 24 de Julho, which also houses many important and useful addresses for the tourist. None of the once-popular budget accommodation in the old downtown area can be recommended anymore as better, cleaner and safer establishments have sprung up elsewhere.

Rich history, pleasant location and a vibrant population have made Maputo a city well worth exploring. Coming from the South African border of Rossana Garcia or from the north of Mozambique, you would enter the city down the western end of Av 24 de Julho. Watch out for the traffic lights at all intersections, there's only one per corner and if you're in front of the queue, you might not see it. The roads are fairly well signposted, but badly potholed in places. To head downtown and to the port, turn right at Av Karl Marx or Av Vladimir Lenin (communism was big after independence). The main road out of this busy area is Av 25 de Setembro. Heading east, you will pass through what is becoming a new fast-food and shopping area with Nando's, Pizza Inn, Debonairs Pizza, Steers, Standard Bank (with an ATM and currency exchange) and Mobil service station all along the left-hand side of the road. On the right-hand side is the original fairground site, which is being redeveloped.

Av 25 de Setembro becomes the Marginal at a large traffic circle (Praça Robert Mugabe). Then, going straight ahead along the edge of the sea, you follow the coast past the Clube Naval. Walking and stopping along this area can be risky, and while some local families do use this section of the Marginal, be careful if you decide to walk or jog here.

At the Praça Robert Mugabe, turning left and heading up the hill brings you to the presidential palace (hidden to your left) and Av Julius Nyerere, which is a major street running through the heart of the upper city. This wide avenue takes you into town past the Polana Shopping Centre (not to be confused with the hotel of the same name) on the junction of Av 24 de Julho and Av Julius Nyerere, the modern Hotel Avenida, trendy bars and restaurants, and the magnificent old Polana Hotel.

After the Polana Hotel and the presidential offices on your right you will come to another traffic circle, and either road leading down the hill from here will reconnect you with the Marginal.

## Walking Maputo

The main tourist sights are all around the older part of town and can be seen on a walking tour. (Care should always be taken when walking around the city as petty crime and muggings are relatively common even in daylight hours.) Start at the top of Av Samora Machel outside the imposing **Cathedral of Nossa Senhora da Conceicao** – if you have a car, park it safely outside the Hotel Rovuma next door. Take off down the road and you will pass the **Casa de Ferro** (Iron

House). This prefabricated iron building was designed by Gustave Eiffel (of 'Tower' fame) as the governor's residence, but was too hot and stuffy to be of any use to him. Behind this folly is the **Jardim Tunduru** (botanical gardens). It's a little overgrown and in need of some pruning, but I think it's great that it survived Mozambique's recent turmoil. The buildings further down Av Samora Machel are also in need of some freshening up, especially the block on the right-hand side of the road, which is a real gem, just crying out for restoration. Down at the bottom, on the left, just above the harbour, is a fort built by the Portuguese in the mid-19th century and still in pretty good shape. And across the road is the **Praca 25 do Junho** where a regular Saturday craft market is held. Turn right here and wend your way through the narrow streets to the railway station on Praca dos Trabalhadores – its impressive dome was also designed by Eiffel (one of its platforms is home to a decent jazz café). Head one block up and into Av 25 de Setembro where you'll find the **Central Market**. Curios, fruit, vegetables, almost anything can be found here, but watch your valuables – pickpockets rule! Back up Av Samora Machel brings you to the end of this little circuit and back to your car.

## Around Maputo

There are other interesting excursions that can be made from Maputo. The **Hotel Costa do Sol** is at the far end of the Marginal (6 kilometres past the Southern Sun Hotel) and is a great place for a meal or sundowner on the wide veranda overlooking the beach and curio sellers. As well as prawns, chicken and steak (all around 500 MT), they serve a mouth-watering selection of chilled desserts, fresh pastries and good coffee. They also offer accommodation upstairs – comfortable singles cost 1 600 MT and doubles 2 400 MT, including breakfast. Tel 82-277-5878, e-mail: res@teledata.mz. Please note that it is not feasible to head further north up the coast from here, simply because the off-roading can be extremely dodgy for the casual traveller without sound 4×4 skills; rather head back into town and take the main road out of Maputo.

Another pleasant excursion is to **Inhaca Island** 35 kilometres offshore. Unfortunately, the old public ferry that used to run from the Catembe ferry jetty is no longer in operation. It was slow and cheap and gave you time to appreciate Maputo's skyline and get to know your fellow passengers. The new alternative is a luxury ferry that runs Saturdays and Sundays at 08h00 from the Porto de Pesca (the fishing harbour at the bottom of Av Samora Machel) and costs 1 800 MT. For bookings, tel: 21-49-7483 or 84-404-0710. There is a marine biological museum and research centre on the island where studies are made of the prolific marine life around the island. The coral reefs (some of the most southerly in the world) teem with colourful fish and are easily accessible from the shore – a paradise for snorkellers. Over 300 bird species have been recorded on Inhaca, including the crab plover, mangrove kingfisher and greater frigate bird. Accommodation is available at the **Inhaca Lodge**,

The Southern Sun in Maputo provides a welcome refuge.

tel: 21-30-5000. Double rooms cost 7000 MT in low season, 8800 MT in high and include dinner and breakfast.

Catembe, just across Maputo Bay, is also worth a visit, if only to get out across the water and view the city's skyline. It's dirt cheap (20 MT), takes just 15 minutes and leaves about every two hours (or when the vehicle deck is full). When you reach the other side, drop into one of the little restaurants for prawn and beer bargains. There is a restaurant within walking distance to the right of the ferry-landing on Catembe called **Retiro**, which serves great seafood, pregos and chicken.

## Top-end accommodation in Maputo

As with any fast-developing city, places come and go. Maputo has seen the opening of some fine new hotels, the refurbishment of others and the downfall of an entire area. The following are worth considering.

At the top end of the market is **Hotel Polana**, 1380 Av Julius Nyerere, tel: 21-49-1001, fax: 21-49-1480, e-mail: info@serenahotels.com, website: www.serenahotels.com. This elegant five-star hotel in a superb location overlooking the sea is like the Mount Nelson in Cape Town and the Old Cataract Hotel in Aswan – a magical mix of colonial and African charm with world-class comfort and service. Pool, tennis court, bowling green, gymnasium, restaurants, bars, business centre and casino, the Polana has it all. The hotel has recently been renovated and new rates have not yet been announced.

The **Hotel Avenida**, 627 Av Julius Nyerere, tel: 21-49-2000, fax: 21-49-9600, e-mail: bookings@hotelavenida.co.mz is modern, classy and sophisticated. This hotel has great facilities for the visiting businessman – conference centre, business rooms and health club. Standard rooms are 10000 MT single,

12000 MT for a double and breakfast is included.

The **Hotel Cardoso**, 707 Av Martires de Mueda, tel: 21-49-1071, fax: 21-49-1804, e-mail: info@hotelcardoso.co.za, website: www.hotelcardoso.co.mz, is extremely well positioned, offering stunning views over the city, bay and beyond. Centrally situated, it also has a large pool and pleasant gardens. Prices start at 4650 MT single and 5200 MT double, including breakfast.

The **Southern Sun**, Av de Marginal, tel: 21-49-5050, fax: 21-49-7700, e-mail: maputo@southernsun.com, website: www.southernsun.com is situated out of the town centre and right on the beach. It is a smart hotel that has been tastefully decorated and has all the facilities a businessman or holiday-maker could need. The deluxe or standard rooms cost 6000 MT single and 6700 MT double, breakfast included.

## Mid-range accommodation in Maputo

The most centrally situated of the hotels in the mid-range accommodation is the **Rovuma Hotel**, 114 Rua da Se, tel: 21-30-5000, fax: 21-30-3960, e-mail: reservas.africa@pestana.com, website: www.pestana.com. Opposite the cathedral, the Rovuma has 200 rooms, an outdoor pool, sauna, gymnasium and large conference and banqueting rooms. A standard room costs 4650 MT single and 5150 MT double, with breakfast.

The **Bahia Hotel**, 737 Rua Patrice Lumumba, tel: 21-36-0360, fax: 21-36-0330, e-mail: girassolbahiahotel@visabeira.co.mz, is just down the road from

## Camping in Maputo

Be aware that no camping is permitted within the confines of Maputo.

the Hotel Cardoso and has similar great views, a pool and gardens. Comfortable singles cost 4550 MT and doubles 4950 MT.

The **Hotel Villa das Mangas**, 401 Av 24 de Julho, tel: 21-49-7507, fax: 21-49-7078, is conveniently situated and has well-appointed rooms around a central courtyard with pool. Singles cost 2800 MT and doubles 3200 MT.

The **Residencial Augustijn**, 204 Pereira Marinho, in the foreign-embassy suburb of Sommershield, tel/fax: 21-49-3693, e-mail: t.theunissen@tvcabo.co.mz, is a small guesthouse that is furnished with antiques and Persian carpets. Rates are 2500 MT single and 3200 MT double, negotiable for longer stays.

The **Hotel Terminus**, 587 Rua Francisco Orlando Magumbwe, tel: 21-49-1333, fax: 21-49-1284, e-mail: info@terminus.co.mz, website: www.terminus.co.mz, is just a few blocks back from busy Av Julius Nyerere in the Polana district. This quiet garden-set establishment offers free high-speed internet access, with breakfast included in the price of 2900 MT double.

The old Parque de Campismo (campsite) has been redeveloped into the **Kaya Kwanga**, Av Marginal, tel: 21-49-2706, fax: 21-49-2704, e-mail: miramar.kayakwanga@tvcabo.co.mz, website: www.kayakwanga.co.mz. This park resort has a hotel, residential accommodation and conference facilities, but no longer offers camping. Air-conditioned chalets cost 1 800 MT single and 2 250 MT double, while for longer stays you can rent a small house that sleeps four for 36 000 MT per month.

**Mozaika**, 769 Av Agostinho Neto, tel: 21-30-3939, fax: 21-30-3965, e-mail: mozaika_guesthouse@hotmail. com, website: www.mozaika.co.mz, has been billed as Maputo's best-kept secret. This small luxury guesthouse is also set in a garden suburb and is popular with NGO workers for longer stays. With a pool, bar and good security, they charge from 2 700 MT to 3 200 MT single/double.

The **Monte Carlo**, 620 Av Patrice Lumumba, tel: 21-30-4048, fax: 21-30-8959, e-mail: info@montecarlo.co.mz, website: www.montecarlo.co.mz, is another hotel in the conveniently situated Av Patrice Lumumba. This one offers value for money at rates from 1 200 MT double.

## Budget accommodation in Maputo

The **Pensão Martins**, 1098 Av 24 de Julho, tel: 21-32-4926, fax: 21-42-9645, is a clean, safe, well-run hotel with a pool, bar, restaurant and off-street parking – and, in this price range, it is a real find in Maputo. En-suite single rooms cost 1 600 MT and doubles 1 900 MT, and include a continental breakfast.

**Maputo Backpackers**, Quarta Avanida, Costa do Sol, tel: 82-467-2230, e-mail: 843989335@vodamail. co.mz, is a little way out of town along the Marginal at Costa do Sol, but is situated in a clean, uncluttered house down a quiet side street. Dorm beds start at 380 MT and a double room will cost you 1 350 MT.

**Fatima's Backpacker**, 1339 Av Mao Tse Tung, tel: 21-30-2994, 82-414-5730, fax: 21-49-4462, e-mail: fatimas@ tvcabo.co.mz, website: www.mozam-biquebackpackers.com was the original budget accommodation in Maputo and is now resting on its laurels. It's clean enough, laid-back, and has a communal kitchen and full notice board, but I didn't feel the vibe. Dorms cost 450 MT, singles 900 MT and doubles 1 050 MT.

The **Pensão Alegre**, 1371 Av 24 de Julho, tel: 21-30-7742, is pretty basic, but at least it has safe off-street parking, and only charges 650 MT for a single and 1 150 MT for a double, with shared ablutions facilities.

**Pensão Central**, Av 24 de Julho (between Vladimir Lenin and Olaf Palme), tel: 21 424476, is a little dingy, but safe and clean, with guarded street parking. Rooms with shared facilities cost 520 MT single and 720 MT double.

The **Base Backpackers**, 545 Av Patrice Lumumba, tel: 21-30-2723, 82-452-6860, fax: 21-31-3750, e-mail: thebasebp@tvcabo.co.mz is a newish place run by husband-and-wife team Luis and Francisca. It is conveniently situated in Av Patrice Lumumba, with a fabulous view of the bay from the deck. Internet, laundry and off-street parking – a nice place. Dorm beds cost 350 MT and double rooms 950 MT.

## Eating out in Maputo

There are so many restaurants catering to all tastes and budgets in Maputo that I cannot even attempt a list of recommendations. What I can do is highlight certain streets or areas that are worth checking out. The best street for cafés and restaurants is **Av Julius Nyerere**, south of the Polana Hotel. Here you will find piri-piri chicken, spicy Thai food, Indian cuisine, seafood restaurants, coffee shops, pizzerias, as well as ice-cream and pastry shops. A right turn down Av 24 de Julho will take you past more restaurants and several fast-food outlets selling pizzas and pies.

**Feira Popular**, the old fairground on Av 25 de Setembro, has closed for redevelopment and the malls are already across the street, where many South African fast-food outlets have set up shop. Nando's, Pizza Inn, Debonairs Pizza and Steers are all on hand to satisfy your wildest fast-food fantasies. Also down in the baixa are **Zambi**, a well-priced, high-quality, gourmet restaurant on the Marginal behind the old Feira, and the **Waterfront Restaurant**, close to the large roundabout at the point where Av 25 de Setembro turns into the Marginal. There is also a Spur Steak Ranch on the Marginal, out past the Southern Sun, though to get there you will pass several decent quality and reasonably priced local restaurants on the right. In the same area as the Spur is the casino, which houses a decent cocktail bar and a branch of the South African Meat Co. restaurant chain.

All the large hotels have excellent restaurants, but those on a very tight budget should drop into any of the open-air markets for cheap and tasty plates of food.

## Nightlife

The **Bar Africa** on Av 24 de Julho has live music and the **Club Maritimo** sometimes plays cool jazz. **Mundos** is a good late-night pub and restaurant in Av Julius Nyerere and if it's disco, dancing and action you crave, then check out **Coconuts** on Av 25 de Setembro. The red-light district of Maputo is in Rua de Bagamoyo, a small street with four or five bars and a strip club. It is also a hang-out for prostitutes, so stay away if you disapprove!

## Shopping in Maputo

There are several interesting and useful shopping malls. The first is the **Shoprite Centre** (S25°57.120 E32°34.751) on Av Acordos de Lusaka, the road to the airport. Fully fenced and secure, with lots of free parking, the centre offers a Shoprite supermarket that stocks all the food and drink you can think of, as well as hardware, camping gear, motor oils and magazines. You can pay in meticais, dollars or rands (but at a poor exchange rate). There is also a pharmacy, bank, ATM, sports shop, fast-food outlet, Woolworths, CNA stationers, cellphone operator and Total petrol station.

Another shopping complex is the **Polana Mall**, on the corner of Av Julius Nyerere and Av 24 de Julho. A smart up-market place, it has an ice-cream parlour, bank and exchange bureau, delicatessen and cellphone shop on the ground floor. On the first floor you will find a modern internet café, hairdresser, tobacconist, pharmacy, optician, small superette, bookshop (with a small selection of English books) and clothing shops. The second floor contains a café, DVD rental shop, curio outlet and a mouthwatering chocolate emporium.

Just across the road from the Polana Mall in Av 24 de Julho, and next to the Piri Piri Chicken Restaurant, is a very clean and well-stocked butchery, delicatessen and fish shop. And for larger items and appliances, a big new Game Store has opened along the Marginal on the way to Costa do Sol. There is a good Portuguese supermarket, **Luz**, on the same road, which stocks a range of Portuguese wines, imported sausages, cheeses, hams and chouriço, as well as home decor, gifts and dry goods.

There is also the new **Maputo Shopping Mall**, which contains a wide array of shops from South Africa. Brands such as Mr Price, Mr Price Home and Sheet Street vie with shops stocking beautiful Indian fabrics, and everything in between. This shopping centre also has a variety of restaurants, and a great ice cream and juice bar.

The markets of Maputo deserve special mention. The main **Mercado Municipal** on Av 25 de Setembro stocks just about everything in the fresh food line, while the **Janeta Market**, at the intersection of Av Mao Tse Tung and Vladimir Lenin, stocks more in the line of household goods and second-hand clothing. The most entertaining, though, is the huge and chaotic **Xipamanine Market** out west on the Rua dos Imaos Roby. Hardware, spare parts and furniture crowd around the scary-looking stalls of dismembered animal parts, herbs and medicinal plants, all for muti (traditional medicines). The **Saturday Craft Market** on Praca 25 do Junho, at the bottom of Av Samora Machel, is another interesting place to visit for its wide selection of hand-crafts from all over Mozambique. All these markets have a criminal element, so don't visit them wearing expensive jewellery or accessories, don't flash your money, and don't be tempted to change money or buy illegal substances.

Take the ferry across the bay to Catembe for great seafood and the best view of Maputo's skyline.

## Public transport

Instead of one large sprawling bus station, long-distance buses in Maputo leave from the companies' separate depots. Here is a list of the main ones:

**Transportes Oliveiras**, tel: 21-40-5108, is out on Av 24 de Julho, just past the big traffic circle (Praca 16 Junho), and can be reached by *chapas* heading west out of the city along the main thoroughfare. They have an extensive network in southern and central Mozambique and run express or local buses. Tickets are sold on the premises on Av 24 de Julho.

Transportes Virginia, tel: 21-42-1271, operates mainly in southern Mozambique and leaves from the Hotel Universo on the corner of Av Eduardo Mondlane and Karl Marx.

TSL goes as far as Tete and Nampula and leaves from the Praca dos Combatantes at the end of Av das FPLM (accessible by *chapas* heading out of town along Av Vladimir Lenin).

The closest thing to a bus station in Maputo is **Junta**, the sprawling stretch of Av de Mozambique heading north out of the city. All buses on their way north must pass through this area, and it is indeed possible to board here, although you are better off catching them at their depots.

Even though there is a very inexpensive city bus service (no rides cost more than 5 MT), most residents use *chapas*, which seem to go everywhere (and cost 12 MT). Routes are called out by the conductor and you hop on and off when you like. Taxis, recognisable by their yellow roofs, stand outside all the bigger hotels and also up and down the length of the busy avenues (choose one with a meter and make sure that it's turned on).

The Laurentina Brewery has moved from the corner of Av 25 de Setembro and Albert Luthuli, but this is still the area to head for to pick up a minibus taxi to Swaziland or South Africa. **Intercape** luxury buses travel daily between Johannesburg Station and the offices of Tropical Travel in Av 24 de Julho, and **Translux** runs a similar service that turns around at Simana Travel in the same street. The Mozambique-based service, **Panthera Azul**, is at 273

## Maputo at your service

◆ Fresh rolls (rather than loaves of bread) are found at bakeries all over town. A couple of the more prominent ones are: **Nautilus** (corner Julius Nyerere and 24 de Julho), **Aziz** (Av Samora Machel) and the in-store one at **Shoprite**.

◆ You will probably be able to have laundry done where you are staying but if this is not possible, use the centrally situated **EcoSec Lavandarias**, at 413 Av 24 de Julho, tel: 21-49-5574. They charge 80 MT for a kilogram of washing and also do dry-cleaning.

◆ Curios can be bought at all Maputo's markets, but also outside hotels Cardoso, Polana and Costa do Sol, and on the traffic island at the corner of Av Julius Nyerere and Av 24 de Julho – where everything seems to happen!

◆ Most of the accommodation establishments, from budget to top end, offer **internet** access and facilities. Otherwise, there are a couple of internet cafés along Av 24 de Julho and Av Julius Nyerere.

◆ **DHL** is on the corner of Samora Machel and 25 de Setembro.

◆ The **Public Information Bureau** (BIP) is on the corner of Av Eduardo Mondlane and Av Francisco Magumbwe, tel: 21-49-0200, fax: 21-49-2622, e-mail: bip@teledata. mz. They sell city maps and books, some in English, but are closed 12h30–14h00.

Av Zedequias Manganhela. Prices are all around 950 MT one way.

## Driving in and around the capital

There are many service stations at which to fill up with fuel. The Mobil garage next to the Polana Hotel also has a car wash, and another Mobil opposite the Hotel Cardoso can repair punctures and pump tyres. There is also one down in Av 25 de Setembro next to the fast-food outlets (petrol costs 37 MT a litre, and diesel 31 MT). For vehicle spares, try one of the many small shops down Av Karl Marx, and for tyres, shocks, bearings and batteries try Bandauto Continental at the unfashionable end of Av 25 de Setembro, between Said Barre Av and Fernandos Farinha. Camping gas can be refilled at Mocacor in Av Karl Marx, just below Av 24 de Julho. The Toyota dealer is at 141 Rua do Logo Amaramba, tel 21-40-0405, fax: 21-40-0471, e-mail: sales@toyota.vir-conn.com. For help with your Nissan, contact Motorcare Mozambique, Rua Paulinho dos Santos; tel: 21-31-2931, fax: 21-31-2930, e-mail: info@moz. motorcare.com, website: www.motor-care.com. Mitsubishi is represented by Tecnica Industrial, 2803 Av 24 de Julho, tel: 21-42-8078 and Ford is at 47 Av Samora Machel, tel: 21-32-0123.

For car hire, visit **Europcar**, tel: 21-49-4982, fax: 21-42-6077, at the Polana Hotel, or **Avis** at the corner of Julius Nyerere and Mao Tse Tung, tel: 21-46-5498, fax: 21-46-5493. They also both have offices at the airport.

## Banking

For best rates and complete safety, change money at a *cambios*, which you will find dotted all over town. SA Cambios is at 118 Av 24 de Julho and No's Cambios is in the same street, between Pensão Alegro and Hotel Santa Cruz. Halfway down Av Samora Machel, just below the bakery, is the Maputo Cambios, and there are others in Av Julius Nyerere. Banks change money, but take a long time doing it, and hotels do so at a lower rate. Don't use the street – it is illegal, and you could be ripped off.

## Health and safety

For medical emergencies, head straight for the **Sommershield Clinic** (S25°57.576 E32°35.769), 52 Rua Pereira do Lago, just off Av Kim Il Sung, tel: 21-49-3924. It is open 24 hours a day and always has doctors and specialists on call. Expect to be charged upfront, but credit cards are acceptable. Just down from the Santa Cruz Hotel, in Av 24 de Julho, is a large yellow building that houses the **Clinica Bathesda**. You might have difficulty communicating without some Portuguese, but they are equipped for most emergencies. Alternatively, they will be able to refer you.

Pharmacies are dotted around town, with the old favourites, 24 de Julho, Julius Nyerere, Shoprite Centre and the Polana Shopping Mall the best.

There is a dentist on Av Julius Nyerere, above the Spicy Thai Restaurant, and another at the top end of Av Patrice Lumumba – check their supplies of Novocaine first!

### Language issues

You should get by speaking English, but for helpful Portugese words and phrases see pages 200–203.

# 13

# North to Inhambane

To get to the EN1 and places north, head out of Maputo on Av 24 de Julho, across Praca 16 de Junho (this is like a history lesson), and to the highway intersection (S25°56.535 E32°32.353) with the EN4 road that extends from the South African border. This intersection is well signposted (to Xai-Xai). Turn right into Av de Mozambique (EN1) and fight your way through the chaos of taxis, trucks and trollies that crowd this busy part of town. If you were coming down from the South African border and bypassing Maputo, you would turn left here.

Lagoons, protected bays and sailing dhows epitomise the coastline north to Inhambane.

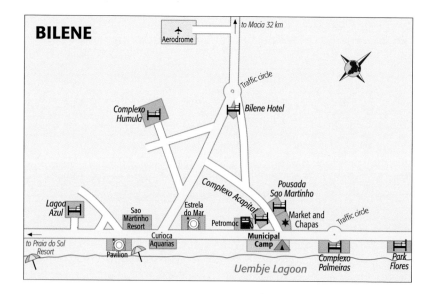

**BILENE**

to Macia 32 km

Aerodrome

Traffic circle

Bilene Hotel

Complexo Humula

Complexo Acapital

Pousada Sao Martinho

Lagoa Azul

Sao Martinho Resort

Estrela do Mar

Petromoc

Market and Chapas

Traffic circle

to Praia do Sol Resort

Pavilion

Curioca Aquarias

Municipal Camp

to Praia do Sol Resort

Complexo Palmeiras

Park Flores

Uembje Lagoon

Please note that it is not feasible to leave Maputo via the Marginal out north, past Costa do Sol, as the route is simply too precarious for anyone with less-than-expert off-roading skills. Fuel is available at large Petromoc and Mobil service stations, and on your right as you leave this area, a large branch of Trentyre will be able repair punctures and sell you new tyres.

A feature of the road north is that it's always just inland from the coast, so to reach any of the country's many seaside resorts, you have to turn off and head down to the coast. The bigger resorts have better roads leading to them, while others can be reached only with a 4×4 vehicle.

## The EN1 north

Roadworks along length of the EN1 are a regular occurrence, so be careful and adhere to the speed limits and stop/go signals.

The first turn-off is reached after only 30 kilometres and is to the **Marracuene Lodge**. Four-wheel-drive is necessary to travel the sandy 4.5 kilometres down to this camp (follow the signposts). A small bar and restaurant overlooks the Incomati River and visitors can launch boats here to fish or bird-watch in the river's delta. Neat, comfortable, self-catering chalets have bedding, mosquito nets, hot and cold water and fully equipped kitchens. The four-person or two-person accommodation costs 600 MT per person (dinner, bed and breakfast 1400 MT). A large campsite offers shady, but sandy, sites at 200 MT per person. To book, tel: 84-484-9230, website: www. marracuenelodge.co.mz.

A good overnight option when travelling north is **Casa Lisa**, 46 kilometres from Maputo. Just 1 kilometre off the highway, the turn-off to the left is well signposted at a small road-side snack bar called Ultra City (S25°35.024

E32°40.029). Expertly run by Paul and Liz Hallowes, Casa Lisa has a comfortable bar, good food and a swimming pool. It offers camping in a well-grassed area (each with its own thatched lapa) for 250 MT per person, and attractively decorated, self-contained chalets with mozzie nets at between 500 MT and 700 MT per person per night. For bookings, tel: 82-304-1990.

The EN1 north continues in fairly good condition through **Manhica**, where you will find a bank, pharmacy, small shops and a garage for fuel and minor repairs. There is also the **Laurentina Hotel** in the main street. Clean en-suite double rooms cost 800 MT per person and 600 MT for rooms with shared facilities (the rooms facing the street could be noisy). This is a busy and popular spot for

a drink on the patio, doughnut or samoosa in the café, or good local specialities in the air-conditioned restaurant, where the menu boasts 'Steak Poll' and 'Suckling Ping'.

Passing over the Incomati floodplain, you travel through sugar-cane fields to the town of **Macia** (144 kilometres from Maputo). Macia has a Petromoc service station/mini-market on the left as you come into town, and in the centre are a market and restaurants. You will also find the turn-off (S25°01.626 E33°05.776) to the seaside resort of **Bilene**. Turn right here to travel the 32 kilometres of good tar down to the coast, but be warned that it can be quite depressing to see the road-side stalls selling wood, charcoal and illegally harvested indigenous plants, dying in the harsh sun.

## Bilene

Bilene is situated on the **Uembje Lagoon**, which is separated from the sea by a narrow line of sand dunes. Only sometimes open to the sea, the lagoon is not great for swimming, but fine for most forms of boating and water sports. Known as Sao Martinho during colonial times, it has always been a popular holiday destination and therefore has a good selection of accommodation. Bilene is entered at a traffic circle, where you will also find the **Bilene Hotel** – a bit far from the beach, but solid and modern, with a large, airy bar and restaurant. A suite for two persons costs 1 500 MT, a four-person self-contained bungalow 3 000 MT, and for six it costs 4 000 MT. For bookings, tel: 282-59014, fax: 282-59012. Dubai World Africa

Fishing in Moz is not generally hi-tech!

announced in February 2008 that it would invest $200 million in upgrading the Bilene Hotel into a five-star eco-resort with 500 new villas and a golf course. Drive the 1.5 kilometres down to the lagoon and turn left, continuing to beyond the little circle at the Complexo Palmeiras until you reach the Park Flores Camp. We'll start here and work our way back.

**Park Flores** is a basic, unpretentious little outfit with a small bar and an even smaller store. The sandy, but neatly raked and shaded campsites cost 250 MT per person (some have electrical points). There are also small rondavels that contain only two beds for 880 MT and larger four-bed rondavels with equipped kitchens for 1440 MT. All ablutions are shared.

Back at the circle on the Marginal is the smarter **Complexo Palmeiras**. Spread out under shady trees along the waterfront are neat little brick-built chalets with verandas right on the sand. The chalets sleep four people, with linen and daily servicing, but are not self-catering, with no cutlery or crockery. They do, however, each have fans, a fridge and braai facilities and cost 2800 MT out of season and 3200 MT in season. The rondavels are similar to the chalets, but sleep two people and cost 2200 MT and 2800 MT (in and out of season). Camping facilities are available under shade above the beach (some electrical points) at 200 MT per site, plus 200 MT per person per day in season. Out of season, they charge the per-person rate, but not for the site. There is a comfortable bar, restaurant with a pool table, standard menu

## The tax man

Remember that a general marine tax is applicable throughout Mozambique:

- boat in a lagoon    500 MT
- boat in the sea     650 MT
- jetski              350 MT

There is also a diver's tax of 150 MT.

and even an espresso machine. For more information, tel/fax: 282-59019, Mozambique cell: 82-304-372, e-mail: palmeira@virconn.com.

Working our way back still further, we pass the extremely dodgy **Municipal Campsite** opposite the Petromoc service station. Stuck between the main road and the lagoon, this camp has no fences, even less security, and ablutions that are shared with the public. On the corner opposite the campsite is a small market where you can catch public transport back to Macia or Maputo.

Just up this side street are two small hotels that face each other. On the far side of the road is **Pousada Sao Martinho** where a house for four people, with fridge, hotplate, microwave, kettle, all utensils, fans and a comfortable veranda, will cost you 3000 MT per day, or a squeaky-clean double room in the main block 1050 MT. Set in pretty gardens, there is a swimming pool and bar/restaurant with pool table. For details, tel: 82-490-1440.

Across the road, the **Complexo Acapital** has neatly tiled double rooms with air-con and TV, but no en-suite bathrooms, for 1350 MT. For information, tel: 82-404-8700.

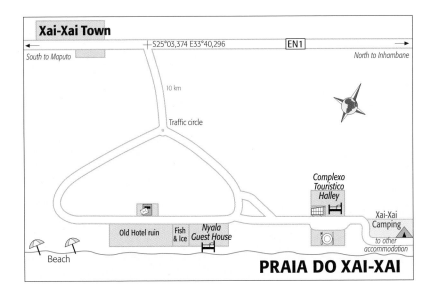

**Xai-Xai Town**

—S25°03,374 E33°40,296 | EN1

← South to Maputo

North to Inhambane →

10 km

Traffic circle

Complexo
Turístico
Halley

Xai-Xai
Camping

Old Hotel ruin | Fish & Ice | *Nyala Guest House*

to other
accommodation

Beach

**PRAIA DO XAI-XAI**

Working still further south down the main road, there are the Estrela do Mar, Carioca and Complexo Aquarias restaurants. A little further down, on the inland side of the road, is the large, refurbished and very secure **Sao Martinho Resort**. It consists of a group of brick-built bungalows that cost from 2 000 MT for a three-bed, non-self-catering unit, to 3 000 MT for a six-bed, self-contained one. It is run together with the beach pavilion bar and restaurant across the road, where you have to book in and pay. For bookings and further information, tel: 282-59001 or 82-880-2900. Just past the pavilion, up a side street away from the beach, is the **Lagoa Azul** complex. Small chalets sleeping four, with a small kitchen, cost 2 200 MT and a larger two-bedroomed house with elegant lounge and dining room, plus fully-kitted kitchen costs 4 800 MT. For details, tel: 282-59006.

To get to the more up-market **Praia do Sol Resort** (S25°17.500 E33°13.855), we have to keep heading south along the Marginal and then follow the signs through the houses. There are two options: one for 4×4s and the other for standard vehicles. Both bring you to an attractive group of wooden chalets dotted across the dunes, all with stunning views of the lagoon. A restaurant, bar, water sports centre and swimming pool are linked by wooden walkways, and chalets sleep two, four or six people. Rates vary between 2 600 MT and 3 500 MT per person in and out of season and include dinner, bed and breakfast. Contact Leo Rogers, e-mail: leo@pdsol.co.za or in South Africa on tel: +27-(0)82-570-4300 and in Mozambique on tel: 82-319-3040, website: www.pdsol.co.za.

Away from the beach, off the road back to the traffic circle, is the exclusive **Humula Complexo**. Accommodation

## Water world

Southern Mozambique features numerous coastal lakes and lagoons. The most prominent are the Uembje Lagoon at Bilene, Lake Inhampavala north of Xai-Xai, Lake Quissico just outside Quissico town, and Lake Poelela, crossed by the EN1 just south of Inharrime. Separated from the sea by narrow strips of dune (only Uembje at Bilene is open to the sea), they are shallow, with brackish water, and contain a variety of freshwater fish species. Birds love them too – Lake Quissico is particularly popular, with over 50 species recorded here.

is in large, comfortable two-bedroomed houses furnished with the latest in fridges, stoves and furniture. Each house has a private garden and carport and costs 4600 MT a night for four people. Motel-style double rooms with air-con, TV and fridge are 1860 MT a night. This is an attractive and secure complex set in beautiful gardens. For more information, tel: 21-314-576, e-mail: info@humulahotel.com, website: www.humulahotel.com.

Boating and water sports are the things to do here and all resorts offer launching facilities at a fee of around 80 MT for a jetski and 110 MT for a single-engined boat.

Head back up to the EN1 at Macia and turn northeast. As you leave town, opposite the Mobil petrol station, you will pass the turn-off left (S25°01.511 E33°06.099) to Chokwe, Massingir and the South African border at Pafuri in the north of the Kruger National Park. This is becoming a popular route as the Transfrontier Park develops around Massingir and the new border post west of there. Before leaving town, stop to buy some delicious cashew nuts from the street vendors (the average price is 225 MT a kilogram). Just before the town of Xai-Xai, you cross the bridge over the Limpopo River. No toll is charged when heading north, but coming the other way, motorists are charged 20 MT for a car and 40 MT for a pick-up.

## Xai-Xai and surrounds

Xai-Xai town (pronounced *shy-shy*) is fairly large with most amenities – bank, pharmacy, general dealers, fast food, transport depots and a reasonable hotel on the main street opposite the central square and gardens. The **Hotel Kaya Ka Hirva** has clean, large, airy rooms upstairs, with TV and air-con, for 700 MT single and 1200 MT double. With your own bathroom, it costs 1350 MT for a double. There is a restaurant at street level. For details, tel: 282-22391.

On the other side of town, up on the hill, is a hospital and, just past it, the turn-off right to Xai-Xai beach (S25°03.374 E33°40.296). It is a short 10 kilometres down to the rather forlorn and neglected resort. Although Xai-Xai suffered heavy damage during recent floods, it is still inexplicable that, with so much development up and down Mozambique's coast, this beautiful spot has been passed over by promoters and tourists. A large, old derelict hotel dominates the main beach, but accommodation is available next door (northeast) at **Nyala Guest House**. An en-suite double room with TV and air-con costs 1 650 MT and there is a communal kitchen for the use of all guests. For information, tel: 282-23043 or 82-301-4640, fax: 282-22658, e-mail: saminvestment@teledata.mz. Fish and ice are sold from the small house situated between the derelict hotel and Nyala.

Northeast, off the ring road that runs around Xai-Xai beach, is the **Complexo Touristico Halley**. The hotel is set back slightly from the beach and hosts a disco in season. Not new, but still clean and neat, they have en-suite sea-facing double rooms for 1 900 MT or back-facing for 1 500 MT, including breakfast. For information, tel: 282-35014, fax: 282-35003. On the ground floor, there is also a general dealer (Estrela do Mar) that sells basic foodstuffs, and across the road, on the beach, is a restaurant that is also part of the complex.

Just past Halley's is the **Xai-Xai Camping and Caravan Park** with a variety of accommodation options. Camping is 250 MT per person, basic reed huts cost 900 MT for two people and 1 500 MT for four, and a rustic, self-catering bungalow with fridge, stove and accommodation for four is 2 500 MT. There is a bar and restaurant, but security in the camp is poor. For further details, tel: 282-35022 or 82-712-6520, fax: 282-35016.

## On to Inhambane

Back on the EN1 heading north, and approximately 65 kilometres from Xai-Xai town, you will reach Chidenguele

### Timbila jam sessions

The unique music of Venancio Mbande and his 32-piece *timbila* orchestra can be heard most Sunday afternoons at his house in Zavala, 27 kilometres north of Quissico. You can turn up to the sessions uninvited, but will be made to feel especially welcome if you bring along some cold beer. Look out for the yellow Chopi Music Centre sign just north of the village of Guilundo – Venancio's house is set back about 100 metres on the right side of the road.

village. To reach the beach at **Paraiso de Chidenguele**, turn right here and follow the signs. The five-kilometre road skirts a huge inland lake (see page 94) and ends high above the beach, where solid thatch-roofed bungalows dot the well-wooded dunes. The bungalows have fridges, stoves and even Weber braais and are linked by wooden walkways. They cost between 3 800 MT for a four-sleeper out of season to 6 700 MT for an eight-sleeper in season. Overnight en-suite accommodation is also available at between 1 100 MT and 1 500 MT per person. This is a pristine stretch of coast where the fishing is unmatched (rock, surf, fly, paddle-ski or deep-sea) and regular competitions are held here. The walls of the bar are covered with photographs to prove how good the fishing really is, and the restaurant serves delicious (surprise!) seafood meals. For enquiries, tel: 282-67001 or 84-390-9999, e-mail: clare@thereservationgroup.com, website: www.chidbeachresort.com.

Following the EN1, the potholes are bad around Zandamela as we head north again. Just on the other side of Quissico there is a turn-off (S24°42.920 E34°44.916) to the **Praia Mar e Sol 4×4 Bushcamp**. A well-signposted, but very sandy track winds down through thousands of coconut palms and crosses the enormous lake (look out for the interesting fish traps at the bridge) to climb up the dunes again to a well-laid-out 4×4 bushcamp. Flushing toilets, showers and thatch-shaded sites offer some luxury, but it is still very isolated. Camping is the only option and it costs 350 MT per person. For information, tel: 82-272-7530, website: www.praia-maresol.com.

Back on the EN1, beware of speed traps when passing through small towns. The local *transitos* have an old, well-used, hand-held radar that is used with devastating – and profitable – effect.

## Inharrime and north

Inharrime is not the most attractive of places to stop, but it does have a decent Galp service station and a dingy-looking hotel. About 10 kilometres out of town is the turn-off left down to Zavora Beach. This is a reasonable 17-kilometre road through rows of coconut palms with only the last section a bit sandy – just passable with two-wheel-drive. You will spot the lighthouse in the distance as you get closer. The beach is pleasant and there is good snorkelling, but most visitors come for the fishing. **Zavora Lodge** is the only budget tourist accommoda-

tion, but it is a little run-down. Self-catering bungalows that sleep four cost 4 000 MT per day in season and the larger six-sleeper houses are 4 500 MT. Camping is charged at 460 MT a person (charged for a minimum of 4 in season). Mosquitoes are a big problem, as is poor security. For details, in South Africa, tel: +27-(0)13-750-0431, or e-mail: zavaralodge@mweb. co.za, website: www.zavoralodge.com.

About 57 kilometres north of Inharrime, at Lindela, the road forks. Keep left and stay on the EN1, continuing up through Maxixe to Vilankulo, after that swing right for Inhambane and all its surrounding beaches and popular resorts.

## The versatile coconut

The coastal strip of Inhambane province is blanketed by about two million coconut palms. Each *Cocos nucifera* plant produces over 20 kilograms of coconuts annually, from which oil is extracted for soap, hair products, perfumes, cosmetics and confectionery. The trunk is also tapped for its sap, which is used for the production of palm wine, while the fronds are used for roofing material or woven into mats. When no longer productive, the palms are chopped down and the trunk used for valuable building timber. Look out for home-made coconut-ice sweets sold in markets and on the street. Made with desiccated coconut and raw brown sugar, it's delicious.

# 14

# Inhambane and surrounds

The district of Inhambane, including the beaches of Jangamo, Tofo and Barra, is the most popular destination for tourists in the entire Mozambique. But it wasn't tourism that brought Arab trading dhows to this large protected bay at Inhambane as early as the 10th century. These traders brought beads, salt, cloth and ceramics in exchange for gold and ivory.

With its uninterrupted views and balmy climate, Inhambane is a prime holiday destination.

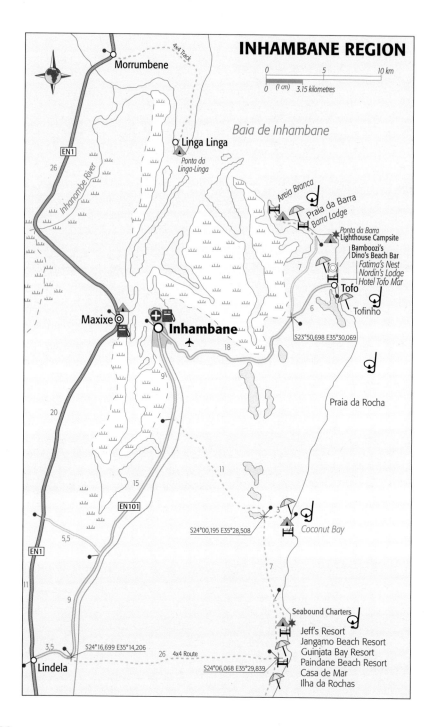

# INHAMBANE REGION

0         5       10 km

0    (1 cm)    3.15 kilometres

Morrumbene

4x4 Track

EN1

26

Inhanombe River

*Baia de Inhambane*

Linga Linga

*Ponta da
Linga-Linga*

*Areia Branca*

Praia da Barra
Barra Lodge

*Ponta da Barra*
Lighthouse Campsite

Bamboozi's
Dino's Beach Bar
*Fatima's Nest*
*Nordin's Lodge*
*Hotel Tofo Mar*

7

Tofo

6

*Tofinho*

Maxixe

Inhambane

S23°50,698 E35°30,069

18

9

*Praia da Rocha*

20

11

15

EN101

3

S24°00,195 E35°28,508

*Coconut Bay*

5,5

EN1

7

11

9

Seabound Charters

Jeff's Resort
Jangamo Beach Resort
Guinjata Bay Resort
Paindane Beach Resort
Casa de Mar
Ilha da Rochas

3,5

S24°16,699 E35°14,206

26   4x4 Route

S24°06,068 E35°29,839

Lindela

Trade increased with the arrival of the Portuguese and the town prospered. Gold dwindled, ivory soared and in the mid-18th century Inhambane was one of the first Mozambican ports to establish a trade in slaves. It developed into the third-largest town in the country after Maputo and Beira, and the beautiful colonial buildings, which can still be seen today, were built. Now a bit of a backwater – even the main EN1 highway bypasses it – it slumbers in faded glory.

## Beach resorts of Jangamo

Before we reach Inhambane itself, we will explore the beach resorts the area has to offer. The first turn-off (S24°16.699 E35°14.206), to Praia de Jangamo, is just 3.5 kilometres past the EN1 fork and is signposted to Sol de Ligogo, Ilha de Rochas and Paindane Resort. This is very definitely a 4×4 route and not easy to follow, but saves going the long way around via Inhambane. The sandy track winds through the bush, passing villages, huts and fields of manioc. It is signposted, but because the signs are generally high in trees and there are so many forks in the track, it is difficult to follow. You are, however, rewarded with one of the best bits of off-roading you're likely to do in Mozambique – a 4×4 route you'd pay good money to drive if it was in South Africa and a good test of you and your vehicle.

Follow the signs for Paindane and, after about 26 kilometres, you will reach the gates (S24°06.068 E35°29.839) of this large, well-run resort. Spread over an attractive palm- and bush-covered slope, **Paindane Beach Resort** can accommodate up to 500 people at the height of season. The lively bar and restaurant, high on the hill, overlooks a beautiful beach. Protected by an offshore reef, the beach is perfect for swimming and snorkelling, and launching boats, too.

There is a variety of accommodation options. Self-catering chalets come in four-, six-, seven- and eight-bed versions and include all linen and a fully equipped kichen. Their verandas offer great views of the sea, and the cost is about 800 MT per person per day during high season. Basic camping is 400 MT per person per day with bright, clean ablution blocks. For more comfortable camping, hire a *baracca* – thatched, open-sided structures with a cement floor, wash-up sink and tap. These can be used as camping kitchens, living rooms or a protected place to pitch your tent under. They cost an extra 1 200 MT a day. The ultimate in camping, though, must be the *casitas*. These are similar to the *baraccas*, but have their own toilet, hot shower, kitchenette with gas cooker and electric plug, and cost an extra 1 500 MT a day. The above rates are all for in-season – there is a 40% discount for out-of-season. There is also a water sports centre on the premises. For reservations and more info, tel: +27-(0)82-569-3436, fax: +27-(0)13-750-3202, e-mail: paindane.sa@mweb.co.za, website: www.paindane.com.

On the beach south of Paindane are a couple of low-key, difficult-to-reach resorts. Some naughty people ride along the beach at low tide, but this is illegal and you are liable to be fined 20 000 MT if caught by the *maritimos*. About 5 kilometres down, as the seagull flies, is the small, ecologically friendly **Casa de Mar**. Des Dandridge has reed huts in the dunes overlooking the beach and can be contacted in South Africa, tel: +27-(0)83-789-5522 or +27-(0)31-266-4716, e-mail: casademar@iafrica.com, website: www.casademar.co.za.

A couple of kilometres further down the beach is a larger, sprawling collection of reed huts and campsites that is **Ilha da Rochas**. Set among the bushes on the dunes overlooking a small offshore rock island, they can be reached on tel: 82-410-5460, or contact Michelle in South Africa on +27-(0)11-893-3110 or +27-(0)83-272-2224.

Back in **Praia de Jangamo**, there are three more popular resorts. The first, just 3.5 kilometres north of Paindane, is **Guinjata Bay**. This large, attractive, up-market complex overlooks a bay and small headland and has a beautiful beach and protected boat- launching area. The restaurant is one of the most attractive I've seen in a lodge in Mozambique, and there is a nautically themed bar and surprisingly well-stocked little shop (booze, batteries, toiletries, fishing and snorkelling gear, as well as basic foodstuffs, charcoal and ice). They offer fly-in packages to Inhambane and diving and fishing excursions from their on-site water sports centre. Catered accommodation costs from 2 700 MT a person for diner, bed and breakfast in low seson to 3 400 MT a person for full board in high season. Self-catering is available in chalets that sleep between four and 16 people. The four-bedder costs 4 600 MT

in low season and 7 160 MT in high. Camping is available under protective *baraccas* equipped with water and electricity for 320 MT per person per night in low season and 480 MT per person plus 1 800 MT per site per night in high season. For bookings and more info, tel: +27-(0)13-741-2795 or +27-(0)83-283-6918, fax: +27-(0)13-741-3149, e-mail: reservations@guinjata.com, website: www.guinjata.com.

Next door to Guinjata is the **Jangamo Beach Holiday Resort**. Although it was once a top spot, it was experiencing management problems and going downhill fast when I last visited. Accommodation was available in the main building at 800 MT a person, while four-bed cabanas cost about 3 000 MT each. Contact Jangamo Beach in South Africa, tel/fax: +27-(0)13-750-2439, e-mail: allan.whitehouse@worldonline.co.za, website: www.jangamo.co.za.

Also in Guinjata are **McGyver Self Catering Chalets**, which have one four-sleeper and two six-sleeper chalets, each with a full sea view. Contact owner/manager Lynette Adams on tel: +27-(0)83-588-0217 or +27-(0)11-425-2052, e-mail: lynadams@mweb.co.za. Fishing charters can be arranged. A 4×4 is essential to reach these chalets.

Colin Jefferies has been involved with both Paindane and Guinjata, but has now developed his own place next door called **Jeff's Palm Resort**. Solidly built villas sleep eight people in four en-suite bedrooms around a central open-plan living room. Prices per villa range from 6 700 MT in low season to 8 600 MT in season. Smaller cabanas sleep four in two bedrooms for between

The coastline stretching from Inhambane boasts many picturesque resorts.

2 600 MT and 3 850 MT. All villas and cabanas are fully equipped with bedding, cooking utensils, freezer and gas cooker. For bookings or more info, tel: +27-(0)83-254-4685, tel/fax: +27-(0)13-932-1263, e-mail: jeffsmoz@mweb.co.za, website: www.jeffsmoz.com, or in Moz, tel: 84-690-1310.

Another operation at Guinjata Bay is **Seabound Charters**, run by Ralph and Celeste Jones (the first place on your left if you are arriving from Inhambane). They offer exclusive and personalised fishing charters and are always available, unlike so many advertised fishing concerns that only operate in the height of season. Ralph has good local knowledge and supplies everything you need – rods, tackle, bait and licences. Barracuda and dorado are plentiful, and he charges 6 000 MT a day to fish for marlin, 4 800 MT to fly-fish, and 2 400 MT for a two-hour introduction to fishing. They also have a well-appointed self-catering guest flat that sleeps six in luxury and comfort. It costs 3 900 MT a night, but only 3 000 MT if you are fishing with them. Contact them in Mozambique on tel: 84-314-8730 or in South Africa on tel: +27-(0)73-938-4409.

## On to Inhambane Town

Heading back to Inhambane, the sandy track becomes a harder surface after about 7 kilometres, at the turn-off (S24°00.195 E35°28.508) to **Baia dos Cocos** (Coconut Bay).

A sandy 3 kilometres down through palms and casava fields brings us to the only Mozambican-owned resort in the area. I liked the atmosphere at this low-key resort. The layout is neat and orderly, with grassed terraces and surfaced roads. A small bar and restaurant serves genuine local dishes, cooked by Rosa the chef/manager; the beach has good surf, and it doesn't look like another Jo'burg-let-your-hair-down kind of resort. Prices are reasonable too – with camping costing 200 MT per site and 200 MT per person in low season (double in season), reed-hut *casitas* for two at 1800 MT to 3000 MT, rondavels for four at 3300 MT to 6000 MT, and chalets that sleep six at 5700 MT out of season and 9000 MT in season. Chalets and rondavels are neat, brick-built units, fully equipped with hot water, fridge, hotplate and all kitchen utensils. For information, tel: 82-311-7250 or 293-20882, e-mail: reservations@coconutbay. co.za, website: www.coconutbay.co.za.

The main road to Inhambane is intersected (S23°56.693 E35°23.894) just 11 kilometres from the Coconut Bay turn-off and Inhambane town is just 9 kilometres further on. Av Eduardo Mondlane ushers you in along the waterfront, past the hospital, and to the jetty in the centre of town. Here you can catch the regular passenger ferry (every 20 minutes or so) across the bay to Maxixe on the mainland (3.5 kilometres and it takes about 40 minutes by sailing dhow). Dhows will also ferry you to Linga Linga or the two small uninhabited islands in the bay, Ratos and Porcos. Just past the jetty, on the waterfront in Rua 3 de Fevereiro, is **Pensão Pachica**, a clean,

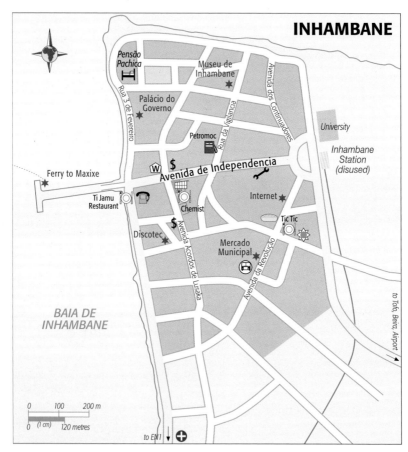

## The Museum of Inhambane

This museum is in Av da Vigilancia, off the Av da Independencia. It has a good collection of old photographs dating back to the early colonial period and a full range of artefacts, including farming implements and musical instruments.

quiet house offering double rooms with mozzie nets and immaculate linen for 3 000 MT or dorm accommodation for 250 MT. Safe parking is available in the backyard, there is a fully-equipped kitchen, and info and help with local excursions is available too. For details, tel: 82-355-9590, e-mail: farolturismo@teledata.mz, website: www.barralighthouse.com.

Up the wide Av de Independencia, which runs from the jetty, you will find a general dealer, bank for changing money and an ATM, petrol station and the old train station at the top. Turn right at the traffic circle here and you will head out of town towards Tofo and Barra.

But further right around the circle brings you into Av da Revolucao. This street has all the action, with an internet office, bakery, restaurants and a bustling market – stock up here before you head out to the beaches again. *Chapas* also leave from here to Barra, Tofo and the main EN1 highway at Lindela (to connect with the intercity buses). If you plan on staying over and want to rave it up, try the **Discoteca Zoom**, Rua da Chimoio (behind the Casa da Cultura), which is open from 18h00 till late.

They offer a bar, pool table, snacks and a night club, so for the lowdown, tel: 82-424-9140.

## Tofo

The road passes the airport on its way out of Inhambane, and after about 18 kilometres (S23°50.698 E35°30.069) you will reach the Bar Babalaza. Turn off right here to Tofo, or carry on straight to Barra. This popular crossroads spot can become quite crowded as expats and holiday-makers pop in for sun-downers or a bite to eat (they also sell ice). The tarred road continues for another 6 kilometres down to Tofo and ends at the market and *chapas* stand, opposite the main beach. Because of its easy access, this beautiful spot is visited by local Inhambane residents over the weekends to picnic and play soccer on the sands. The laid-back lifestyle at the campsites, resorts and hotels of the area draws foreign visitors from far and wide too, particularly backpackers, but Tofo is spread out enough to handle them all.

Left of the market is the neat little double-storeyed **Hotel Tofo Mar**. With secure and shaded parking in the street (where they will also wash your car for you), they offer sea-facing double rooms for 3 200 MT (single 2 100 MT). A kettle with tea and coffee is supplied, and breakfast is included. They also have cheaper non-sea-facing rooms or more expensive air-conditioned suites. For bookings, tel/fax: 293-29043, e-mail: info@hotel-tofomar.com, website: www.hotel-tofomar.com.

Just across the road, on the corner, is **Mundos**, a motel-styled establishment offering air-conditioned en-suite rooms with three beds and kitchenette (not equipped). Excellent security, shaded parking and a spacious bar/restaurant makes this a good, simple, value-for-money option. Just up the side street is **Casa de Comer** restaurant. They not only offer delicious Mozambican and French cuisine, but serve the best espresso in town.

Heading north along the coast brings us to more places to stay. The first is **Nordin's Lodge**. Although a little run-down, with poor security, they do have a great position right on the beach and only charge 5 600 MT for a four-bed chalet. **Fatima's Nest** is next. This well-known place has seen better days and is now looking a bit tatty. With a bar/restaurant on the beach, communal kitchen and very basic ablutions, they charge 300 MT for camping, 450 MT for a dorm bed, and 900 MT single, 1 050 MT double in small reed huts. Book through Fatima's in Maputo.

Next along is **Dino's Beach Bar**, a great, multilevelled, vibey spot with cool music, cold beer and hot pizzas. There is also a shop selling hand-made shirts, skirts, trousers and bikinis made from the colourful local cloth – the resident tailor will make anything to order while you take refreshments at the bar. There is also a wi-fi internet café on the upper level, which offers light snacks, milkshakes and fresh fruit smoothies. At the end of this sandy track (1.5 kilometres from Fatima's) is **Bamboozi's**. They offer camping, have a small swimming pool and A-frame chalets with equipped kitchens. A very large, airy rondavel serves as a dorm and they also have small reed huts. The funky ablution block has hot water and the big open-air communal kitchen is well equipped. Huts cost 600 MT a person, dorms 520 MT and the three-sleeper chalets are 3 000 MT, and camping is 480 MT a person. For information, tel: 293-29040, e-mail: reservations@bamboozibeachlodge.com, website: www.bamboozibeachlodge.com.

Not far from Bamboozi's is a horse-riding stable, run by Volker. He has 10 horses and offers lessons and rides along the beach or through the coconut plantations. Your first ride will cost 500 MT, but the price decreases with subsequent bookings or if you are in a group. Contact Volker, tel: 82-308-0300 or 82-391-5680, or book through Tofo Travel, website: www.tofotravel.com.

There are also three dive operations in Tofo. **Diversity Scuba** is situated in the village behind the market and near to the Casa de Camer restaurant, tel: 293-29002, e-mail: info@ diversityscuba.com, website: www. diversityscuba.com. Another dive shop operates from near Dunes Bar and is called **Tofo Scuba**, tel: 293-29030 or 82-826-0140, e-mail: tofoscuba@ teledata.mz, website: www.tofoscuba. co.za. And last but not least is **Liquid Adventures** situated at Bamboozi's (see Bamboozi's website for details). All offer PADI courses, have equipment to hire and will show you the area's wide variety of marine life, including mantas, whale sharks, dolphins, humpback whales and turtles.

Also in Tofo are **Tofo Beach Cottages**, seven self-catering cottages, in various sites around Tofo and Tofinho. The cottages offer rustic-style basic accommodation. Some of the cottages are adjacent to each other, which offers flexibility when accommodation is required for a large group. Casey (the owner/manager) and Raule see to the well-being of guests. The cottages are equipped and serviced and cater for groups of between four and eight persons. Each cottage offers the basics, including cutlery, crockery, bedding and furnishing. Tariffs range between 1800 MT per night and 5200 MT per night, depending on season and size. Potential visitors can check availability and make a reservation on their website: www.tofo.co.za, or contact Christa de Villiers at e-mail: bookings@tofo.co.za or tel: +27-(0)72-129-4278 or Casey on tel: 82-426-5840 (office hours).

A few hundred meters before you get to the village of Tofo turn right, to **Casa Barry Beach Lodge**. This well-run and organised resort is situated right on the beach, where self-catering chalets shelter under whispering casuarina trees. The costs are 5245 MT for four people, and 6540 MT for six. Basic four-bed reed bungalows cost 1200 MT a person. The restaurant has a spacious wooden deck overlooking the beach and serves tasty snacks, food and drinks all day. It is a large, professionally run resort in a good position. Contact them, tel: 293-29007 or, in South Africa, +27-(0)31-767-0111, e-mail: peggy@dbnmail.co.za, website: www.casabarry.com.

Casa Barry Beach Lodge is also home to the now famous **Foundation for the Protection of Marine Mega Fauna**. Dr Andrea Marshall and Dr Simon Pearce run the Foundation and all of its marine research from Casa Barry Beach Resort. The project aims to study and protect manta rays along this stretch of coast. As many as 30 mantas have been spotted on a single dive, and this site boasts the only recorded observations of their mating and birth in the world. Contact Andrea in Mozambique, tel: 82-352-1030 or in South Africa, tel: +27-(0)82-478-9251, e-mail: andrea.marshall@uq.edu.au. The researchers provide three interactive talks each week in the Casa Barry big-screen room for anyone interested in the marine life and their research in Tofo.

Behind them on the hill is **Paradise Dunes**, a collection of solidly built holiday homes that sleep four, six or eight in comfort and style. The kitchens are particularly well equipped, with both fridge and freezer. Two-bedroomed houses cost 1680 MT a night out of season and 2400 MT in season, three bedrooms 2520 MT to 3600 MT, and four bedrooms 3360 MT to 4800 MT. Book through Tofo Travel, tel: 293-56188 or 82-426-5840, e-mail: info@tofotravel.com, website: www.tofotravel.com.

The small residential area of **Tofinho** has a Frelimo monument to fallen heroes on the headland, near to where unfortunate victims of the colonial era were thrown into a sea cave to be drowned by the rising tide. The waves off the point here make this Mozambique's best surfing spot, and the breaks known as 'Backdoor' and 'Monument' are spoken of around the world. **Turtle Cove Lodge** is a couple of blocks back from the beach (signposted). It offers dorm

Beach driving is strictly forbidden, except at certain boat-launching sites.

beds at 320 MT and accommodation in reed chalets for 400 MT a person, en-suite double rooms are 1100 MT and camping is 200 MT a person. Lazy hammocks and a star-gazing platform make this a great chilling spot. Contact Charles, tel: 82-430-2880 or Nic at Mozambique Connections in South Africa, tel: +27-(0)11-803-4185, website: www.mozcon.com.

Another place that offers accommodation in the area is the **Blue Roof**. Nice double-bedded, self-contained cottages (with fridge, hotplate and utensils) overlook the best surfing spots and are a bargain at 1500 MT a night per cottage. Contact Blue Roof, tel: 82-818-2470 or book through Fatima's in Maputo.

## Barra

Back at Bar Babalaza, turn right onto a good dirt road and head towards Barra. After 5 kilometres there is a turn-off to the right that will take you to the lighthouse at **Ponta da Barra** (signposted to Farol da Barro 4×4 Campsite). You will need a 4×4 for this 2.3-kilometre track, but you'll

be rewarded with one of the most beautiful sights along this coast. The lighthouse is situated on a high bluff with a fantastic view back along the beach towards Barra Lodge.

There is also a picturesque campsite that you can stay at here, which shares the spot and the view. **Lighthouse Campsite** is run by Dennis Adams and, although it is a bit rustic, there are plans to renovate the old governor's weekend retreat into a more permanent bar/ restaurant. The ablutions are fine and the security good. Dennis is an imaginative cook and only serves filter coffee, no instant. He allows no quadbikes, no jetskis and no loud music. In season, he charges 520 MT per person, while out of season it is 360 MT. His son Derrick organises occasional one-week tour packages from Johannesburg (check the website for more details). For more information, tel: 84-389-5217, or in South Africa, +27-(0)73-313-2456, e-mail: farolturismo@teledata.mz, website: www.barralighthouse.com.

From the lighthouse, take the short cut to the beach towards Barra Lodge (stay on the sand track road and not on the beach). There are a number of lodges along this stretch. First up is **Barra Estates**, which can accommodate 38 people in two-, four- and six-bed chalets, all fully equipped for self-catering. They also have two large entertainment areas with fully equipped kitchens (including fridges and freezers), a pub and large covered decks with views of the sea. Rates start at 1 200 MT for the two-bed chalets, 2 400 MT for four-bed chalets and 3 600 MT for six-bed chalets. For further details, visit website: www.barraproperties.com, e-mail: info@barraproperties.com or contact Anton van Huyssteen on +27-(0)13-753-3474 or +27-(0)82-460-2139, or the on-site manager Miguel on tel: 84-878-1370.

Next up you will find **Barra-Cuda Lodge** on the beach. This self-catering lodge sleeps a total of 60 people in houses that can accommodate four to 16 people. Each house is fully equipped with bedding, fans, mosquito nets, en-suite rooms as well as beds in the lounge areas. They are fully equipped for self-catering with fridges and freezers, diningroom tables and chairs, stoves, and a gas braai for every unit. All cutlery, crockery and pots are supplied. Prices vary from 2 800 MT to 22 000 MT per unit depending on the size of each unit. For more information, tel: +27-(0)82-321-3439, or go to the website: www.barra-cuda.com.

Also on Lighthouse Road are **Montanha Lodge** and **Montanha Valley** (www.montanhalodge.co.za). These are comfortable self-catering wooden *casitas* and chalets available for holiday rentals. The lodge is nestled in a palm plantation behind the primary dune, 300 metres from beach and has a restaurant, bar and swimming pool. Chalets are serviced daily and have 24-hour electricity and borehole water. Contact Susan Lee, tel: +27-(0)82-572-6275, e-mail: info@mozmate.co.za. Rates range from two–four-sleeper *casitas* at 1 600 MT per night to eight–ten-sleeper chalets at 5 200 MT per night in the low season and 4 000 MT to 7 200 MT in the peak season.

In the same area, **Cowrie Lodge** (www.upandgo.co.za) has great views of the Barra coastline and beyond, and provides traditional *casitas* with privacy, security, 24-hour electricity, borehole water and serviced chalets. Contact Susan Lee, tel: +27-(0)82-572-6275, e-mail: info@mozmate.co.za. Rates range from 780 MT per person per night in the low season to four-sleeper chalets at 4 800 MT per day in the peak season.

**Bay View Lodge** and **Bay View Estate** (S23°47.129 E35°29.901) are situated on the beach, in brick and thatch one- and two-bedroomed, fully equipped self-catering units. Bedrooms are air-conditioned and en-suite, linen and bathroom towels are supplied and all units are serviced daily. In addition to the chalets, there is a large house that can sleep 16 persons in eight air-conditioned bedrooms. Rates are from 2 400 MT for a one-bedroomed unit in low season to 10 000 MT for a six-sleeper two-bedroomed unit in December. Contact tel: +27-(0)82-902-4628, e-mail: info@bayviewlodgemoz.com, website: www.bayviewlodgemoz.com.

Also along this stretch of coast is the complex that consists of Barra

Lodge and Flamingo Bay (about 1 kilometre apart). **Barra Lodge** (S23°47.509 E35°30.646) is the largest of the three and the first along this road. Built right on the beach, the lodge nestles among coconut groves, and all the accommodation has sea views. There is also a beach bar, large exotically shaped and landscaped swimming pool, games room, activities centre and a 60-seater restaurant. They offer sailing trips on a 33-foot catamaran, snorkelling and scuba diving, quadbike trails, fishing and horse-riding. This is a big professional operation that can tailor-make your holiday, wedding or honeymoon, depending on your needs.

Twin-bedded *casitas* with en-suite shower and toilet are 4160 MT per person, dinner, bed and breakfast in low season, and 4860 MT in high season; self-catering two-bedroomed cottages that sleep six have big verandas and cost 6220 MT and 9000 MT. The lodge has constructed a wooden walkway over a nearby mangrove swamp, which gives an interesting glimpse of life in the tidal zone. They also offer fly-in packages and good dive packages. For reservations in South Africa, tel: +27-(0)11-314-3355, fax: +27-(0)11-314-3239, e-mail: info@barraresorts.com, website: www.barraresorts.com. Alternatively, you could contact Barra Lodge locally, tel/fax: 293-20561.

Next up are the **Ocean View Chalets** that offer self-catering in comfortable chalets right on the beach. All units come fully equipped with fridge, stove, cutlery, crockery and linen, and there is also a restaurant on the premises. Rates start at 2400 MT for a four-bed chalet in low season and rise to 7000 MT for an eight-bedder in high season. Contact them through ocean_view_barra@mozbookings.com and view the website at www.mozambiquetravelservice.com.

The newest and best lodge along this stretch (or any other stretch, for that matter) is the magnificent and exotic **Flamingo Bay Resort**. Conceived and constructed by Dave Law of Barra Lodge, it consists of 20 luxury chalets built on stilts over the waters of a protected bay. The spacious main building is built on a small island and the whole complex is interconnected by wooden bridges and walkways. Chauffeur-driven golf carts ferry you around. Guests can go diving off the porch of their chalets or swim in the pool that gave Dave so many headaches while he was building it. Contact Barra Lodge for bookings and more information on what Flamingo Bay has to offer.

Finally, right out on the tip of the Barra peninsula, in an unbeatable location, is **Areia Branca Lodge**. The lodge is built under coconut trees, and the chalets are situated on the lagoon side of Barra peninsula. Areia Branca has 17 two-bedroomed (sleep six) self-catering chalets at 450 MT per person per night in low season and 3 800 MT per chalet per night in high season. Camping is 210 MT and 380 MT per person (high and low season). Each campsite has a thatched canopy with an electrical plug point and a light. For reservations and more info, contact Joey, tel: 82-716-4820, e-mail: areiabranca@tdm.co.mz, website: www.areiabranca.co.za.

# North to Vilankulo

From Inhambane, you have to retrace your steps to rejoin the main road north (EN1). This can be done by driving down to the main intersection at Lindela or by turning right 24 kilometres south of Inhambane. This 5.5-kilometre short cut is a good dirt road that joins the EN1 about 20 kilometres south of Maxixe and saves about 12 kilometres on the road.

Murals are a fairly common form of artistic expression, and you will see them on many walls in Mozambique, especially in and around the towns.

**109**

## Maxixe

Maxixe (pronounced *masheesh*) is a pretty little waterfront town situated just across the bay from Inhambane. The Shell service station on the south side of town has a small shop, air for pumping your tyres and sometimes even unleaded petrol.

The **Campismo de Maxixe** is in the centre of town, on the right just before the ferry jetty. This pleasantly situated campsite is on the water's edge and has good security. Brick-built bungalows for two with en-suite facilities cost 700 MT per night, cottages that also sleep two but have shared ablutions cost 800 MT a night, while campsites (most have electric plugs) are 170 MT a person. For further information and enquiries, tel: 293-30351.

Just past the jetty, in a welcoming cool garden under huge flamboyant trees, is the Stop Restaurant. This is a good spot to break your journey for a bite to eat or something cool to drink, and they also do takeaways. Across the road from the jetty is another petrol station, bank, cellphone shop and closed-down hotel. A few blocks north on the left-hand side of the road is the **Residencial Tania**, which offers bright and clean accommodation on the second floor of a rather dirty and dingy building. En-suite rooms cost 750 MT single and 850 MT double. Contact the Residencial Tania, tel: 293-30059.

The road north of Maxixe is very badly potholed, but they are working on it. After about 30 kilometres, you reach the little town of Morrumbene; turn right here to visit fascinating Linga Linga.

## Linga Linga

Situated at the end of the peninsula jutting into the northern side of Inhambane Bay, Linga Linga is the site of an old whaling station. Accessible only with 4×4 or by boat from Inhambane, Maxixe or Morrumbene, there is good birding and fishing in the area and, if you're lucky, you might even spot a dugong. White sandy beaches to relax on and the popular **Linga Linga Lodge** for accommodation – what more do you want for a few days of chilling? Self-catering cottages range from 3 150 MT a night for a four-bed chalet in low season to 3 850 MT in high season. Book through www.mozambiquetravelservice.com.

## Massinga

Just before reaching Massinga, you will cross the Tropic of Capricorn – you are now officially in the tropics. For food and accommodation in Massinga, you need only one name – **Dalilo's**. The restaurant of that name is in the centre of town and the hotel is on the left-hand side of the main street a few blocks up. Plain double rooms with shared facilities cost 500 MT, en-suite with bedroom and a little veranda is 750 MT and, for 1 500 MT, they'll throw in a TV, air-con and fridge. For details, tel: 293-71043.

## Morrungulo

About 8 kilometres north of the centre of Massinga is the turn-off right to Morrungulo, and 13 kilometres down a good dirt road brings you to the gates and reception of **Morrungulo Holiday Resort** (S23°14.047 E35°29.401). This is a well-established and well-run place with neat lawns under large shade trees. A small wetland area has good birdlife and tame crested guineafowl roam the camp. The beach is at your chalet's doorstep and the whole place is spacious enough not to get too crowded. Four-sleeper, fully-equipped chalets cost 3000 MT and upwards. Camping is 300 MT a person and another 600 MT if you want the comfort of a *barracca*. For more information, e-mail: morrungulo@1wayafrica.com, website: www.morrungulo.co.za.

There are two other establishments in this area. Just before you reach the Morrungulo Resort, there is a turn-off on the left that leads to **Baobab Lodge**. This is the backpacker's alternative for the budget-conscious traveller. High on a hill overlooking the bay, this rustic, locally run spot offers camping at 200 MT in season and 130 MT otherwise, and two-bed reed huts with shared ablutions cost 1 000 MT and 800 MT.

The other camp is much smarter. **Sylvia Shoal Resort and Adventure Divers** is signposted off the road down to Morrun-gulo and is set among grassed dunes just above the beach. They offer bungalows with bathrooms and kitchenettes that sleep two, but are equipped for six so that extra family and friends can camp next to the bungalow and share with you. Bungalows range between 2 100 MT and 3 700 MT (seasons) and camping is between 400 MT and 450 MT a person. *Baraccas* cost an extra 320 MT to 800 MT. The dive operation offers all the usual scuba courses, as well as snorkelling and fishing. For more info and bookings, contact tel: +27-(0)83-270-7582 or +27-(0)71-319-6788, e-mail: merle@stfrancis.co.za or lesley@stfrancis.co.za, website: www.mozambique1.com.

## Pomene

Resisting the local kids' cries of 'Sweeeeets' on the drive back up to the EN1, continue for only a quarter of a kilometre up the main road, and turn off again (S23°15.281 E35°22.280) for the drive down to Pomene. The kids along this road are far more discerning than those down the Morrungulo road, for instead of begging for sweets, the cry is for 'Chocolaaaate'. This is also a rougher road, especially the last 9 kilometres, which are very narrow and sandy. Beautiful coastal dune forest gives way to a mangrove swamp and you end up dodging rather large land crabs as you wind your way down to this gloriously isolated spot. The sea breaks gently onto an endless sandy beach, while birds feed in the lagoon just behind you. A river forms a mangrove-ringed estuary and it's a birder's paradise. Sparsely populated and unspoilt, this is also a good spot to look for the illusive dugongs. Fortunately, 20 000 hectares of the surrounding area was declared the **Pomene Reserve** in 1972 and this wonderful ecosystem of mangroves, dunes and lagoon with its birds and marine life is protected.

The road runs all the way to the headland at the end of the bay where the empty shell of what was once the Pomene Hotel stands, begging to be renovated. The view from here is magnificent and when it is once more made habitable, I would love to be one of the first guests.

But back along the beach (more 4×4 driving) is the very comfortable **Pomene Lodge**. The resort offers all the amenities such as restaurant, bar and curio shop, as well as organising diving and fishing activities. Self-catering cottages have their own toilet and shower with hot and cold water, as well as cutlery, crockery, a two-plate gas cooker, freezer, mosquito nets and bedding. Costs range from 4 000 MT for a three-sleeper out of season to 5 750 MT a day for a six-sleeper in season. Camping costs 550 MT per person per day. Pomene Lodge is owned and operated by the folks at Barra Lodge, so for bookings and info, contact their South African office, tel: +27-(0)11-314-3355, e-mail: info@barraresorts.com or website: www.barraresorts.com or www.pomene.co.za.

Slightly inland, near to the airstrip (850 metres long and a great way to visit the area if you are lucky enough to own a plane) is the new **Pomene View Lodge** (S22°56.945 E35°35.145). Solidly built with bricks and mortar (one gets a little tired of all the quaint rustic bamboo huts sometimes), it sits high on a hill and overlooks one of the best views in Mozambique. Created by the friendly father-and-son team of Clint and Dave Krause, Pomene View has big shade trees (the grass is still struggling), large braai boma, wooden deck with the famous view and a swimming pool. They offer walks through various habitats where the birding is outstanding (fish eagles, flamingos and kingfishers, to name

a few of the common ones). The spacious accommodation is fully equipped to sleep five and costs 1 800 MT to 2 700 MT, depending on season). They can be contacted through tel: 84-465-4572, email: dave@pomeneview.co.za, website: www.pomeneview.co.za.

On the drive back to the main EN1 highway, stop at a little marshy lake along the way (S23°12.003 E35°23.043). This lily-covered waterway is another fine birding spot.

Yet another accommodation option in the Pomene Bay area is **Casa Rei** on the north bank of the estuary. Ray Preen is an experienced Springbok fisherman with two world and 18 South African records to his name and is passionate about conserving his little piece of paradise. It's difficult to reach, as the road is not the same as for the south-bank resorts (Ray's very detailed instructions for the three-hour, 65-kilometre route take up no less than two foolscap pages). Accommodation is in six self-contained camps on the water's edge, each equipped to cater for up to eight people. Each camp has four two-bed reed huts, a living-room lapa, kitchen, shower and toilet. Cooking is over an open fire and lighting is by paraffin lamp, but you are allocated trained staff to do everything for you. Bring all you need, and relax, relax, relax. For info and bookings, tel: +27-(0)82-882-0067 or +27-(0)82-344-2677, e-mail: paul@casarei.co.za, website: www.casarei.co.za.

The road on up to Vilankulo is often badly potholed, but work is in progress. No reliable fuel is available until you get into the town of Vilankulo itself.

# 16

# Vilankulo and the Bazaruto Archipelago

About 146 kilometres from the Pomene turn-off, you will reach the poorly signposted road down to Vilankulo – you will recognise it by the large radio towers and small market that has sprung up (S21°59.825 E35°08.710). The countyside around here is pockmarked with small, round lakes, the origin of which, some believe, is a meteorite shower. Just before reaching Vilankulo, you will pass the turn-off (on the right) to the airport (fly-in options are available, so see Chapter 9) and, about 18.5 kilometres down, you will reach the main T-junction in Vilankulo town. Turn right for the market, village shops and fuel, or left to reach the harbour and most of the accommodation and restaurants. It is not a large town, but is quite spread out.

Trek-net fishing keeps the markets of Vilankulo well stocked with fresh fish.

## Introducing Vilankulo

If you start your tour of Vilankulo by turning right, you will run straight into the municipal market a couple of blocks down, passing small restaurants and a bakery on your right and a bank and pharmacy on your left. This is not only the hub of most commercial activity, but also where to go for public transport. Buses to Maputo and Beira leave in the early morning, but make local enquiries for the latest info. Turn left at the market and head down to the town's fuel station. This is also the part of town where you can stock up with supplies if you are going across to the islands or heading further north up the coast. Drive back around the block and stop at the Mozambicano bakery for fresh bread, pastries and coffee before making your way back to the central intersection.

Heading down the main street away from the market area, you will pass a fuel station on the left, opposite the new fresh produce market (turn right further on if you need the hospital). A little further down, on the right, is the turn-off down to Complexo Bimbi, then Café Edson and Motel Darcia, the Deli and Talho Butchery. The popular Na Sombra restaurant and rooms are next on your left, then there's the Luxus building with take-away, shops and rooms upstairs. Opposite, you will see Taurus supermarket, just before a bank (with ATM). Curios and fresh fish are sold at the T-junction, where this road runs up against the bayside beach.

Turn left here. The road follows the beach, with its boatbuilders, until you reach the new Hotel Pescador, and Casa Rex restaurant and accommodation. Across the road is the Ka Massingue Snackbar and the Maritime Office (the place to go to arrange a boat-launching licence). Next is the Vilankulo Conference Centre, shortly followed by the Aguia Negra Resort and, finally, the Vilankulo Beach Lodge.

Back at the junction, you could turn right to pass the Saverite supermarket, Smugglers bar, restaurant and accommodation and then carry on to the Hotel Dona Ana. This beautiful old hotel is currently being restored and is situated on the headland of the little Vilankulo harbour, with boats bobbing in the bay on one side and a palm-fringed beach on the other. Dhows and ferries to the islands leave from the little jetty here. Swing right and continue down the beach front. You will pass Sail Away and then reach Vilankulo camping on your right. A little further on is the Tropical Restaurant on your left and Casa Josef on your right. Look carefully to spot the little lane that leads off right to the Zombie Cucumber (all will be revealed later...). This beachfront road will eventually lead you past Dolphin Dhow and Transport, Margie's Tourist Services with book exchange, tours and transfers, and Veranda restaurant and rooms, to Baobab Beach Backpackers and Odyssea Dive.

To reach the southern beaches of Chibuene, turn right upon entering town and, soon after you see the cellphone towers, onto a gravel road opposite Vilankulo Madeira. After 5 kilometres, you will begin to see signposts on the left, indicating Dona Soraya restaurant and rooms,

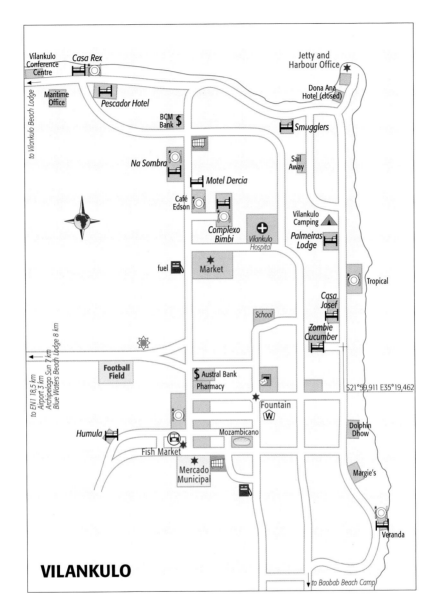

**VILANKULO**

Vilankulo Conference Centre
Casa Rex
Jetty and Harbour Office
Maritime Office
Pescador Hotel
Dona Ana Hotel (closed)
BCM Bank
Smugglers
Na Sombra
Sail Away
Motel Dercia
Café Edson
Vilankulo Camping
Complexo Bimbi
Vilankulo Hospital
Palmeiras Lodge
fuel
Market
Tropical
Casa Josef
School
Zombie Cucumber
S21°59,911 E35°19,462
Football Field
Austral Bank
Pharmacy
Fountain
Humula
Mozambicano
Dolphin Dhow
Fish Market
Mercado Municipal
Margie's
Veranda
to Baobab Beach Camp

to Vilankulo Beach Lodge

to EN1 18,5 km
Airport 3 km
Archipelago Sun 7 km
Blue Waters Beach Lodge 8 km

Archipelago Resort and Dive Bazaruto, Casa Guci restaurant and chalets, Blue Water Beach restaurant and accommodation and, finally, Vila dos Sonhos. Mozambique Horse Safaris operate on this beach too and they collect from town and southern lodges.

Vilankulo is growing rapidly – get up-to-date information from www.vilankulo.com or www.vilanculos.org.

## Overnight in Vilankulo

There is a lot of accommodation on offer in Vilankulo – in fact, it starts 13 kilometres from the EN1, before you even reach the town. A turn-off to the left (S21°59.971 E35°17.072) is signposted to the Archipelago Sun and the Blue Water Beach Resort, both about 7 kilometres down this dirt road and nicely isolated from the hustle and bustle of Vilankulo town. **Blue Waters** is a well-tended, secure spot with grass and shade just above the beach. Compact en-suite, self-catering bungalows that sleep two cost 3 000 MT, larger four-sleeper bungalows are 4 500 MT, and six-sleepers cost 5 200 MT. There is also camping at 400 MT a person. Contact, tel: 82-807-5750, South Africa, tel: +27-(0)78-618-1969, e-mail: brian@vilanculosresorts.com, website: www.vilanculosresorts.com.

The nearby **Archipelago Sun** used to be called Baia do Paraiso, but has been considerably upgraded and now has 18 large houses, each one fully equipped for six people. Sea-facing units cost 7 000 MT and others are 6 000 MT a night. There is a water sports centre on site. For bookings, +27-(0)21-683-6444, e-mail: reservations@ archipelago-resort.com, website: www. archipelago-resort.com.

Nearby **Casa Guci** offers accommodation, a restaurant, a pool and reputedly the best pizzas in Vilankulo. Contact Uli on tel: 82-868-6540. Also nearby is **Vila dos Sonhos**, which offers the most discerning self-catering accommodation on the bay, with an eight-passenger island-hop boat for hire. Nightly rates are 14 000 MT for up to eight residents.

For bookings, tel: 84-307-4130, e-mail: landco@tdm.co.mz.

The other accommodation areas are the main beach and town centre (for value-for-money options), and the smarter up-market resorts north of town. We start down at the southern end of the beach at the **Baobab Beach Camp**. Past its sell-by date and with bad security, I hope that it might one day be renovated. The cost of camping is 200 MT, dorm beds cost 300 MT and small reed huts with a double bed cost 600 MT. Contact Mandy, tel: 82-731-5420 or 82-865-0210.

Still on the beachfront, but more central, is the totally different **Zombie Cucumber** – now this is how a backpackers' lodge should be run! Set in a pretty garden, down a narrow lane (S21°59.911 E35°19.462), there is both privacy and good security. Sabrina and Grande run this clean and compact little camp very well and offer dorm beds at 330 MT, and two-bed A-frame chalets at 980 MT. The shared ablutions are spotless, a washing service is offered and they cook a delicious special daily meal. Info and assistance are offered for all local activities – contact them on tel: 82-804-9410, e-mail: steph@ zombiecucumber.com, website: www. zombiecucumber.com.

Just up the road, also opposite the beach, is the old-established **Casa de Josef e Tina**. Situated on a large grassed property, it has en-suite reed rondavels for two people at 1 000 MT, and 1 500 MT for four people. Communal cooking is available in an open-air kitchen. There is also a large, self-catering house that offers accommodation

The islands and reefs of the Bazaruto Archipelago are protected as a national park.

for up to eight in well-equipped luxury for 4000 MT and camping is 200 MT per person. Contact, tel: 293-82140, e-mail: info@joseftina.com, website: www.joseftina.com.

The next place along this beach-front road is **Palmeiras Lodge**, set in exotic tropical gardens with a pool. Bed and breakfast in free-standing, en-suite chalets costs 3150 MT double. There is also a large, self-catering and serviced villa with backpackers' dorm accommodation for 500 MT per person. Palmeiras is managed and operated by the folks at Smugglers and they can be contacted on tel: 82-753-8980 or 84-829-2126, e-mail: smugglers@teledata.mz, website: www.smugglers.co.za.

Next door is **Vilankulo Camping**. With well-grassed sites under whispering casuarina trees, this spot is also past its prime, with poor security and scruffy ablutions. They were closed for business when last I visited, so check before booking on tel: 293-82043.

Continuing to the end of the beach-front, you will reach the **Hotel Dona**

**Ana**. This well-positioned place just can't stay closed forever, so watch the space...

Following the road around the harbour brings you to **Smugglers**, popular with families, locals and overland tour groups. There is a clean, casual and reasonably priced restaurant, vibey bar with darts, a pool table and international dance music. A secure, residents-only back garden with neatly trimmed lawns contains the accommodation. This consists of rows of rooms each with two beds, a table and fan, and leads out onto a veranda overlooking a swimming pool. The costs are 1500 MT double. Two double en-suite rooms are also available at 2250 MT. Laundry can be organised as well as just about anything else going on in Vilankulo. Contact Smugglers, tel: 82-753-8980, e-mail: smugglers@teledata.mz, website: www.smugglers.co.za.

At the central junction, swing left and away from the harbour to take the main road through town. Pass the bank on your right and you will spot

**Na Sombra**, one of the nicest locally flavoured restaurants in town. From continental breakfasts to evening grills and everything in between, this is the place in which to linger. There are also rooms – a bit basic and old, but jolly and clean. All have a fan and share facilities at a cost of 500 MT single, 700 MT double and 1000 MT for a four-bedder. There can be some noise from the bar at night. For the low-down, tel: 293-82090, or Oliver on tel: 82-762-4350.

Further down the road, on the left, is the **Motel Dercia**, behind Café Edson. A little garden, secure off-street parking, small en-suite A-frame chalets for 850 MT and plain double rooms for 670 MT make this a good budget option. For bookings, tel: 293-82070.

The final in-town accommodation is signposted off left further down the street. **Complexo Bimbi** is like a small village with two-bedroom and three-bedroom houses, each with air-con and TV in a quiet, secluded garden compound. Four-bedders cost 2800 MT and six-bedders 3500 MT. Contact the complex, tel: 293-82105.

## The resorts of Vilankulo

Heading back to the central junction, take a sharp left to follow the harbour road around to reach the up-market resorts of Vilankulo. First up on the left is the classy, new **Hotel Pescador**. Beautifully decorated, with views of the bay and islands, this compact luxury hotel offers air-conditioned comfort, bar, restaurant and sparkling pool. Rates range from 2400 MT to 4200 MT per person, sharing, and they can be

contacted on tel: 293-82312, e-mail: pescadormoz@hotmail.com, website: www.amazingmozambique.com.

Next up on the right is **Casa Rex**, recommended for a good, well-served meal in gracious surroundings. Casa Rex also has limited accommodation. Charmingly decorated with custom-crafted wood furniture, the rooms have views of the bay. The en-suite rooms with double bed cost 3300 MT, and a luxury suite is 5400 MT – all per person, with a single supplement of 900 MT. For bookings, tel: 293-82048, e-mail: info@casmaratrading.com, website: www.casa-rex.com.

Last, but definitely not least, is the recently renovated **Vilanculos Beach Lodge**, 5 kilometres from the town centre. From the secure parking area down to the main building with bar and restaurant, through the gardens and past the pool to the beachside dive and marine centre, this lodge feels welcoming and comfortable. The en-suite chalets all have great views from their own private balconies with rates from 4785 MT. For the latest information, tel: 293-82388, fax: 293-82314, e-mail: beachlodge@teledata.mz, website: www. vilanculos.co.za.

Finally, for bookings of all accommodation and activities, and information on transport and health issues, contact the **Vilankulo Tourist Information Office** behind the municipal offices. Tel: 82-525-0457.

## On the road in Vilankulo

**Vilankulo Service Centre**, beyond the bank and facing the harbour – formerly known as Dirk's/Sueine Centre/

VIP Nissan – is now run by Martina, tel: 82-627-2681/84-521-4559. Nearby is the workshop of **DTM Diesel**, tel: 82-758-5660, for general repairs, and **Dodo** has a new workshop on the road between the municipality and the Marginal beach road, tel: 82-891-4050. For mechanical repairs to boats or wet bikes, contact John at **Flamingo Marine**, tel: 82-501-0482, or Alfred, tel: 82-894-1907.

## Off to the archipelago

Vilankulo has always been a jumping-off point for the Bazaruto Archipelago and has struggled to keep tourists interested in staying in the town. The larger resorts to the north and south of town are making it very tempting with their water sports but, of course, most visitors want to get to the islands, or at least onto the water. **Sailaway Dhow Safaris** is situated one street back from the beach, near to Hotel Dona Ana, and offers day trips as well as two-, three-, and four-day dhow safaris. The day trips are to Magaruque Island, where you are free to snorkel the reef or wander the beaches. The cost per person of 2 160 MT includes dhow transport, park entry fees, use of snorkelling equipment and a seafood lunch on the beach. Overnight safaris visit Bazaruto, Benguerra and Magaruque, where you can snorkel the reefs and hike the islands. The cost of 3 900 MT per person per day includes tented accommodation, park entry fees, all meals, use of snorkelling equipment, and dhow transport. Each sailing dhow has a crew of three – captain, cook and translator/guide – and also has life jackets and a stand-by motor. For further

details, contact Sailaway tel: 293-82385 or 82-387-6350, e-mail: david@sailaway.co.za, website: www.sailaway.co.za.

Another highly recommended operation is **Dolphin Dhow Safaris**, run by the energetic Junior Cassamo. Situated along the main beachfront with beautiful views of the sea and islands, they offer not only dhow trips, but taxi and car hire, horse riding and accommodation. Their wedding proposal package (if you're in need of such a thing) is guaranteed to elicit a yes, and then you'll need their full honeymoon package! A double en-suite room costs 1 500 MT, a four-sleeper family room 2 000 MT, and dorm accommodation is 300 MT. Day trips to the islands are around 2 250 MT per person and overnighters cost 3 000 MT. Contact Junior on tel: 82-462-4700 or 293-82466, e-mail: dolphindhowvlk@yahoo.com, website: www.dolphindhow.ning.com.

The world-renowned **Bazaruto Archipelago National Park** consists of five pristine islands – Bazaruto, Benguerra, Magaruque, Bangue and Santa Carolina – all situated 10–20 kilometres offshore between Vilankulo in the south and Inhassoro in the north. The park is managed by the National Directorate for Conservation Areas in the Ministry of Tourism, in collaboration with the WWF and the Endangered Wildlife Trust. Bazaruto is the largest island, Bangue the smallest, and uninhabited. Santa Carolina, previously the most popular and known as Paradise Island, currently has no tourist facilities. Famous for the rich marine life around the islands – dugongs, whales, turtles and 2 000 fish species – there is

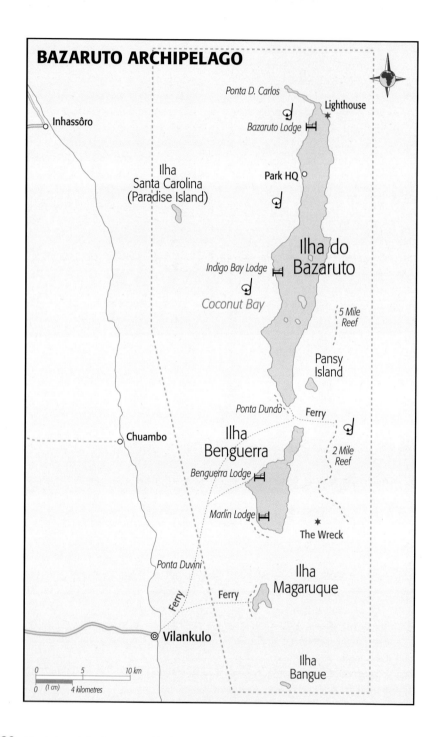

# BAZARUTO ARCHIPELAGO

Ponta D. Carlos

Lighthouse

Inhassôro

Bazaruto Lodge

Ilha
Santa Carolina
(Paradise Island)

Park HQ

Ilha do
Bazaruto

Indigo Bay Lodge

Coconut Bay

5 Mile
Reef

Pansy
Island

Ponta Dundo

Ferry

Chuambo

Ilha
Benguerra

2 Mile
Reef

Benguerra Lodge

Marlin Lodge

The Wreck

Ponta Duvini

Ferry

Ilha
Magaruque

Ferry

Vilankulo

Ilha
Bangue

0        5        10 km

0   (1 cm)   4 kilometres

also a list of over 180 birds to be spotted here, including the crab plover and olive bee-eater, which tunnels its nest into the sand dunes. Add to all this the fresh-water crocodiles that inhabit the lakes on two of the islands and you have a truly unique fauna. Camping is prohibited in the park, and there is accommodation only on Bazaruto and Benguerra. Park entry tickets (at a cost of 300 MT per entry per person) must be bought prior to visiting, and are available at the National Park office behind Pastelaria Mozambicana or from registered tour operators. If visiting with your own boat, there is an additional fee of 200 MT.

## Accommodation in the Bazaruto Archipelago

The accommodation on the islands is understandably rather exclusive and expensive. **Indigo Bay** on Bazaruto Island is a large resort offering water sports, cultural tours, sandboarding, island drives and horse-riding. Full-board rates (in-cluding transfers from Vilankulo) start from 14 000 MT per person a night sharing. For reservations, tel: +27-(0)11-463-6313, e-mail: enquiries@raniresorts. com, website: www.indigobayresort.com.

**Marlin Lodge**, on Benguerra Island, is a pretty lodge constructed from Mozambican hardwoods and elevated on stilts to overlook the bay. There are excellent fishing and diving facilities, and full-board rates start at 19 000 MT a person a night sharing. For details, tel: +27-(0)12-809-3594, e-mail: reserva-tions@mantiscollection.com, website: www.marlinlodge.co.za.

Another up-market option on

Benquerra Island is **Benguerra Lodge**; tel: +27-(0)11-452-0641, fax: +27-(0)11-452-1496, e-mail: reservations@ benguerra.co.za, website: www.ben-guerra.co.za.

## On to Inhassoro and beyond

The EN1 continues north from the Vilankulo turn-off through the Tamane gas fields (which are not especially conspicuous) until, after approximately 49 kilometres, you reach the Inhassoro turn-off (S21°34.370 E35°04.266). There is an impressive little tyre shop here, in case you need to have a puncture repaired.

It is another 14 kilometres down a single-lane tar road to the coast and Inhassoro. On the way down, at S21°33.970 E35°06.074, the road crosses a shallow river and wetlands, which is a good spot for aquatic birds – we spotted openbill stork and African jacana. A T-junction as you enter Inhassoro gives you the choice of turning either left into the Complexo Turistico Seta, or right into town.

**Seta** has 14 chalets in leafy, park-like surroundings. Two-sleepers cost 2 000 MT, four-sleepers 3 000 MT and six-sleepers 4 300 MT. A large airy bar/restaurant overlooks the beach, and boat launching as well as trips to the islands can be arranged. Contact Seta on tel: 293-91000 or 82-302-0990, fax: 293-91002, e-mail: hotelseta@hotmail.com. A campsite is also entered through the Seta complex. It is well situated above the beach, with trees and grass, but has ablutions that must date back to colonial days. Cost is 350 MT per day per person.

## Rough ride to Kruger

An interesting alternative route back to South Africa from Vilankulo is the rough two-day ride that heads west from the Vilankulo area to Pafuri in the northeastern tip of the Kruger National Park. With the only fuel (diesel and petrol) along the way available at Mabote (after 170 km) and about another 700 km beyond that to the next garage in South Africa, make sure your vehicle has sufficient range to tackle this route before leaving Vilankulo. A good dirt road turns off west from the EN1, about 32 kilometres south of the Vilankulo turn-off and goes to Mabote. From there, it is a sandy track (don't deviate, as the area has not yet been cleared of all landmines) as far as Machaila, and it then improves again as it heads southwest to cross the railway line at S Gorge de Limpopo and reach the Limpopo River at Mapai. There is no bridge at Mapai, just a drift through the river, so this route is best travelled in the dry season.

During the wet season, the river is too deep and the crossing is dangerous or impossible. A small, leaky pontoon ferry is operated by the local villagers. It only just supports a 4×4 vehicle after it has been offloaded (luggage travels separately). A risky crossing that costs 2 000 MT, plus another 200 MT for the luggage, but it's a unique experience and one of the most exciting that you're likely to have in your travels through Mozambique. Check the level of the Limpopo River with the Pafuri Border Police by calling them on tel: +27-(0)13-735-8936. A poor dirt road runs up along the Limpopo from the crossing through beautiful countryside to the Mozambique-South Africa border at Pafuri. On entering South Africa, you are in the Kruger National Park and can then choose your route south through the park or straight out to Makhado (the town previously known as Louis Trichardt) via Thohoyandou.

A right turn at the T-junction brings you into the small village of Inhassoro, which has grown rapidly in recent times and now has two banks with ATMs, two bakeries, a supermarket (Super Ana) and a hardware store (Kangela). In addition there are two fuel stations, two wholesalers and markets stocking fresh produce and fish. There is also an internet café and various bars and restaurants. Visit www.inhassoro.org or contact the team running the local tourist information on info@inhassoro.org.

Here you will also find **Inhassoro**

**Beach Lodge**. Situated on the beach front with good tarred-road access, the lodge has 12 double, en-suite chalets with air-con and TV. There are a further 10 bungalows that sleep four and are equipped for self-catering with fridge, stove, cutlery, crockery, TV and air-con. The campsites are serviced with power points. Chalets cost 1 375 MT to 2 750 MT (depending on the season), bungalows 2 750 MT to 3 850 MT and camping is 275 MT a person a day. For info and reservations, contact them at e-mail: info@inhassaoro.org, website: www.inhassoro.org.

The ferry across the Limpopo at Mapai is not guaranteed!

Slightly further along the beach to the south of Inhassoro town, **Dugong Investimentos** has a three-star self-catering establishment with four eight-sleeper lodges and six five-sleeper chalets. All accommodation is air-conditioned. Dugong has a pool, braai and laundry facilities and is in the process of completing construction of a residents' bar and restaurant. Eight-sleepers cost 7 050 MT to 10 500 MT per night and five-sleepers cost 3 000 MT to 4 200 MT, depending on the season. Contact Dugong on tel: 84-389-1471 or 82-456-7170, e-mail: dugonginv@vodamail.co.mz, website: www.dugong-mozambique.com.

Other accommodation in Inhassoro includes Goody Villas, Ilala Beach Lodge, El Hacienda, Beach Lodge, Pensão Inhassoro, Casa Luna, Canta Libre, Captain Lee and Billfish Lodge. Details of all of these and activities such as the CADSAS fishing tournament that takes place in Inhassoro can be found on the town's tourism website: www.inhassoro.org.

And if you're looking for the vibe in Inhassoro, head north up the beach for a short way to Johnson's Bar for good food and drink.

Back at the EN1, there is a large Total service station just north of the Inhassoro turn-off (no unleaded petrol). This is the last fuel for the next 180 kilometres (at Muxungue, then another 160 to Inchope).

The 62 kilometres to the bridge across the Save River is reasonably well tarred and runs through more gas fields. There is a small toll payable when crossing the Save bridge, and be careful of the checkpoint there – the officials may want to search your vehicle. The BP garage at Muxungue is reached after another 106 kilometres, where you can buy all fuels (including unleaded).

The road has some bad potholes beyond the Buzi River, but after another 95 kilometres you reach Inchope and the big crossroads (S19°12.477 E33°55.983) of the EN1 and the EN6, the highway down from Mutare in Zimbabwe to Beira.

# 17

# Beira

Whether driving from South Africa via Masvingo and Birchenough Bridge or from Harare, you would have to travel through Mutare to reach Beira. Mozambique's second largest city is like a neglected stepchild. Rundown and economically stagnant now, it will hopefully surge ahead when (and if) Zimbabwe sorts itself out.

Beira's skyline bears no resemblance to New York's.

## From Mutare

If you decide to stay over in Mutare, I would suggest you look up Anne Bruce on the corner of 6th Ave and 4th St (S18°58.257 E32°40.463), the best budget accommodation left in town – a friendly house with a homely atmosphere in a quiet street, and within walking distance of everything. Contact Anne, tel: +263-(0)20-63569. The nearby Holiday Inn has a Spur Steakhouse located on the premises.

When leaving Mutare, head down Herbert Chitepo Street to the corner of Robert Mugabe Avenue, turn east and go down, past the offices of the Automobile Association of Zimbabwe, across the little river. Turn right into Park Road and at Number 52 you will pass the only other budget accommodation option in town, the **Homestead Guesthouse**. A historical old building that was the first school in the area, it is set in large grounds with lots of safe parking. Keep on Park Road, driving through the industrial area and take the left turn signposted to Beira.

Machipanda border post, 10 kilometres from Mutare, is usually not very busy and mostly free of the hustlers that make so many border posts a chaotic nightmare. Leaving the Zimbabwean side should be quick and painless, and the Mozambique side is clean and orderly, with polite and honest officials (see page 54 for details on crossing the border into Mozambique and make sure that you have all the necessary documentation). A good road leads away from the border, and 75 kilometres from Mutare (S19°03.515 E33°17.340) you will pass the turn-off

that leads north to Tete (see page 193). Chimoio is a further 22 kilometres.

## Chimoio and Inchope

It's hard to believe that Chimoio is actually the fifth largest in Moz, but it does have all the amenities, such as banks, fuel, general dealers, bars, restaurants and hotels – you'll spot them when driving through. The **Hotel Inter** on Av 25 de Setembro offers luxury double rooms with TV, air-con, courtesy tea and coffee and breakfast for 2 900 MT double. They also have a comfortable bar and safe overnight parking. Contact them on tel: 251-24200, e-mail: interchimoio@gmail.com, website: www.interhotels.co.mz. On the other side of town, on your way out, you will find the big, new Shoprite Centre. The supermarket stocks everything, the Hungry Lion serves take-aways, and there is also a bank and pharmacy. The parking area is fenced off and patrolled by guards and next door is a smart new Total service station.

The EN6 highway continues east following the railway line and clusters of big, old mango trees (they say you can trace the ancient slave routes by following the concentrations of these trees), and after 63 kilometres you will reach the intersection with the EN1 at Inchope. There is fuel here, but no accommodation or much of anything else, just the inevitable sprawl of an informal market and *chapas* blocking the road. North leads to the Gorongosa National Park, Zambezi River and Nampula, and south takes you down to Maputo. Let's carry on straight to Beira…

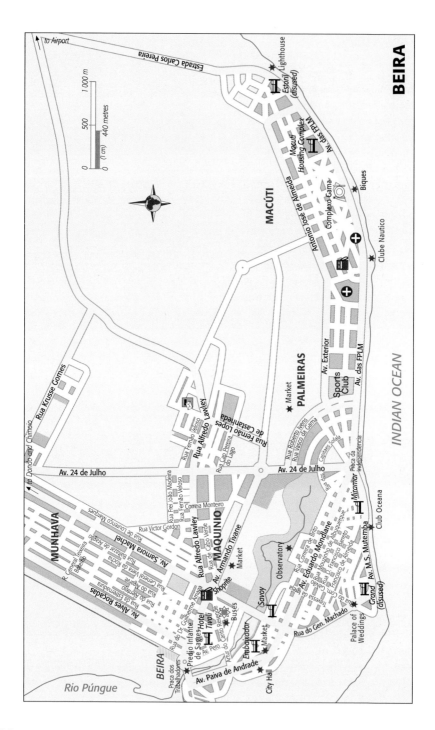

**BEIRA**

to Airport

Estrada Carlos Pereira

Estoril Lighthouse
(disused)

Macúti
Housing Complex

Av. das FPLM

Macúti
Biques

Antonio José de Almeida

Complexo Gama

MACÚTI

Clube Nautico

INDIAN OCEAN

Av. Exterior

Av. das FPLM

Market

Sports
Club

PALMEIRAS

Rua Krusse Gomes

Rua Fernão Veloso

Rua Alfredo Lawley

Rua Fernão Lopes
de Castanheda

Rua Cap Pereira
do Lago

Rua Roberto Ivens

Rua Vasco Da Gama

Capitães Sofala

Rua Aos Capitães

Praça da
Independencia

Av. 24 de Julho

Av. 24 de Julho

to Dondo and Chimoio

Av. Samora Machel

Rua Frei João Madeira

Rua Fernão Veloso

Correia Monteiro

MAQUINIO

Rua Victor Gordon

Rua Alfredo Lawley

Rua de Cabo Verde

Rua Armando Tivane

Market

Club Oceana

Miramar

MUNHAVA

to Lourenço Marques

R. Central Ferreira
Botelho

Rua General Vera da Rocha

Rua da Alfange

Rua de Alentejo

Rua Baltazar de Arêgo

Av. Alves Roçadas

Av. Eduardo Mondlane

Observatory

Rua Correia de Brito

Rua Moutinho de Albuquerque

Rua Francisco Barreto

Rua Com. Galião

Travessa da Igreja

Rua Francisco de Almeida

Rua da Pessaia

Av. M.S. Mutemba

Grand
(disused)

Palace of
Weddings

Rua do Dr Guilherme Amúge

Predio Infante

Av. Pero Canto

Artur do Canto Resende

Hotel
Tivoli

Savoy

Shoprite

Buses

Embarcadon

Market

Rua do Gen. Machado

de Sagres

Praça dos
Trabalhadores

Predio Infante

BEIRA

Av. Paiva de Andrade

City Hall

Rio Púngue

1 000 m

500

0 (1 cm)  440 metres

0    500    1 000 m

Club Oceana

## On to Beira

It's only another 135 kilometres to Beira, but the road deteriorates with numerous potholes and bumps in the road. Enter the outskirts of Beira passing under the flyover – the only one in Beira, make a mental reference of this landmark.

The City of Beira is situated at the mouth of the Pungue River that rises in the eastern highlands of Zimbabwe and it is this location as a port town that led to the city's existence. The original port was 30 kilometres to the south and was known as Sofala (today known as Nova Sofala – rather confusingly, the province of which Beira is the capital is now known as Sofala as well) and was the principle sea port of the Monomatapa Kingdom.

The establishment of the port of Beira in 1890 heralded the collapse of Nova Sofala, and in 1891 Beira became the headquarters of the Mozambique Company that had been granted a 50-year concession over the territories that now make up the provinces of Sofala and Manica. The company had full rights over the territory including the levying of taxes, issuing of currency and public administration. Elevated to the status of city in 1907, Beira's administration along with its territories reverted to the Portuguese government in 1942 when the concession was not renewed.

As remains the case today, Beira's main economic activity was based on its location serving the trade routes to neighbouring Zimbabwe, Malawi and Zambia. Beira's decline started after Mozambique's independence when the government decided to close her ports to what was Rhodesia, in support of the Zimbabwean independence movement and in respect of international sanctions. The Mozambican civil war compounded Beira's problem, with rail and road links along the Beira Corridor often being targeted and thus reducing vital trade.

From the late 1980s, vast improvements were made, but unfortunately the current difficulties in Zimbabwe have hampered growth in recent times. Despite this, the port remains the primary economic driver in Beira and plays a vital role for its landlocked neighbours. Major investments have been made recently, including new fuel and grain terminals, upgrades to the fuel transport pipeline to Zimbabwe, refurbishment of the railway line to Zimbabwe, reconstruction of the railway line to Malawi and central Mozambique, and a new coal terminal is projected to begin construction soon.

Manufacturing and industry are still in their infancy in Sofala province, as in much of the rest of Mozambique, but change is gradually taking place, driven by the growing economy. While Beira still appears careworn and rundown and has many problems to overcome before it returns to its tourist heyday of the mid 70s, the hospitality industry is developing all the time and the city can offer visitors an enjoyable stay. To the uninitiated Beira can be quite a confusing city to drive in, with many traffic circles (called *praças*) and small, sometimes one-way, roads leading off them. It is further complicated by a lack of road names displayed, and a lack of road signs giving directions. For ease of reference we will take a large circular route to orient you. Bear in mind Beira's shape (see the map on page 126), which makes it difficult to orient yourself by the water, as the sea/Pungue River is on three sides of you so you always seem to be facing it!

After passing under the flyover as you enter the city, the EN6 becomes Av Samora Machel, which will take you right into the heart of town. The first traffic circle you reach is Praça 7 de Outubro, which has a Shoprite supermarket on your right as you enter the circle. Head straight across the Praça 7 de Outubro taking care to also obey the traffic lights that control access to the circle, and you will reach the next traffic circle – Praça de Continuadores. Carry on straight, crossing a small bridge to reach the next traffic circle – Praça de Juventude. Taking a right here will put you on the main street of downtown Beira, but for now keep straight, going through a set of lights (suspended above you on wires!) and at the second set of lights you have reached Av Eduardo Mondlane (recognisable because it is surfaced with interlocking bricks). Turn left onto Av Eduardo Mondlane and this route will eventually loop all the way around back to the flyover on the EN6.

Having turned onto Av Eduardo Mondlane, you are now in one of the oldest parts of the city with some of the houses here dating from the founding of the city over 100 years ago. On your left you will pass the Catholic Cathedral, some of the stones from the original fort in Nova Sofala were used

to build it. Further on along Av Eduardo Mondlane you will come to Praça 3 de Fevereiro, which you should go straight across. The brick paving on Av Eduardo Mondlane ends as you enter this circle. As you exit the circle, have a look up on the right at the mural of St George and the Dragon by well-known sculptor and artist Garizo de Carmo, a famous son of Beira.

Continuing along Av Eduardo Mondlane, you will pass the Governor's Residence on the right before reaching the Praça de Independência on the seafront. At this circle Av Eduardo Mondlane becomes Av das FPLM (which stands for Mozambican Liberation Armed Forces). Go across the circle onto Av das FPLM and travel along the seafront through the suburb of Palmeiras. After a few kilometres you will pass the hospital on your left, bear left, leaving Av das FPLM to continue and turn into a dirt road. As you leave Av das FPLM you come to another traffic circle with a fuel station on it, and continue straight across the circle, onto Av Martires da Revolução which travels through the residential suburb of Macuti.

As you leave the built-up area you will come to the lighthouse on your right and the derelict shells of the Estoril and Dom Carlos hotels on your left. These once-beautiful hotels in the most sought-after positions have recently been sold to developers but it will be a considerable time before they reopen. At this point Av Martires da Revolução becomes Rua do Aeroporto.

Rua do Aeroporto continues through rice fields, past a motocross track and

Monte Verde Night Club, both on your left, until it reaches Beira International Airport on your right. Continue past the airport and further along the same road you reach the flyover under which you drove to enter Beira.

With an improved understanding of the layout of the city you can now turn left back to Beira city centre or right to Zimbabwe.

## Exploring Beira

Beira's main attraction is its beaches, the best being in Macuti extending from Clube Nautico all the way to the Macuti shipwreck and beyond. As in many countries there can be petty theft on the beaches in Mozambique, so it is best to avoid taking valuables to the beach and leaving your belongings unattended. The beaches in front of Biques and Clube Nautico are most often frequented by tourists.

To access these sections of beach, at the hospital bear right on Av das FPLM and you will come to **Clube Nautico** on your right. After Clube Nautico, Av das FPLM becomes a sand road that runs parallel to Av Martires da Revolução and rejoins it just before the Dom Carlos Hotel. This section of the road can be tricky and often needs a 4×4 in some of the sandy sections. Biques is situated about halfway along the sand section of Av das FPLM.

Of particular interest are the lighthouse and the shipwreck, which was beached in front of the lighthouse to protect it from erosion, both of which are in front of the **Dom Carlos Hotel**. There are also various informal bars in this area serving cold beer.

In the northern coastal areas a white face mask, known as *musira*, is used to protect and beautify the skin.

Away from the beaches, to visit downtown Beira, begin at Praça de Juventude and turn right onto Rua Major Serpa, which is the main street downtown. Within a block of Rua Major Serpa you will find travel agents, the main LAM airline office, a private clinic (Clinica Aviçena), shops, banks and the movie house (English films with Portuguese subtitles). Worth a visit, especially on a hot Beira day is the bakery on the first floor of the Bulha Shopping Centre (on Rua Major Serpa), which is air-conditioned, has clean public restrooms and a good selection of pastries and snacks.

At Praça de Juventude, behind the petrol station, is one of Beira's most remarkable historical landmarks, the **Casa dos Bicos** (Pointed House). It's less attractive from the outside, but when you walk inside, the sheer scale of the freestanding winged roof cast in concrete sections cannot fail to impress. Sadly the building is disused and various attempted adaptations have detracted from the original open design, conceived by sculptor Garizo do Carmo.

Behind the Bulha Shopping Centre, near the main mCel office, is the **central market**. This has two floors, with fresh produce and fish on the ground floor and a selection of craft and curio stalls on the first floor. The market is a great place to stock up on cheap fruit and vegetables; the fish and seafood available here are not guaranteed to be fresh. Crafts and curios can be sourced at the central market, in front of Clube Nautico, in front of Biques, near the Dom Carlos Hotel and at Galeria de Sá on Av Eduardo Mondlane.

Continuing along Rua Major Serpa, away from Praça de Juventude and towards the port, the central prison – an imposing fortress-like building just off the town square, is on your left. Opposite the prison is the main TDM office, which also houses an internet café. There is another internet café in the Teledata building behind the prison. Also in this area is the Praça de Município which, while sadly run down, has some interesting architecture, a coffee shop, Barclays Bank and, just off the square, one of the largest of a selection of great second-hand clothes shops run by ADPP. Clothes are donated by people in Western countries and find their way to Mozambique in large bales, where they are unpacked and sold for very low prices, a great way to source vintage and sometimes unused designer clothing!

Continuing on Rua Major Serpa, travel through a traffic circle, with the Praça de Metical on your left. This Praça, as the name suggests, is home to several banks (including Standard Bank) and an exchange bureau. At this circle the road becomes Av Poder Popular, which ends at the **provincial courthouse**, on the left, and Manica Freight Services Building – **Casa Infante de Sagres**, both of which are interesting examples of Beira's architectural past. From Casa Infante de Sagres you can see the fishing port, the main port (entry is restricted) and the arch of the impressive railway station nearby.

To see further examples of Beira's historical architecture, from the Praça de Independência take Rua Dom Franciso Gorião along the sea front until you reach the derelict **Grand Hotel**. This condemned building has become home to hundreds of families who live there with no water, electricity or sanitation. Opposite the Grand Hotel is the **Wedding Palace**, Beira's official wedding venue decorated with a mural depicting life from the womb to the grave. Also in front of the Grand Hotel is a sculpture that resembles an upturned hand, which was made by Garizo do Carmo, the same man who designed the St George mural on the Praça 3 de Fevereiro and the impressive Casa dos Bicos.

Other things to do include a visit to **Clube Nautico**, tel: 23-311-720, e-mail: clubenauticobeira@gmail.com, across from the hospital on Av das FPLM. Beach access through the club and entry to the club's restaurant costs 20 MT per day. In addition, the club

Biques bar, restaurant and campsite are right on the beach in Beira.

offers various sporting activities including a clean swimming pool (cost 150 MT per day), floodlit tennis courts (cost 100 MT per hour), gym (daily membership permitted) and options to hire water sports equipment. There is also a ramp for boat launching and retrieval (cost 100 MT per launch).

The **Golf Club** on Rua Correia de Brito, tel: 23-328-508, welcomes non-members, and although the course is not your typical championship course, it does offer a challenging and entertaining nine holes, and is one of the few courses where a crab might steal your ball (free drop permitted if this happens)!

## Overnight in Beira

There are not many hotels from which to choose in Beira, especially in the luxury class. Here are some of the best, in diminishing order of price and comfort...

It is difficult to believe that the rather plain and basic **Hotel Tivoli**, 363 Av de Bagamoyo, tel: 23-32-0300, fax: 23-32-0301, e-mail: h.tivoli_beira@teledata.mz, website: www.tdhotels.pt, is the best Mozambique's second-largest city can offer. This centrally situated establishment also offers conference facilities and charges 3 300 MT to 4 300 MT (single and double) for rooms and 4 900 MT to 5 500 MT for a suite (all inclusive of a buffet breakfast). Across from the Tivoli is the neat and compact **Beirasol Guesthouse**. Their smallish en-suite rooms all have air-con, cable TV and fridges and the excellent Monaco restaurant is next door. Double rooms cost 1 500 MT.

Not very central, but extremely comfortable and excellent value for money, is the **Macuti Housing Compound**, Av dos Martires da Revolucao, tel: 23-31-1988 or 82-509-2810, fax: 23-31-1804, e-mail: mhcadms@teledata.mz (S19°50.861 E34°53.375). Like a small village, it is set in the walled security of a large garden compound. The complex offers tennis courts, swimming pool and a sauna to complement its flats and houses. One-bedroomed flats cost 2500 MT per night and three-bedroomed houses are 5000 MT (discounts for longer stays).

The recently renovated three-star **VIP Hotel** is centrally situated in Rua Luis Inacio. Prices range between 2875 MT and 3250 MT (single and double) and there are also suites available. Contact them on tel: 233-40100, fax: 233-22002, e-mail: hotelbeira@viphotels.com, website: www.viphotels.com.

**Royal Guest House**, 1311 Av Eduardo Mondlane, tel: 23-324-030, is another popular choice for business travellers and is often busy, so book in advance. The rooms are spacious and air-conditioned, there is a TV lounge and a pool, and the suite has its own jacuzzi. Prices are 2300 MT for a twin room and 2500 MT for a family room. Prices include internet access and laundry. The owners also operate a fully equipped, self-catering guest flat available for long- and short-term rentals.

**Hotel Infante** is a nice little multi-storeyed hotel on Rua Jaime Ferreira, tel: 23-32-6603, in the heart of town. En-suite, air-con and breakfast costs 950 MT single and 1250 MT double. Take away the air-con, and you'll be charged 900 MT and 1000 MT. If you want to sample some of Beira's night life, the Aquarius Club and Africa Bar are just across the road.

Just off the traffic circle at the intersection of Rua Major Serpa Pinto and Samora Machel is the basic, but clean **Hotel Savoy**. A double with your own bathroom costs 1050 MT, and if you're prepared to share facilities, a single will cost 400 MT and a double 800 MT. For reservations, tel: 23-32-9302. The **Hotel Miramar**, tel: 23-32-2283, is just off Praca da Independencia in Rua Vilas B Truao. A little dingy, it has double rooms with air-con for 700 MT and without for 450 MT. But I've saved the best for last. The new **Jardim das Velas**, 282 Av das FPLM, is out at Macuti beach near the lighthouse. Built in an attractive Mediterranean style, this complex boasts six double rooms and another six family rooms with kitchenettes. There is good security, fine views of the beach and all accommodation has air-conditioning and TV. Mr and Mrs Jakov make you feel very much at home and charge 2850 MT for the double rooms and 3300 MT for the family rooms, tel: 23-31-2209, e-mail: jardimdasvelas@yahoo.com.

The only campsite in Beira is at **Biques** (S19°51.043 E34°53.094), where a sandy spot with poor ablutions and dodgy security will cost you 200 MT per person, but you do have a great beach and pub on your doorstep to compensate. For info, tel: 23-31-3051, fax: 23-31-2451, e-mail: biques@teledata.mz.

## Eating out in Beira

The Beira restaurant scene is improving all the time with new restaurants opening and old favourites upping their game. Note that some restaurants close one day per week, often on Mondays.

**Anselmo's**, Av Martires da Revolução (by the Dom Carlos Hotel), is a *barraca* (traditional bar/restaurant, made using poles, bamboo etc.) that is popular with Mozambicans and expats alike. It's a perfect place to experience traditional Mozambican informal dining, with wobbly chairs and plastic tablecloths, but they serve excellent seafood, bought daily from the local fishermen, prepared over coals. As well as impressive seafood platters, Anselmo's offers a variety of good-quality, well-prepared grilled meats – call Inocent on tel: 82-428-7240.

**Beira Sol**, opposite Hotel Tivoli, is another typical Portuguese-style eatery, serving dishes such as pork with clams, tel: 23-236-420 or 82-533-3337.

**Biques**, Av das FPLM, tel: 23-312-451, is a large, thatched establishment that includes a restaurant and pub on the beach and is popular with expats. It has pool tables, screens international rugby, and serves large English breakfasts, pizzas and a variety of pub meals and draft beer.

**FatBelle** is at Clube Nautico de Beira, Av das FPLM, tel: 23-313-384. Arguably the best location in Beira and set right on the beach within Clube Nautico, this restaurant offers a wide range of snacks, meals and pastries. Non-members pay 20 MT a person to enter the club's premises. The restaurant is open from early morning to late evening, and caters throughout the day. The beach terrace is a top spot for sundowners, and the restaurant is one of the most popular in Beira.

**Restaurante Bar Solange**, 836 Av Eduardo Mondlane, tel 23-322-992, has a friendly bistro-style atmosphere and is very popular, particularly on weekend evenings. Owners Solange and Rui offer a good range of well-prepared meat and fish dishes, including local and Portuguese meals, pizzas and pasta.

**Restaurante Kanimambo**, tel: 23-323-132, just off Rua Major Serpa, is an excellent owner-managed Chinese restaurant offering a wide variety of oriental meals. Charles and Barbara combine their Taiwanese and Chinese heritage to offer specialities including Szechuan Beef, Teriyaki Chicken and spicy Kung Pao dishes. Closed on Saturdays.

**Restaurante Pic-Nic**, 123 Rua Costa Serrão, tel: 23-323-806, is a Beira institution and one of the oldest restaurants in town, where little has changed since the day it opened. This restaurant serves a range of traditional Portuguese dishes.

**Restaurante 2+1**, 180 Rua 8B Maquinino, tel: 23-312-113, is a popular and reasonably priced lunch venue that also serves evening meals, including a variety of Mozambican and seafood dishes.

**Pizzeria Itália**, Av Eduardo Mondlane near the Praça de Município, tel: 82-781-4188 offers simple, good-quality pizza from a wood-fired oven, served in a relaxed, informal outdoor environment.

**Restaurante Wing**, Macuti Housing Complex, Av Martires da Revolução, tel: 23-312-520. This well-established restaurant has been in business for almost 20 years and is still one of the most

Fresh fish is always on the menu in Beira.

popular, offering a varied menu that includes some Macao-style Chinese food, pizza and a good prawn cocktail.

## Out and about in Beira
Mozambican nightclubs follow the Mediterranean culture and only really get started late, with most people dining late and then going on to bars and clubs until the early hours of the morning. Beira is no exception, with most clubs opening around 11 pm and only getting interesting from midnight.

The two top nightclubs in Beira are **Complexo Monte Verde**, on the Rua do Aeroporto (next to the motocross track), tel: 23-301-651, and **Centro**

**Hípico** (near the flyover), situated in the horse riding club. Both are very busy over weekends and on public holidays. Music is a mix of western, Portuguese-African kwasa-kwasa and Brazilian dance music, with live local bands sometimes featured.

Between dinner at one of the restaurants mentioned above and visiting a club, people often head for drinks to **ABC** (Art Bar Cafe), situated behind the movie house on Rua Major Serpa, or to FatBelle at Clube Nautico or Biques.

Also popular with locals are Africa Bar, Aquarius and Miramar.

For shopping, the best place to start is the **Shoprite Centre** at the intersection of Samora Machel and Armando Tivane. This supermarket is the best stocked in Beira, with groceries, meat, bakery, dairy products, fruit and veg, hardware, some camping gear and even sim cards and airtime for your cellphone. Some of the other services in the complex include a takeaway, pharmacy, photo lab and an ATM. Next door is a large BP service station.

There is also a small supermarket out in Macuti near the Housing Compound and other small general dealers dotted around the city.

For seafood, it is best to buy direct from local fishermen on the beach, checking for freshness, or ready-frozen from Pescamar or Remar, both of which are on Av Armando Tivane near the port.

Good-quality meat and chicken is available from a South African run butchery, called Carnes da Beira, situated just off Av Armando Tivane, two blocks after Shoprite, in the direction of the port, in front of the Maquinino Market (not to be confused with the central market).

All the major banks are represented in Beira and have ATMs. These include various branches of BancABC, Barclays, BCI, BIM and Standard Bank, which are found all over the city and are easily identifiable. Western Union money transfers can be received at Standard Bank.

There are also three major *cambios*: **Câmbio Dragão** on Praça de Metical; **786 Câmbios** at 31 Rua Machado dos Santos, off Av Armando Tivane; and **Multi Cambios**, just around the corner in Rua Açores. *Cambios* generally give the best rates, are fast, safe and efficient and don't charge commissions.

Beira has many fuel stations including BP, GALP, Petromoc and Total, offering diesel and unleaded petrol. The city also has a variety of pharmacies, which are easily identified by a green cross displayed outside. The best is **786 Farmácia**, next to 786 Câmbios at 31 Rua Machado dos Santos, off Av Armando Tivane.

**Clinic Avicena**, 326 Av Poder Popular, tel: 23-32-7990, fax: 23-32-7988, e-mail: avicena.clinic@teledata.mz, is best for medical emergencies, as they have an ambulance, doctors, X-rays and a laboratory for malaria tests.

## On the road in Beira

The airport is contactable on tel: 23-30-1071, and **LAM**, the Mozambican airline, has an office there, tel: 23-30-1024. The car-hire firms are also out at the airport. **Avis** is on tel: 23-30-1263, e-mail: avis@teledata.mz, and **Imperial Car Rental**

may be contacted on tel: 23-30-2650. *Chapas* run along most main routes in town and cost only 15 MT a ride. Marcello runs the traditional sort of taxi service, tel: 23-32-2921 or 82-324-9130. Intercity buses have their depots between Avs Daniel Napatina and Bagamoyo. The TSL and Oliveiras lines have daily buses to and from Maputo in the south, and Nampula in the north. There is also a bus to Tete.

Beira is well endowed with motor dealerships. Landrovers are supplied by **Setec Auto**, 539 Av Eduardo Mondlane, tel: 23-35-2257, e-mail: setecauto@teledata.mz, while Toyota is represented by **Toyota de Mozambique**, 2575 Av Base N'Tchinga, tel: 23-32-4329, fax: 23-32-3794, e-mail: toyotabeira@teledata.mz, and Nissan by **MozAuto**, 72 Rua Machado Santos, tel: 23-32-3739, fax: 23-32-3734. **CALS Motors** in Av Base N'Tchinga fix suspensions, shocks and springs as well as doing general mechanical repairs, Contact Luis Teixeira, tel: 82-556-2390. **Shakrani Motors** – at the roundabout that boasts the giant plastic Coke bottle – stocks general spares, filters, lubricants and tyres, as does **Sena Centro** in Rua Antonio Enes, tel: 23-32-4430. For used nuts, bolts and anything else, try the sprawling market on Armando Tivane, and for tyres and puncture repairs, the BP garage at Shoprite.

And finally, if you are heading up to **Gorongosa National Park**, drop in at their offices in the Predio Infante de Sagres (Manhica Freight Building), 1 Av Poder Popular. They have the latest info and you can make bookings there. For information, tel/fax: 23-32-0346, e-mail: gorongosa@teledata.mz.

# 18

# Gorongosa National Park and on to Quelimane

Av Samora Machel is the way out of Beira and onto the EN6. It is 33 kilometres to Dondo, where there is a customs checkpoint (S19°34.599 E34°43.356) and the turn-off onto the old road north (the EN213 is signposted to Cheringoma). This road is very bad, but at Muanza you can turn left for a novel, back-door entry to Chitengo Camp in Gorongosa National Park. It continues up to Inhaminga (turn left here for Mount Gorongosa) and eventually joins the EN1 just south of Caia on the Zambezi – a rough, tough road that is now only used by keen birders looking for those elusive 'mega-ticks'.

On the road in Gorongosa National Park…

## On to Gorongosa National Park

Staying on the EN6, the following 41 kilometres to Tica is badly potholed and even deteriorates to poor gravel as it crosses the marshy area around the Pungue River.

About 135 kilometres from Beira, you will reach the intersection (S19°12.477 E33°55.983) at Inchope where the EN1 crosses the EN6. Turn north here onto a good tarred road. The speed limit is a low 100 kph, with long stretches of 80 kph.

After another 44 kilometres you will reach the turn-off right (S18°56.041 E34°07.980) to the Parque Nacional da Gorongosa. A good, single-lane gravel road, with solid little bridges that date back to 1936, runs down 11.3 kilometres to the main gate. The smart and efficient staff will book you in, and 17 kilometres further is Gorongosa's only camp, Chitengo (S18°58.740 E34°21.084).

## Chitengo Camp

Make your way to the office and pay the entrance fee of 200 MT per adult plus 200 MT per car, per day. An additional fee of 500 MT per vehicle per day is payable for self-drive game-viewing within the park. Although Chitengo Safari Camp is open all year round, the park encourages visits between April and November (the dry season), as during the rainy season the internal road network in the park becomes impassible

The entrance to Gorongosa National Park.

# GORONGOSA NATIONAL PARK

and entrance to the park may be restricted. Gorongosa is at the southern end of the African Rift Valley. The park's sweeping landscapes and exciting plans to rehabilitate it and return it to past glory make this place worth a trip.

**Chitengo Safari Camp** offers nine modern and comfortable double cabanas – a total of 18 separate double rooms equipped with mosquito nets, air-con and en-suite bathrooms (with hot showers). Breakfast is included in the room rates, which are from 2500 MT single and 2990 MT double. The park's camp-

ing area includes recently remodelled bathroom facilities with hot showers. To book, tel: 23-535-010 or 82-302-0604, e-mail: travel@gorongosa.net.

Activities include guided safaris with trained game guides along the park's 150 kilometres of gravel roads, during which you may visit the famous **Lion House** (S18°54.256 E34°22.607) and **Hippo Terrace** (S18°54.812 E34°31.032). Other attractions include the limestone gorges of the Cheringoma Plateau, Lake Urema and its surrounding wetlands, and the beautiful Murombodzi waterfall descending from Mount Gorongosa. These activities can be planned when booking and you should contact the park to ensure availability of guides.

Wildlife remains skittish but recent game surveys indicate the presence of lions, elephants, buffalos, leopards, hippos, crocodiles, zebras, sables, kudus, nyalas, waterbuck, impalas, bushbuck, reedbuck, oribis, Lichenstein's hartebeests, warthogs, bushpigs, cervals, civets, genets, chacma baboons and vervet monkeys.

Morning and evening game drives are offered for 780 MT per person and self-drive game-watching (for a fee of 500 MT per vehicle per day) is also an option.

Chitengo has two swimming pools, a gift shop and laundry service. Meals in the Chitengo Restaurant are served buffet style as well as à la carte. The restaurant is open 06h00–21h00.

## Beyond Gorongosa

Back on the EN1, continue north through the town of Gorongosa (not to be confused with the national park of the same name). Local buses and minibus taxis travel this route, so stay alert – especially for the dopey goats that graze along the sides of the road. The region is hilly and to the east you will see the impressive **Mount Gorongosa** (turn right in Gorongosa town). These mountains are definitely worth exploring, particularly if you're a keen birder – the green oriole is endemic here.

About 280 kilometres from Inchope, and 32 kilometres before the Zambezi River, (S18°02.361 E35°11.684), turn off

right to James White's camp, the only accommodation along this stretch of road. James owns the Catapu Sawmill and adjoining **Mphingwe Camp**. He also has a 25 000-hectare forestry concession and conscientiously plants three trees for every one he cuts down. The camp consists of rustic cabins built of solid local hardwood and fitted with furniture made at James's own factory. James is also very proud of the 75 species of birds and the 240 species of indigenous plants on his property. The Mphingwe restaurant offers homecooked food with a range of grills as well as daily specials and has a well-stocked bar. Camping and self-catering are not permitted. The cabins are 650 MT single and 850 MT double. More comfortable en-suite cabins are 900 MT single and 1 300 MT double. Contact them on tel/fax: 23-302-161 or 82-301-6436, e-mail: tctcatapu@gmail.com, website: www.dalmann.com.

From the turn-off to Mphingwe Camp, it is about 32 kilometres to the town of **Caia**. This is a good, tarred road with little traffic, no roadblocks and a pleasure to drive.

At Caia (S17°50.030 E 35°20.561), the road branches off north up to the old railway bridge across the Zambezi at Sena. Built in 1934, it is – at 3.7 kilometres – the longest rail bridge in Africa. Please note that the bridge is being repaired and renovated to once more take rail traffic, and vehicular traffic across it has been banned. Backpackers with no wheeled encumbrances may cross on the backs of local bicycle taxis.

Were you to turn off south here, you would pass the lonely site of

Mount Gorongosa is a birder's paradise.

Mary Moffat-Livingstone's grave at Chupanga Mission on your way to **Marromeu**, the Zambezi estuary's best birding site (contact the offices of the sugar mill in Marromeu for info on bed-and-breakfast or camping, tel: 23-960-014). A new fuel station has opened in Caia for petrol and diesel. There is also a small shop for basics and a Standard Bank with 24-hour ATM for cash.

## Caia Bridge

At long last the ferry across the Zambezi has been replaced by a new bridge. This is the Armando Emilio Guebuza Bridge, an impressive sweeping structure crossing the Zambezi and its floodplain from Caia to Chimuara on the other side. The bridge has a toll, which at the time of writing was 100 MT for a car. But,

I must say, I'll miss the old ferry – it was pure Africa! Muddy banks crowded with little stalls, offering the traveller food, drink, accommodation and other, more dubious, pleasures. Buses, trucks and 4×4s jostling for position in the queues. Fat mamas carrying scrawny chickens and skinny men pushing overloaded bicycles. Girls washing clothes

## Casualties of war

It's horrifying to think that during the the 17-plus years of the civil war, 14 000 buffalo and 3 000 elephants were eradicated from Gorongosa – and that's not counting the many other species that were brought to the brink of extermination here.

in the shallows, dugout canoes drifting serenely by, and always that one vehicle stuck on the ferry ramp, holding up the loading process. People shouting advice, the ferry churning up mud, and somehow everything sorted itself out. It was a precious tableau that has gone forever now.

On the other side of the bridge **Cuacua Lodge** offers accommodation and meals in a setting overlooking the river. Stone-built chalets cater to individuals and groups. The restaurant offers meat dishes from the farm on which the lodge is situated. Accommodation ranges from 2250 MT to 4800 MT per chalet, depending on size – some chalets can accommodate up to six people. Cuacua also offers camping for 300 MT per person. For more information,

tel: 82-312-0528, e-mail: cuacualodge@gmail.com.

Continuing up the EN1 you drive the 165 kilometres to **Nicuadala** and the chance to refuel. At the stop sign and intersection here you have the choice of turning right (south) to the coast at Quelimane or left (north) to continue up to Nampula and beyond.

## On to Quelimane

The 37-kilometre road to Quelimane is good tar, but the swarms of cyclists transporting heavy loads of charcoal are a menace. Coconut-palm plantations stretch as far as the eye can see, but go largely unharvested.

Quelimane is the capital of Zambezia province and the little coastal town is quite busy, but I can't help thinking that,

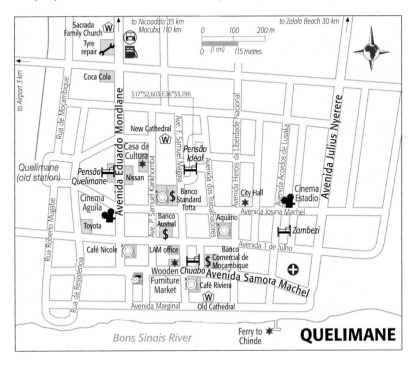

as the roads improve inland, so the reason for its existence as a small port will diminish. Its history is similar to that of Beira – gold, ivory and slaves – but with the added importance of a river and canal that once connected this town to the Zambezi River. David Livingstone was appointed the British Honorary Consul to Quelimane in 1858, and later started his exploration of the Zambezi from here.

The town is entered down yet another Av Eduardo Mondlane. Passing the Sacrada Familia Church, carry on straight to reach a BP garage and bus depot (to all routes south and north of Quelimane) on your left. The tyre-repair shop across the road does well as the roads are so badly potholed. At the Coke warehouse further down on your right is the turn-off (left) to **Zalala Beach**. This is a pleasant 33-kilometre run down to the beach on a tarred road through palm plantations, but find out if the **Complexo Turistico Kassi Kassi** has reopened before trekking all that way for nothing.

Further down on your right, opposite MozAuto Nissan, is the Pensão Quelimane and a couple of blocks further you run into Av Samora Machel. Turn left and cruise through town, passing the furniture craft market on your left, then the Hotel Chuabo, and the Riviera restaurant across the road. The Marginal along the waterfront is one block to the right and the rest of town is up to the left. At the end of Samora Machel, you will run into Av Julius Nyerere where a left turn will get you going in the direction of Zalala Beach again.

## Out and about in Quelimane

The top place to stay in town is the **Hotel Chuabo**, tel: 24-21-3181, fax: 24-21-3812, a smart eight-storeyed building in Av Samora Machel. Comfortable air-conditioned rooms with TV cost 3000 MT single and 4800 MT for a double. There is a grand restaurant on the top floor with a terrific view, but it was sad to see a staff of eight waiters standing around 20 tables decked with starched linen and polished silver and not a patron in sight.

**Pensão Quelimane** is on the way into town in Av Eduardo Mondlane. It is near the bus depot, but probably a bit out of the public-transporter's price range, with singles costing 450 MT, doubles 600 MT and twin beds 700 MT. Clean en-suite rooms with fridge and air-conditioning cost 1600 MT single, 1300 MT double and 2000 MT for twin beds.

The **Hotel Zambeze** on Av Acordos de Lusaka has a nice garden, courtyard and off-street parking. En-suite singles cost 450 MT and doubles 600 MT.

**Pensão Ideal** (S17°52.603 E36°53.196) is difficult to find as it is not signposted, but it gets my vote as Quelimane's best value-for–money establishment. It is on Av Samuel Magaia, just below the big 'new' cathedral. Neat, well run and down a quiet side street, they have a small bar/restaurant, which serves the locals in the neighbourhood. Singles cost 300 MT, doubles 400 MT and a large double with bathroom is 600 MT. For bookings and information, tel: 24-21-2731.

But be warned, there are often water shortages in and around Quelimane, so your en-suite bathroom isn't always

View of Quelimane from Hotel Chuabo.

much use to you, no matter where you are staying.

The best place to eat is **Café Riviera**. This old-style, pre-independence-type restaurant has an extensive menu, a good selection of wines, pastries and cakes, and the choice of inside or pavement dining. Pizzas, ice cream and espresso coffee – pinch me, am I in the sticks of northern Mozambique? Another option is **Restaurante da Estação**, an authentic Italian eatery also serving great pizza.

Other places to eat are at the above-mentioned hotels, with the Chuabo definitely the best of the bunch. Also look out for **Café Nicole** on Av 1 de Julho and **Pica-Pica Takeaway** opposite Chuabo Hotel.

To change money in Quelimane, try **Meizel Cambios** in Av 1 de Julho or the **Standard Bank** on the corner of Josina Machel and Samuel Magaia (look out for the huge bats that roost in the palm trees across the road).

**MozAuto Nissan** is on Eduardo Mondlane, opposite Pensão Quelimane, and the Toyota dealership is one block west on Rua da Residencia (this street also has other spares and tyre shops). General motor spares can be found at **Zambeze Pecas** in Samora Machel (tel: 24-21-4623). The hospital is in the block between Acordos de Lusaka and Julius Nyerere and for beautiful hand-crafted wooden kists and furniture go to the corner opposite the Café Riviera – but bear in mind that you need a special licence to export large timber products like these from Mozambique.

# 19

# North to Nampula

If you are leaving Quelimane in the early morning, look out for weaving bicycles in the mist. And if you're headed for Nampula (about 520 kilometres), then prepare yourself for a bumpy and difficult ride – the road is bad and the navigation tricky. From Nicoadala, the road comprises 30 kilometres of good tar to Namacurra, a pleasant enough town but no sign of fuel or accommodation.

The Makonde people are famous for their carved masks, like this one in Nampula.

## Mocuba and beyond

We continue for another 77 kilometres to **Mocuba**, on good, new tar. Both diesel and petrol are available as you enter town. Just before the fuel station, is the difficult-to-detect turn-off left (S16°51.356 E36°57.901) that doubles back and eventually takes you through to Milange in Malawi.

Passing the aerodrome, carry on straight to a fork, keep left, carry on through the traffic circle with the monument with a large metal star in the centre and take the double-laned Av 25 de Setembro to a large church on the right. With the police station opposite, swing left and drive across the traffic circle with the fountain in the middle (S16°50.420 E36°59.116). This is the main street, and if you carry on through town you will cross a long bridge over the Lugela River and, thankfully, say goodbye to this confounding place.

But maybe you need food or accommodation. The **Pensão Cruzeiro**, tel: 24-81-0184, couldn't be more central as it is situated in the main street just below the fountain circle. It's the main bar and restaurant in town and has clean two-bed rooms with bathroom for 700 MT.

If you have the courage to navigate your way back to the southern entrance to town, you could try the grandly named **Pensão Estralagem Pariaso 2000 Mocuba**, a simple, clean and secure little motel-style establishment off left at the star monument traffic circle. There is a bar/restaurant and the double rooms cost 500 MT, and 650 MT with bathroom.

The road north from here to Alto Molocue starts out as reasonable tar, but soon deteriorates with signs of repair work. There are some bad potholes as you approach the turn-off (at 66 kilometres) to Gurue. Keep straight on, and about 100 kilometres from Mocuba, the road becomes a single dirt track to cross the bridge at Nipiodi. From here it is back onto tar again, but a similar dirt track bridge crossing awaits you at Naiopue. More deviations occur where new bridges have been built, but I would avoid this road in the wet.

On approaching Alto Molocue, turn left off the tar and drive into the centre. The rather scruffy **Pensão Santa Antonio** is on your right. They offer safe parking and double rooms for 380 MT, or 600 MT with en-suite bathroom. Across the square is the neater **Pensão Fambo Uone** with a cool veranda that faces the dusty square and rooms that cost about the same as Santa Antonio. The compact little town centre has basic foodstuffs, bar and restaurant, but not much else (and no fuel when I was there). To get out of town, cross the river and wind your way up the other side, past the hospital, and head for a big church and a house that looks like a fort. Keep right when approaching the church (left would take you to Gurue and Cuamba) and head out of town through the administrative centre and past the communications tower.

Two roads run parallel between Alto Molocue and Alto Ligonha and, depending on how the rebuilding of the northern route is progressing, you might be directed onto the southern one. This is a wide dirt road in reasonable condition, but don't look at a compass while on this road, because it will just scare you. At times you are heading directly south, when you know you should be heading north – but have faith and spare fuel! About 20 kilometres past Alto Ligonha you will cross the narrow bridge over the Ligonha River and enter Nampula province. A very courteous police roadblock will check your papers and you're off on a good tarred road to Nampula town. But there is still no fuel available along this stretch, and you start eyeing the 20-litre yellow drums filled with blackmarket fuel with new appreciation. Hopefully, you won't need them as you make your way through the fantastically shaped granite hills and koppies. The ruins of a classic old colonial church on a hill heralds the approach to Nampula.

## Gurue

The highland town of Gurue is a good opportunity to get away from the coastal heat. Set among rolling hills and tea plantations, it has a high rainfall and a fresh and invigorating climate. Walking and climbing are worthwhile pastimes and there are waterfalls and caves to visit. The best place to stay is the newly restored Pensão Gurue, which also has a restaurant. Singles cost 500 MT, en-suite doubles 1150 MT and camping 130 MT. Guides are available to take you for walks through the tea plantations, into the mountains and to the waterfalls. Tel: 84-305-8393, e-mail: pensao.gurue@gmail.com.

## Introducing Nampula

Nampula is the capital of the north and Mozambique's third-largest city. Its position at the intersection of the main south–north highway and the railway line from Nacala to Malawi gives it commercial and administrative importance. With a pleasant climate, it is surrounded by impressive insel-bergs, mountainous plugs of volcanic granite that soar up to 1000 metres above the plains. Approaching from the southwest (the Quelimane side), you will spot Toyota and other motor-vehicle workshops as you pass the big water tower and enter town along Av de Trabalho. Keep the railway line on your left until you reach the station, and then turn right into Av Paulo Samuel Kankhomba, Nampula's main street,

which runs all the way down to a traffic circle at the bottom. The city is quite easy to figure out as it is laid out in a grid pattern, with a main inter-section about halfway down where it crosses with Av Eduardo Mondlane.

There are three fairly new hotels in Nampula. **Girassol Hotel** is a 4-star establishment and part of a large shop-ping and business complex. With con-ference facilities and 24-hour services this is the ideal businessman's home. Rates start at 3000 MT single and 3500 MT double, reaching up to 6000 MT for the executive suite. Tel: 26-21-6000, fax: 26-21-9004, e-mail: girassolnampulahotel@visabeira.co.mz, website: www.girassolhoteis.co.mz. Another newly opened 4-star hotel is the **Executive Hotel** near Shoprite.

Rates are similar to the Girassol Hotel, and a swimming pool, two restaurants, well-appointed rooms, conference facilities and an on-site car-hire service complete the picture. Tel: 26-21-9001, fax: 26-21-9004, e-mail: hotel-executivo@tdm.co.mz. The latest new hotel in Nampula is the **Hotel Milenio** situated in Av 25 de Setembo, near the cathedral. Forty comfortable en-suite rooms have air-con and TV and are slightly better value than the above-mentioned two hotels. Tel: 26-21-8877, e-mail: hotelmilenio@tdm.co.mz.

Nampula's old, established hotel is the **Hotel Tropical**, 1 Rua Macombre, tel: 26-21-2232, fax: 26-21-6359, which is situated in a quiet, leafy street behind the National Ethnography Museum. Secure parking, a cool, shaded patio for dining out on, and comfortable rooms make this popular with visiting businessmen and NGO workers. They will also change money at a reasonable rate. Single en-suite rooms cost 2000 MT and doubles 3000 MT. Down Av Paulo Samuel Kankhomba, on the right-hand side, just before Eduardo Mondlane is your next best bet for affordable accommodation – **Residencial Farhana**, tel: 26-21-2527. This establishment is quiet and secure, but it has neither a bar nor restaurant. The rooms all have a bathroom, air-con, TV and fridge and cost 1200 MT single, 1700 MT with double bed and 2400 MT with two single beds. There is secure parking. A block down on the same side of Av PS Kankhomba is the **Residencial a Marisqueira**. Very similar in rooms and price to Farhana, they offer en-suite rooms with TV, air-con and fridge for 1300 MT single, 1800 MT double bed, and 2200 MT for two single beds.

The best value-for-money place in

Shops are few and far between and often closed, so be fairly self-sufficient.

the budget range is further down SP Kankhomba, near the circle at the bottom. **Pensão Parque**, tel: 26-21-2307, charges only 400 MT single and 600 MT double for shared facilities, but is nearly always full. That is because this is a neat and tidy little 'cheapy' in a good position. It also has a small bar/restaurant, patio and roof-top with a view.

There is quite a selection of accommodation in this area. **Pensão Residencial Estrela**, tel: 26-21-4902, is just above Pensão Parque and has reasonable rooms with bathroom, TV, fridge and air-con for 1 000 MT single and 1 300 MT double. Across the road and down the side street next to the market, is the **Residencial Monte Carlo**, tel: 26-21-2769. Large, airy rooms with a bathroom (cold water only) and balcony

overlooking the market cost 550 MT single and 750 MT double. If you were to go around the circle at the bottom of Av PS Kankhomba and turn off right, you would reach the **Residencial Brasilia**, tel: 26-21-2126. A little pricier and more up-market than the last few places mentioned, they have rooms with air-conditioning, TV and bathrooms (with hot water) for 1 150 MT single and 1 300 MT double.

There are two good alternatives to staying in town. The first is the reasonably priced **Complexo Quinta Nasa**, tel: 82-684-5150, fax: 26-21-6994, on the road out of town, going towards Nacala. Take the Av de Trabalho east out of Nampula to the traffic circle (S15°06.743 E39°17.012) and turn right to Nacala, Pemba and Ilha de Moçambique.

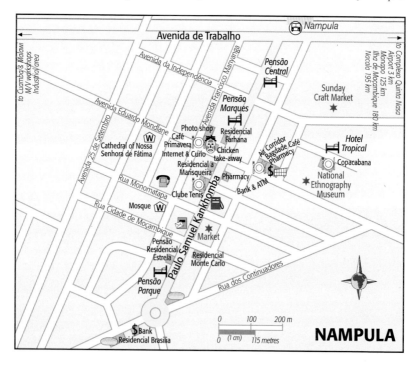

About 3.7 kilometres further, there is a signpost on the right (S15°06.957 E39°19.019) that points you across the railway line and down through small fields and houses. Follow the signposts for 3 kilometres to the gates of Quinta Nasa (S15°07.746 E39°20.014). The complex is quiet and secure and is popular with local conferences and weekenders. Neat, double en-suite rooms cost 900 MT, and larger self-contained bungalows that can sleep up to six cost 1 200 MT double.

The other out-of-town option is much more up-market. Take the Quelimane road out along Av de Trabalho for about 40 kilometres and then turn off right (S15°06.685 E39°13.661) towards Ribaue and Cuamba – the **Apart Hotel** is just along on the left. With modern motel-styled accommodation, swimming pool, resort-styled bar and restaurant all set in well-kept gardens, this is very good value for money at 2 000 MT single and 2 500 MT double. Most suites are newly built and have air-con and satellite TV. For reservations, tel: 26-21-6595, fax: 26-21-6468.

## Out and about in Nampula

Apart from the new hotel dining rooms, the best eating in town is probably at the **Copacabana**, opposite the Hotel Tropical in Rua Macombre. Authentic pizzas and pastas are a speciality, along with great omelettes (try the prawn special). Shaded patios overlook a fish pond, and there is often live music. They also have a good selection of wine, a car guard on duty, and spotless toilets. The **Clube Tenis** is in Av PS Kankhomba and is reached via a short alley next to

Protea Furnishers. A somewhat faded and jaded old place, it is nevertheless very central and the food is hot and the beers cold. Cool and comfortable during the day, it has a disco at night. For late-night pubbing, try the **Bagdade Café** on Av Eduardo Mondlane, two blocks down, east off SP Kankhomba and close to the Standard Bank.

A pleasant sidewalk café for delicious cakes and coffee is the **Café Primavera**, a block west of Av PS Kankhomba on the corner of Av Eduardo Mondlane and Francisco Manyanga. Three doors down is the **Frango King** for grilled chicken and chips takeaways. Bread and pastries are available at the bakery on the traffic circle at the bottom of Av PS Kankhomba or from another *pastelaria* just off the circle next door to the Hotel Brasilia. One of the best-stocked small supermarkets is **Mercado Ideal** situated just below the Bagdade Café in Eduardo Mondlane.

There are two groupings of interesting shops and services in town. The first is on **Av Eduardo Mondlane**, two blocks east of Av PS Kankhomba, where you will find a travel agency, Bagdade Café, a pharmacy, copy shop, Standard Bank with an ATM and the Mercado Ideal supermarket. The wonderful Ethnography Museum is in the next block down. The other grouping is situated west of Av PS Kankhomba on the corner of **Av Francisco Manyanga**. Clustered around this corner is Frango King takeaways, Gett Lda Internet services (20 MT for 30 minutes), SkyNet Couriers and business centre, Café Primavera, and Fotocopiodora for photocopies, photographic processing (digital, too) and even number plates. A big new shopping mall has been built just up the road, opposite the cathedral, which has a supermarket, cinemas, hotel and restaurants. But, the best news for travellers is that a new Shoprite supermarket has opened on the corner of Rua dos Continuadores and Rua de Tete (S15°07.249 E39°15.371).

Fuel is available from BP near the bottom of Av PS Kankhomba or Petromoc 5 kilometres out of town on the road to Nacala. They also have air for your tyres, and a small but well-stocked minimarket. We saw the Toyota workshops as we came into town from the Quelimane side. For info, tel: 26-21-2125, fax: 26-21-3128, e-mail: toyotanpl@teledata.mz. The Nissan dealers, **MozAuto**, tel: 26-21-7144, are also out that way. **Tecnica Industrial** on Av Eduardo Mondlane is the agent for Mitsubishi; contact them on tel: 26-21-3153, e-mail: contjfs@teledata. mz, while the place to go for help with your Land Rover is **Setec Auto**, Rua Industrial, tel: 26-21-7172. You can rent a car from **Imperial** (tel: 26-21-6312) or **Moti** (tel: 26-21-7144), both of which are out at the airport. If you need to contact the airport (out east across the traffic circle at the bottom of Av PS Kankhomba), tel: 26-21-3138.

Transport east to Ilha de Moçambique and north to Pemba leaves from Av de Trabalho, outside the train station. For transport west towards Cuamba and south to Quelimane, head west along Av de Trabalho for about 2 kilometres to the junction where the road turns off to Ribaue and Cuamba. The railways have a daily passenger service to Cuamba

Small towns have big churches in Mozambique although not all are in use.

and a slow, unreliable goods train that runs on into Malawi – a great rail adventure (see page 57 for details).

But we can't leave Nampula without visiting one of the best museums in Mozambique, the **National Ethnography Museum**. Situated in Av Eduardo Mondlane, just below the Standard Bank, it is crammed full of articles and artefacts depicting the past and present cultures of this northern region. On display are weapons, pottery, fishing traps and gear, a small dhow, a great selection of musical instruments and Makonde masks. The Makonde, an important local tribe, are well represented with ceremonial drums and costumes, traditional medicine and jewellery. The exhibits are well captioned, and a guide is also available to show you around – and it's all for free, donations gladly accepted. Behind the museum is a very interesting craft workshop and market where you can watch carvers at work and then buy curios at very reasonable prices.

# 20

# Ilha de Moçambique

To get to the fabulous Ilha de Moçambique, you take Av de Trabalho east out of Nampula to the traffic circle (S15°06.743 E39°17.012) and turn right towards Nacala and Pemba. About 5 kilometres past the turn-off to Complexo Quinta Nasa, you can refuel at the big Petromoc service station. There is a police roadblock fairly close by, but they should simply wave you through.

Boat-building at the little fishing harbour of Santo António, Ilha de Moçambique.

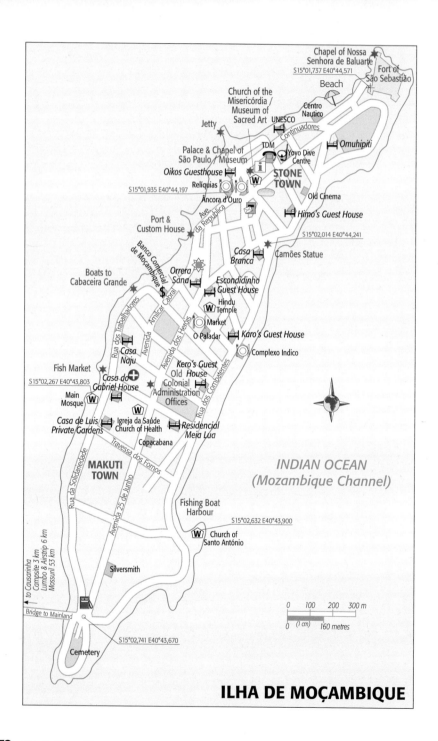

Chapel of Nossa
Senhora de Baluarte
S15°01,737 E40°44,571

Fort of
São Sebastião

Church of the
Misericórdia /
Museum of
Sacred Art

Beach

Centro
Nautico

Jetty

UNESCO

Continuadores

Palace & Chapel of
São Paulo / Museum

TDM

Yoyo Dive
Centre

Omuhipiti

Oikos Guesthouse

STONE
TOWN

S15°01,935 E40°44,197

Relíquias

Âncora d'Ouro

Old Cinema

Port &
Custom House

Himo's Guest House

S15°02,014 E40°44,241

Ave.
da República

Banco Comercial
de Moçambique

Casa
Branca

Camões Statue

Boats to
Cabaceira Grande

Orrera
Sana

Escondidinho
Guest House

Amilcar Cabral

Hindu
Temple

Market

Avenida dos Heróis

O Paladar

Karo's Guest House

Complexo Indico

Rua dos Trabalhadores

Casa
Naju

Kero's Guest
Old House

Avenida dos Combatentes

Fish Market

Casa do
Gabriel House

Colonial
Administration
Offices

S15°02,267 E40°43,803

Main
Mosque

Casa de Luís
Private Gardens

Igreja da Saúde
Church of Health

Residencial
Meia Lúa

Copacabana

Travessa dos Fornos

MAKUTI
TOWN

Rua da Soldariedade

Avenida 25 de Junho

INDIAN OCEAN
(Mozambique Channel)

Fishing Boat
Harbour

S15°02,632 E40°43,900

Church of
Santo António

to Cacorinha
Campsite 3 km
Lumbo & Airstrip 6 km
Mossuril 53 km

Silversmith

Bridge to Mainland

S15°02,741 E40°43,670

Cemetery

0    100    200    300 m

0    (1 cm)    160 metres

ILHA DE MOÇAMBIQUE

## En route to Ilha

A granite hill shaped like a Makonde mask looms on the left as you travel down this upgraded section of the EN8. This is cashew-nut country and young boys offer this delicacy at 300 MT (negotiable) for half a basinful. You will reach the junction town of **Namialo** after 86 kilometres. A left turn here takes you north to Pemba, but we first have to visit Ilha, so continue straight on. You'll reach the roadside town of **Monapo** after 39 kilometres where there is fuel available at a Galp service station (there is no fuel on Ilha de Moçambique). Carrying on straight would take you another 50-odd kilometres to **Nacala**. This large natural harbour is northern Mozambique's most important port. Turn right here (S14°53.533 E40°19.117) and continue on a good tar road through pleasant countryside where baobabs make way for palms again. After another 43 kilometres, you will reach the **Complexo Continental**. Although it offers bar, restaurant, rooms and camping, it is expensive and too far from Ilha to be of any interest other than being at the turn-off to the 1918 British War Cemetery. Turn left here (the aerodrome is across the road) and a short way down you will see a neatly kept walled enclosure (S15°00.980 E40°40.137) on your left. Although it is called the British cemetery, I noticed that most of the graves were of South Africans with names such as Smith, Delport and Geldenhuys from the South African Medical Corp, Supply Corp and Labour Corp. The ride back to the main road passes the old Portuguese Maritime

The grand entrance to the impenetrable Fort of São Sebastião.

Offices and offers beautiful views across the bay to Ilha de Moçambique.

Another 3.6 kilometres brings you to the causeway to Ilha, but before you cross, have a look at the campsite down on the beach to the left. **Causarinha Camp**, tel: 82-446-9900, was popular when accommodation was hard to find on Ilha and it is still the only feasible place to camp. But now that there is such a wide choice of reasonably priced rooms on the island, I don't know why you would want to stay here and not immerse yourself in the history and culture of Ilha (the off-handed attitude of the staff doesn't help either). Camping is right on the beach and costs 160 MT a person plus 200 MT a car per night.

Small rustic bungalows are also available at 350 MT single and 600 MT double. All share the same basic ablutions.

## Ilha's past and present

Ilha de Moçambique was already well established as a trading post, and linked to others on the East African coast such as Kilwa and Zanzibar, by the time Vasco da Gama landed there in 1498. Trade with Madagascar, Oman and Persia to the north, and Sofala to the south, was flourishing. By 1507 the Portuguese had established a permanent settlement on the island and usurped most of the trade. Ilha also served as a valuable replenishment station for the ships and crews sailing between Portugal and their eastern bases in Macau and Goa. The mighty Fort of São Sebastião was constructed in the late 16th century and the island became the capital of Portuguese East Africa. Attacks by the Dutch and later the Omanis were repulsed and the island prospered. As it did, so Stone Town grew in beauty and stature, and the magnificent buildings we still see today were constructed during this time.

Various factors contributed to the decline of Ilha de Moçambique around the turn of the 20th century – the abolition of the slave trade, the rise in importance of Delagoa Bay (Maputo) after the discovery of gold in the Transvaal and even the opening of the Suez Canal, which diverted much of the sea traffic north. So began the slow but inexorable decline and destruction of the island's economy and, with it, its buildings. The population shrunk towards the mid-1900s, only to receive an unwelcome influx during the civil war as many refugees fled to the relative safety of this island. Firewood was scarce, and many irreplaceable carved doors and even furniture were burned.

The declaration of a World Heritage Site by Unesco in 1992 has now focused attention on the island, but problems still plague restoration efforts. Ownership issues make it difficult to assign or accept responsibility for individual buildings, the ultimate usage of restored properties is undecided and, of course, there's always a shortage of money. But despite these problems, there is hope. There is a general consensus that the island's architecture and heritage are too important to ignore. The island is threatened only by decay – at least it doesn't have rampant development to contend with, and tourists are showing interest. I think that the slow but steady increase in tourism will make the islanders realise the value of what they have and encourage the restoration of more and more on the island.

## Introducing Ilha de Moçambique

Although Ilha de Moçambique is an island, it is linked to the mainland by a 3.5-kilometre causeway, which means that – for a toll of 35 MT (pay on the island side) – you can drive a light vehicle across. The bridge is only a single lane, but passing bays are spaced at regular intervals for two-way traffic. Bollards at both ends limit the width of vehicles, keeping trucks and buses off the island (but no problem for cars, bakkies and 4×4s).

Once on the island you will encounter a traffic circle, but follow the road down the centre of the island and set off along Av 25 de Junho through the reed huts of **Makuti Town**. This southern end of the island is the poorer neighbourhood and contrasts sharply with the faded glory of the rest of the island. The first sign of the island's colonial past is the Igreja da Saude Church on your left and then the once-magnificent hospital. It's difficult to believe that anyone would have built such a grand porticoed structure – it looks like it was once a five-star hotel – just to serve as a hospital. But, we must remember that Ilha was the hub of not only the Mozambique colony but the entire sea route between Portugal and the East. The hospital is now no longer operational, except for a small clinic at the back in one of the old wards. The withered gardens of the park across the road show the same neglect. But

don't despair – it's gratifying to find that these historical buildings are still standing, and what is standing can still be restored.

## Stone Town

You now enter the old Stone Town, so called because coral blocks were used as building material. The architecture is a mixture of Old Portuguese and African East Coast, the culture is Swahili and the predominent religion is Muslim. Narrow streets wind between double-storeyed, shuttered buildings, some perfectly restored, painted in pretty pastel shades and sporting rooftop patios, while others are only shells, held together by the roots and vines of wild fig trees. The road forks at a shaded little square where we find the beautifully restored **Escondidinho Guest House** (S15°02.066 E40°44.084). Bear left and continue past more houses and a few poorly stocked shops to the

The underground cisterns in the Fort of São Sebastião still supply water to the island.

The Chapel of Nossa Senhora de Beluarte on the northern tip of Ilha.

**Central Square.** On the left is the police station and on the seaward side the old customs house and disused boatyard, entered through impressive cannon-flanked gates.

Keeping left, pass the inviting Reliquias restaurant. Most streets are one-ways, so keep a sharp look out for them, and if you get caught going the wrong way, use me as an excuse! You now run straight into the historic core of the island, the Governor's Palace, the Chapel of São Paulo (both restored, and now a fascinating museum) and the Church of Misericordia. Still on your left, the old jetty juts far out into the bay. Then there's the island's secondary school. Centro Nautico, which houses the Dugong Dive Centre, overlooks the island's only clean, sandy beach and then, totally dominating the entire northern end of the island, the huge **Fort of São Sebastião.** Swing off to the right and you can continue your trip around Ilha de Moçambique by heading back to the causeway via the eastern (seaward) side.

Right up near the fort is the newly renovated, upmarket **Hotel Omuhipiti** followed by the old, boarded-up cinema. **Casa Branca** guesthouse, with the statue of writer Louis Camoes in front, slips by, as does **Karo's Guest House** and **Indigo** restaurant. The fishing boat moorings are always busy and beg for a photo, with palm trees and the Church of Santo António in the background. You're now back at the causeway, but a quick loop around the Hindu cemetery gives you a good view of the little fort on the island of São Lourenco, just south of Ilha.

## Exploring Ilha de Moçambique

Ilha de Moçambique really doesn't need a museum – the whole island is one –

but the **Governor's Palace** (S15°01.882 E40°44.219) has been renovated and furnished in the opulent 18th-century style of the island's heyday. Or maybe it always looked like this – it certainly looks and feels like the governor just stepped out to inspect the plantations or meet with his mistress. Built in 1610 and last used by Samora Machel on an official visit, this marvellous museum is a blend of Portugal, Arabia, India and China. Each room is filled with authentic period pieces: heavily carved Indian furniture, huge paintings of Portuguese heroes, ornate chandeliers, tapestries, carpets, jewellery and sedan chairs. The kitchen looks like it could still produce a banquet on the immaculately laid table for 22 in the dining room. And with so few tourists on the island at any given time, you'll probably have the museum entirely to yourself. The adjoining **Chapel of São Paulo** still has its original Chinese carved pulpit, and behind the palace is the **Church of the Misericordia** and the **Museum of Sacred Art**, displaying religious paintings and carvings. Opening hours are 08h00–12h00 and 14h00–17h00 and someone is usually happy to show you around – although it would help if you could speak Portuguese (no entrance fee, but donations are appreciated). The museum also contains the offices of the excellent **Tourist Information Bureau**. The pleasant staff here are most helpful with info on accommodation, public transport and anything else pertaining to the island. They offer short tours of the Fort of São Sebastião or whole-day tours of the island, and are open 09h00–12h00 and 14h00–17h00

every day. For information, tel: 26-61-0081, fax: 26-61-0082.

For such a small island, there is much of interest to see on Ilha de Moçambique, and many thick layers of history too – like the **Fort of São Sebastião** on the northern tip of the island (S15°01.737 E40°44.571). This formidable old fortress has not only withstood sieges and attacks by the Dutch and Omanis, but more recently served as a Portuguese bastion during the Mozambique liberation struggle. It is remarkably intact for the oldest complete fort still standing in sub-Saharan Africa, and even the extensive underground cisterns are still used by the islanders for their daily fresh water needs. There is no entrance fee and you are free to wander about the ramparts with their many old cannons, and explore the rooms in the courtyard. Just outside the walls, on the extreme tip of the island, is the **Chapel of Nossa Senhora de Beluarte**. Built in 1522, it is considered the oldest European-built structure in the southern hemisphere, and is the last resting place of many of the 16th- and 17th-century Portuguese bishops.

The little protected bay on the southeast corner of the island is a good place to watch the busy comings and goings of the fishing dhows, and there is always at least one boat being built or repaired on the beach – the ancient tools and methods used are fascinating. Another old craft practised on Ilha is that of the silversmith. Difficult to find in the warren of reed huts in Makuti Town (down the steps, right, off the central road), José Orievas works with four apprentices to create delicate and fine pieces. In a dark room with the only light coming through an open door (no wonder José's glasses are so thick), silver wire is melted, cast, drawn through holes in small plates and hammered on makeshift anvils. Their methods may be crude – smelting is achieved by blowing through a straw across a paraffin flame – but the chains, bracelets and pendants are beautiful, and not very expensive either.

Visit the fish market on the west of the island, just beyond the green mosque. The selection of fresh fish and crustaceans might not make your mouth water (when cooked they will), but you'll get a few good photographs. A little further north (S15°02.100 E40°43.908) is the beach where dhows come and go to Cabaceira Grande (cost 20 MT) and Cabaceira Pequena (10 MT), destinations across the bay. Whether you just want to watch and photograph these ancient crafts being executed, or actually take a trip, drop by at high tide. Unfortunately, the islanders use the beaches as a toilet, so swimming is not an option here. There is, however, one small beach that is reasonably clean, with beautiful white sand. Situated on the north of the island between Centro Nautico and the Fort of São Sebastião, it is popular with the locals who often exercise and play soccer there in the evenings.

## Overnight on Ilha

I struggled to find accommodation on Ilha during my first visit in 1997, but now the visitor is spoilt for choice. The most up-market hotel is definitely the **Hotel Omuhipiti**, set apart from the crowded Stone Town on the northern tip of the island just outside the walls of the famous fort. Renovated to a very high standard and well staffed, the comfortable rooms offer air-con and satellite TV at a cost of 3 000 MT single and 3 500 MT double (including breakfast). It also has an excellent restaurant and safe off-street parking. For more information, tel: 26-61-0101, fax: 26-61-0105.

The next most expensive establishment is **Casa do Gabriel** (aka Patio dos Quintalinhos), a quaint little place in Rua do Celeiro, across the road from the green mosque. This guesthouse has been imaginatively designed and renovated by its Italian architect-owner and is beautifully decorated with local furniture and crafts. The rooms look out over a small plunge pool and intimate garden courtyard, and feature unique ideas such as a bed suspended from the ceiling and a roof that opens for stargazing. A large self-contained room for two costs 1 250 MT, a family room for four, 1 800 MT, and the rooms without *en-suite* bathrooms cost 720 MT single and 830 MT double. Your car will have to sleep outside, but there is a guard. For bookings, tel: 26-61-0090 or 82-419-7610, e-mail: gabrielemelazzi@hotmail.com, website: www.mozambiqueguesthouse.com.

My choice for comfort, position and value-for-money is **Escondidinho**. Over looking a small square in the centre of Ilha, this restored double-storeyed guesthouse has a laid-back atmosphere and big, airy rooms. It also has a wonderful unpretentious restaurant where I had one of my best seafood meals in Mozambique (nine queen prawns followed by fillet of parrot fish – the bill, 500 MT). The swimming pool is set in a pretty garden and displays of dancing by local school children are organised for some evenings. Double rooms with en-suite facilities cost 2000 MT and without, 1000 MT. Parking is in the street but, again, there is a car guard. Contact Escondidinho, tel: 26-61-0078 or 82-674-8420, fax: 26-61-0057, e-mail: ilhatur@teledata.mz, website: www.escondidinho.net. The rest of the accommodation on Ilha de Moçambique consists of at least 10 small guesthouses spread around the island, but the following are just a few worth mentioning:

One of the oldest and most popular establishments is **Casa Branca** on the eastern side of the island behind the statue of Louis Camoes. There are three high-ceilinged rooms that overlook the sea and catch the cooling breeze. There are no private bathrooms, but breakfast is included at 700 MT single and 900 MT double. Flora, the proprietress, is a real go-getter and is busy renovating two more houses inland towards the museum that will offer a small self-contained family unit for 1500 MT a night or double en-suite rooms for 750 MT. For more details, tel: 26-61-0076 or 82-454-3290, fax: 26-61-0089.

**Casa Himo** is a little way up the street from Branca (between the disused cinema and 25 de Junho school) and also faces the sea. This old, established guesthouse is clean and neat and has offstreet parking in the yard. Rooms are without private

## Buses from Ilha

◆ Monapo – 1 hour (cost 45 MT)

◆ Namialo – 2 hours (cost 55 MT)

◆ Nacala – 3 hours (cost 100 MT)

◆ Nampula – 4 hours (cost 100 MT)

◆ Pemba (change at Namialo) – 7 hours (cost 300 MT)

bathroom and cost 900 MT double and 700 MT single.

**Unesco**, tel: 26-61-0126, is my favourite of the 'cheapies' in the Old Town, as no other place evokes the feeling of going back in time as this place does. A big old merchant's house just up the road from the museum, it has storerooms that open to the beach below and bedrooms above that overlook the channel. It is also the offices of Unesco, who are co-ordinating a lot of the island's restoration, and contains some valuable (but unrestored) antiques. With shared ablutions, rooms cost 700 MT single and 800 MT double.

You can't, however, get more central than **Oikos**, tel: 26-61-0096, opposite the museum and in the same block as the Ancora d'Ouro. A bit tatty and no en-suites available, breakfast is nevertheless included at 450 MT single, 700 MT twin beds and 600 MT 'married' (double bed).

The last guest house in the Old Town is **Orrera Sana**, over the road from Escondidinho. Owned by the lovely lady Regina, who runs the general-dealer store under the arches, and managed by her very knowledgeable son Hugo (both of whom speak English well), they have one single room and two doubles, all en-suite and inclusive of breakfast. There are fans in each room, and you have the use of the kitchen for self-catering. Hugo is a very good guide around the island too. The single en-suite room costs 700 MT, the two-bedder 750 MT and the double-bed room 850 MT. Contact Regina or Hugo on tel: 26-61-0136.

I think the best of the Makuti Town bunch of guesthouses is the friendly **Casa Naju**, tel: 26-61-0008, which you will find north of the green mosque and the fish market. Painted in green trim, Naju's is a family business run by a mother and daughter and consists of a general shop and family residence. The rooms are part of the main house and have the neat, clean and tidy touch that only a woman can bring to an accommodation establishment. No private bathrooms here, but good value

at 450 MT single and 850 MT double. Up the central Av 25 de Junho, on the right, just before the Igreja da Saude church, is **Copacabana**. With a busy bar and restaurant in the front, the rooms in this guesthouse might be noisy at night. A double-bedded en-suite room costs only 425 MT, and without bathroom costs 325 MT a person, breakfast included. Up to the church corner and around to the right is the difficult-to-find (come to think of it, they're all rather difficult to find) **Residencial Meia Lua**. Recognisable by its orange-painted trim, this rather neat little free-standing house offers a double bed (for married couples only!) in an air-conditioned room for 700 MT. The single room has no air-con, but costs only 350 MT. They all share the same nicely tiled bathroom.

Continuing across to the east coast

The former Governor's Palace is now a fascinating, well-stocked museum.

and up a couple of blocks, you will find the very basic **Karo's Guest House**, tel: 26-61-0034. For what you're getting – water only in buckets – it's probably a little overpriced at 425 MT single and 700 MT double. Breakfast is another 80 MT. The only place on Ilha where you can camp – and then only in little one- or two-man tents – is **Casa de Luis** (aka Private Gardens). A basic backpackers' joint in the middle of the Makuti *barrio*, it is impossible to describe how to get there – asking for '*O Makutini, Travessa dos Fornos*' will help. Set in a rather damp, smelly yard, at least the rooms are clean and you can use the kitchen. There are three rooms, each with two beds at a cost of 370 MT a bed, while camping is 200 MT a person.

## Eating out on Ilha

You should be able to find somewhere to stay among that lot, and you could also eat at some of them, but there are some great restaurants with an island-style, laid-back atmosphere on Ilha. The best, and one you must visit, is **Reliquias**. Decorated with relics (hence the name) of shipwrecks and treasures from the deep, they offer a full menu, daily specials and a busy bar. You can dine indoors or out in the garden right above the beach. It's popular with tourists and locals alike, so you may have to book – to do so, tel: 26-61-0092.

For a pleasant local dining experience, try **O Paladar**, which you will find on the back corner of the block that houses the central market. Hostess Kiu-Kiu will welcome you for tea, coffee, light snacks, drinks, or a variety of genuine local dishes (it's so diffi-

cult to find anything other than grilled chicken, steaks and seafood in most restaurants). Food is specially prepared, so order an hour ahead by calling tel: 82-455-9850.

I've already mentioned the fabulous food that can be enjoyed at the **Escondidinho Restaurant**, but it deserves another mention. Cooked with care and flair and enjoyed on a cool open-sided veranda, it's especially pleasant on an evening when they've organised the local school dance troupe to perform. For bookings, tel: 26-61-0078. **Centro Nautico** is more of a bar than a restaurant, but they do serve snacks and light meals to go with the cold drinks that you will sip on their roof-top patio as you watch the sun go down over the channel (life is a slow, easy pleasure on Mozambique Island). The atmospheric old **Ancora d'Ouro** bar and restaurant has reopened again, serving drinks, snacks and meals at all times of the day. Its wonderfully central position opposite the Church of the Misericordia in the old Stone Town entices you to just sit and watch the world go by, as the time goes by…

## Out and about on Ilha

There are few shops on the island, with the only cluster being 'under the arches' in the Rua de Arcos. This is a long building with an arched façade housing a pharmacy, Missinga curios and a small general dealer run by Regina, who also owns the Orrera Sana guesthouse. The most central bakery is unmarked, but on the opposite corner from Ancora d'Ouro and the Church of the Misericordia. They bake in the early morning and close when they've sold out, so don't go looking for bread or rolls in the late afternoon. In the same block as Ancora is a gallery selling art and jewellery. Other supplies can be bought at the central market or at a couple of small shops, where it is said you can also change money. The official currency exchange is at the branch of **Banco Comercial de Moçambique** (S15°02.117 E40°43.959) in a beautifully restored and panelled building on Av Amilcar Cabral.

There is an internet service available at the **TDM** offices just north of the museum. International calls on a good clear line can also be made from here. The **Dugong Dive Centre** is situated at the Centro Nautico on Nankarramo beach, near the Fort of São Sebastião. It offers diving, kayaking and dhow

The Church of Santo António.

trips. This isolated and unspoilt section of Mozambique's coastline offers the opportunity to see turtle nesting, whales, dolphins and a variety of fish and birdlife, tel: 82-454-7810, e-mail: caku@teledata.mz.

In case of a medical emergency, it is probably best to see Dr Rino Scuccato who runs the Escondidinho guesthouse. He has retired from the medical profession, but is very experienced and well connected. If necessary, he can arrange for a transfer to the hospital in Nampula or an airlift out.

The service station on the island side of the causeway will probably not have fuel, but you can buy from hawkers out of cans if you are desperate. In the market behind the service station, small mechanical and tyre repairs can also be undertaken. Minibuses leave from the mainland side of the causeway for various destinations.

There are at least four smaller islands offshore from Ilha de Moçambique – Ilha de Sete Paus, Ilhas Inhaca, Ilha de Goa and Ilha das Cobras. All are uninhabited and most of them are still growing slowly as their coral multiplies. The **Baia de Mossuril** (in which Ilha de Moçambique lies) is ringed with mangroves and small fishing villages, while beautiful sandy beaches such as **Praia da Carrosca** grace the northern peninsula. Down south past Ponta Bajone there is **Baia de Lunga** and more uninhabited coast with inviting beaches. All of this is best reached by boat and the tourism office at the museum would be glad to assist with more information and help in organising a sailing dhow to take you there.

# 21

# North to Pemba

To continue your journey north, you have to retrace your steps to Monapo and then Namialo. Turn north at the intersection (S14°55.421 E39°58.879) onto the EN106. The tarred road here is reasonable, although some sections do have bad potholes. Nacaroa lies 65 kilometres from Namialo and at around 120 kilometres, you'll pass some weirdly shaped granite hills.

Careened fishing boats are repaired at Paquitequete, Pemba.

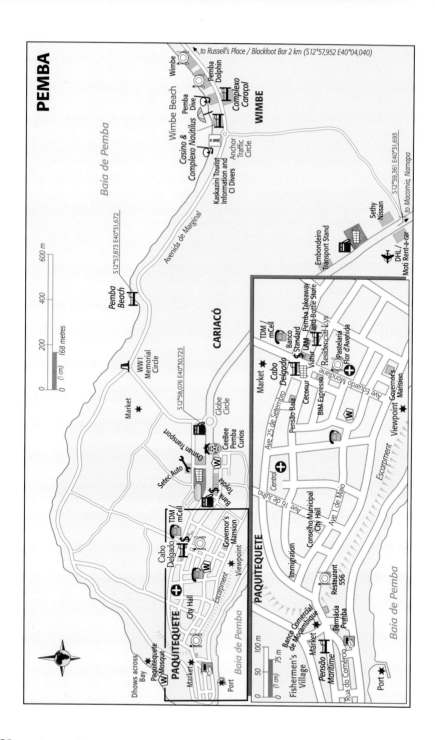

**PEMBA**

to Russell's Place / Blackfoot Bar 2 km (S12°57,952 E40°04,040)

Wimbe
Pemba
Dolphin
Wimbe Beach
Pemba
Dive
Complexo
Caraçol
**WIMBE**
Casino &
Complexo Nautilus
Kaskazini Tourist
Information and
CI Divers
Anchor
Traffic
Circle

*Baia de Pemba*

S12°59,361 E40°31,693

to Macomia, Nampa

Sethy
Nissan

Avenida de Marginal

Embondeiro
Transport Stand

S12°57,873 E40°31,672

DHL /
Moti Rent-a-car

600 m
400
200
0

0   (1 cm)   168 metres

Pemba
Beach

**CARIACÓ**

WW1
Memorial
Circle

S12°58,076 E40°30,723

Market

Globe
Circle

Osman Transport

CeeBee
Pemba
Curios

Setec Auto

Toyota

Bank

TDM /
mCell

Banco
Standard

Pemba Takeaway
and Bottle Store

LAM

Viatur

Residencial Uys

Pastelaria
Flor d'Avenida

Market
Cabo
Delgado

Cecoñur

Pensão Bala

BIM Expresso

Ave Eduardo Mondlane

Governor's
Mansion

Viewpoint

Escarpment

Cabo
Delgado

TDM /
mCell

Governor's
Mansion

Viewpoint

**PAQUITEQUETE**

Ave 25 de Setembro

Central

Ave 16 de Julho

Conselho Municipal
City Hall

Immigration

Ave 1 de Maio

Restaurant
556

**PAQUITEQUETE**

City Hall

Escarpment

Baia de Pemba

Banco Comercial
de Moçambique

Market

Farmácia
Pemba

Pensão
Marítimo

Rua do Comércio

*Baia de Pemba*

Dhows across
Bay
Paquitequete
Mosque

Market

Port

Fishermen's
Village

Port

100 m
50
0   (1 cm)   75 m

Namapa is 146 kilometres from Namialo, and you are able to refuel here. A couple of kilometres further you will cross the important Lurio River, a colourful sight of wide, sandy streams crowded with people washing clothes and enjoying themselves in the sun. At 186 kilometres, at the town of Chiore, carry on straight (do not take the left fork) and you will reach a major T-junction at Metoro (S13°06.345 E39°52.341). On your left is a new tarred road that stretches as far as Montepuez, which then deteriorates and eventually goes all the way west to Lichinga. You take the road right (east) and head for Pemba on a good tar road.

After 13 kilometres on the east-bound road, you pass the turn-off north to Macomia and on to the Tanzanian border and another 53 kilometres further is the dirt-road turn-off north to Metuge, Quissanga and the jumping-off place for Ibo Island. But, keeping to the tar, you carry on straight towards Pemba (the general speed limit is 80 kph, with 50 kph through the towns), and at S12°59.361 E40°31.693 you reach the Pemba airport terminal building.

## Introducing Pemba

A right turn at the airport will take you down to Wimbe Beach, but carry on straight into Pemba for a full circuit of the town and back to Wimbe. Making your way down the hill, you will reach the traffic circle with the globe in the middle. A right turn here leads down to the seafront at the war memorial traffic circle and the very up-market Pemba Beach Hotel, but head straight to the main intersection in town (you will

## Tourist information

Your most useful contact for all tourism services and bookings of accommodation, car rental, water sports, island trips, cultural events and even hunting is Kaskazini, with offices at Wimbe Beach Hotel, tel: 82-309-6990, e-mail: info@kaskazini.com. They are also a mine of information and have an excellent website that covers Pemba and surrounds: www.kaskazini.com.

know it by the Standard Bank, Hotel Cabo Delgado and mCel offices). Turn left here, head up the hill, turn right and stop at the monument to view one of the deepest, most protected bays in the world. The road winds down to the old town and the small dockyard. Head through to the point and stop for a view of the reed-hutted village on the beach (known as Paquitequete). Swing right and around the point, the road passes this village with all its fishing and boat-building activities to come out at the entrance of the vast bay (I was fortunate enough to spot whales here). Follow the seafront to the World War I memorial traffic circle and carry on to pass the Pemba Beach Hotel. You then reach another traffic circle (with a large anchor in the middle) where a right turn would take you back to the airport. Straight on takes you past the Complexo Nautilus and the beautiful palm-studded beaches of Wimbe. This is where tourists and travellers relax and enjoy the best of Mozambique. You carry on past the restaurants and accommodation to the end of the tar, and after 2 kilometres of sandy dirt road (keep left at the fork), you reach Russell's Place, aka Pemba Magic Lodge (S12°57.952 E40°04.040).

## Overnight in Pemba

**Russell's Place** is one of my favourite camps in Mozambique, but was closed for renovations for some time. Renovated and reopened now, it boasts a new kitchen, dorm and swimming pool. The old vibe is still there, as is the famous Blackfoot Bar. Double en-suite chalets cost 1 900 MT and camping is 222 MT per person. Contact Russell on tel: 82-686-2730, e-mail: russellbott@ yahoo.com, website: www.pemba-magic.com.

Heading back into town from Russell's, on the left just before the anchor traffic circle, is **Complexo**

**Turistico Caracol**, which offers smart, clean and comfortable rooms across the road from the main Wimbe beach, bars and restaurants. All double suites have sea views, air-cons, en-suite bathrooms and verandas for 2 000 MT. A suite of two bedrooms, lounge and bathroom, with additional TV and fridge, costs 4 000 MT. There is a small adjoining restaurant called Tipico. For details, tel: 27-22-0147 or 82-688-7430, fax: 27-22-0108, e-mail: sulemane@tele-data.mz. Nearby are two other options. The first is **Residencial Wimbe Sun**, which has clean, air-conditioned, en-suite double rooms for 1 800 MT a night (book through Kaskazini). The other is **Pieter's Place** with comfortable rooms in a garden setting under a majestic baobab tree. En-suite rooms have fans and fridges and cost 1 800 MT a night. Contact the nearby CI Divers for info

Locals trek-fish off the beach at Pemba.

and bookings. Across the road – and on the beach – is **Complexo Nautilus**, which has thatched bungalows under the palms, each with bathroom, fridge and air-con. There is a pool, bar and restaurant and a casino has also opened on the premises. A two-sleeper luxury bungalow costs 3 000 MT, a luxury four-sleeper 4 500 MT, and a standard four-sleeper bungalow 2 500 MT. Contact Nautilus, tel: 82-460-8640, e-mail: nautilushtl@teledata.mz.

Continuing along the seafront on the Av de Marginal we reach the magnificent **Pemba Beach Hotel** (S12°57.873 E40°31.672). From the moment you enter the gates of the extensive grounds and feast your eyes on the bougainvillea-covered main building, you know this is going to be a stylish visit. Huge Zanzibar doors set the mood as East African chic, while bubbling fountains, potted palms and cool, jazzy piped music slow you down to island time. Of course, the art is original, the carpets hand woven and the staff pleasant, friendly and efficient, for this is not just one of the best hotels in Mozambique, but one of the best in Africa. Within the complex is a sports club with swimming pool, tennis courts, gym and a newly constructed small-craft harbour. The Bar Niassa and Quirimba Restaurant are understandably the best in Pemba. The rooms have everything you could wish for at a cost of 5 500 MT per person sharing. The opulent suites cost 15 000 MT. For reservations, tel: +27-(0)11-463-6313, e-mail: enquir-ies@raniresorts.com, website: www.pembabeachresort.com.

From the World War I memorial traffic circle, head up into town and turn right into the main street at the globe traffic circle. The **Hotel Cabo Delgado** is very centrally situated on the corner of Av 25 de Setembro and Av Eduardo Mondlane. Although it looks a little run-down from the outside, the rooms are large and clean. Some have air-con. Singles cost 750 MT, doubles 1 400 MT and a two-roomed suite 2 000 MT. For details, tel: 27-22-0558, fax: 27-22-1552. One block up Av Eduardo Mondlane, turn left to get to the **Residencial Lys**. On a quiet side street, and always with running water, this is better value than the Cabo Delgado. Rooms with private bathroom and air-con cost 1 000 MT single and 1 200 MT double. To book, tel: 27-22-0951, fax: 27-22-0108, e-mail: suleman@teledata.mz. If you were to turn right instead of left off Av Eduardo Mondlane, you would find the **Pensão Baia** at 289 Av 1 Maio. Also in a quiet neighbourhood, the rooms are clean and neat and there is a cheap restaurant and shady patio. A room with two beds and shared facilities costs 700 MT and an air-conditioned room with bathroom costs 800 MT single and 900 MT double. Tel: 27-22-0153.

## Eating out in Pemba

Other than the restaurants at the hotels listed earlier, there are more options for eating out. The best is **Restaurant 556** on the edge of the hill as you drive down to the harbour. With air-con, a great view, soft lights and a cosmopolitan atmosphere, this is the place for a smart evening meal. Prices range from half a chicken 350 MT, rump steak 500 MT to pizza 450 MT. The best place for daytime pastries, coffee and light lunches is the **Pastelaria Flor d'Avenida**, just up from Hotel Cabo Delgado on Av Eduardo Mondlane. There is also a bakery next door selling rolls, bread and pastries. The most popular spot to eat and drink on Wimbe Beach is the **Pemba Dolphin**, just past the Complexo Nautilus. It's more of a beach bar than a restaurant, but they do serve good snacks in a beautiful setting under the palm trees. There are two other restaurants on Wimbe Beach. Heading away from Pemba Dolphin in the direction of Russell's, you will first reach the **Restaurant Wimbe**, which is more of a nightclub really, and then there's the **Restaurant Aquilo Romano**, serving predominantly Italian dishes. For takeaways, drop in at **Pemba Takeaways** at the intersection at Hotel Cabo Delgado.

## Out and about in Pemba

**CI Divers** has a shop in the main Complexo Nautilus building, and offers resort diving courses for 10 000 MT, open-water courses for 15 000 MT and divemaster for 27 000 MT. A guided dive with their equipment costs 1 800 MT and only half of that if you have your own gear. Contact Pieter or Gi-Gi Jacobs, tel: 82-682-2700, tel/fax: 27-22-0102, e-mail: cidivers@teledata.mz,

website: www.cidivers.com. **Pemba Dive** operates from their own lodge and bush camp within a 100-acre coastal nature estate overlooking Pemba Bay. To find them, turn left at the control point 1 kilometre before the airport when approaching the town – it's another 2 kilometres down to the lodge (aka Nacole Gardens). They also have an office on Wimbe Beach. They offer all the normal scuba diving activities, as well as other adventure sports. Accommodation is available in en-suite chalets, which cost 3 000 MT per night, standing tents at 600 MT per person and camping is 300 MT per person. For more info, tel: 82-661-1530, e-mail: pembadive@gmail.com, website: www. pembadivecamp.com.

Martin Visagie runs a sport fishing and diving operation based on his 34-foot boat *St Lazarus*. Whether it's day trips or five- and seven-day packages, he has the gear, tackle and 40 years of experience to tailor an itinerary to suit your needs. Contacts are in South Africa, tel: +27-(0)35-571-0104 or +27-(0)82-936-3599, e-mail: worldcharters@iafrica.com, website: www.world-charters.com.

At the intersection of 25 de Setembro and Eduardo Mondlane across from the Hotel Cabo Delgado, you will find all the major banks (who will change currencies and also have ATM cash machines that accept Visa and Mastercard), and the offices of airline LAM, bottle store and Pemba Takeaways. On the other corner is TDM for public telephones, and mCell for mobile phones and recharge vouchers. Up the road from the Cabo Delgado is a small supermarket, auto-spares, tyres

Don't be tempted to buy sea shells in Mozambique. Rather help keep them where they belong – living on the underwater reefs.

and gas shop, as well as a pharmacy. Behind LAM is the **Viatur** travel agency, tel: 27-22-3431, fax: 27-22-2249, e-mail: viatur@emilmoz.com, and Omar Rent-a-Car. Up the road, on the same side, is the Pastelaria Flor d'Avenida.

Another busy part of town is the section of the main road past the globe traffic circle. There's a garage on the right and further down the road on the right are a few motor-spares shops and the big, well-stocked Osman Jacob Supermarket. Behind the supermarket you will find the Macula bus depot from where buses fan out to destinations such as Mueda, Mocimboa da Praia, Nampula and Nacala. Next door to the bus depot is Trak Auto, agents for Land Rover and Mazda. And ask for Herculano Fario's workshop in the area for repairs to all makes of

machinery. Across the road is Toyota de Moçambique, tel: 27-22-0551, fax: 27-22-0813, e-mail: toyotapmb@teledata.mz. Next up is a bank, and further down on the right is another good bakery.

The old town near the dockyard used to be a hive of activity, but now it's just a traffic jam of trucks ferrying Mozambique's precious hardwood forests to hungry foreign ships. Maybe it's because the old Maritimo Hotel is closed for renovations, but the few remaining shops and bars are mostly deserted. The market is still alive and kicking, and the main post office is still open, but there is not much to keep a traveller down here.

At the airport (just off the main road as you come into Pemba) you will find DHL and the offices of **Moti Rent-a-Car**. They have a range of pick-ups and

Boats dry out at low tide in Paquitequete, Pemba, the largest town in the north.

SUVs to hire. Contact Moti, tel 27-22-1687, fax: 27-22-1688. The airport hosts domestic flights by LAM to Beira and Maputo and international flights to Dar es Salaam and Nairobi. SA Airlink also flies direct to Johannesburg and charter flights flit across to the islands of the Quirimbas Archipelago.

Shortly after the airport, on your right going into Pemba, is **Sethy Nissan**, tel: 27-22-1521, fax: 27-22-0079, e-mail: sethy1@teledata.mz. Further on into town is the big Galp service station for fuel and puncture repairs, where they also have a surprisingly well-stocked minimarket (food, booze and toiletries). Galp also refills gas cylinders, as do Vida Gas near the port and Ceconur in the main avenue in town. For general auto repairs, try **Setec Auto**, tel: 27-22-0323.

There is a private clinic just up the hill from the Hotel Cabo Delgado in Av Eduardo Mondlane and a provincial hospital in Av Base Moçambique (carry on through the Cabo Delgado intersection). For medical assistance, tel: 27-22-1701. You can be tested for malaria at the Centro de Saude de Natite Clinic near Mbangula market. This clinic also has a Cuban dentist with lots of anaesthetic!

There are a couple of internet options in town. The more appealing one is in the Pemba Beach Hotel business centre, which offers a fast, but expensive wireless connection. The other is at Sycamore Services in the big new building in town, opposite the Standard Bank.

And finally, for the best in Makonde masks and traditional jewellery, mats and baskets visit the two branches of Artes Makonde (previously known as Cee Bee Pemba) on the premises of Complexo Nautilus and at the Pemba Beach Hotel.

# 22

# Ibo Island and north to Tanzania

The history of Ibo Island and the Quirimbas Archipelago is similar and linked to that of Ilha de Moçambique. First settled by Muslim traders, the islands were part of a commercial network that started in the Gulf of Oman and stretched down the East African coast – Mogadishu, Kismayo, Lamu, Zanzibar and Kilwa to the north, and Ilha de Moçambique and Sofala to the south. Large trading dhows would sail down the coast, using the northerly winds during November to April, and sail back again on the southerly winds from May to October – the Trade Winds.

The crumbling entrance to the Fort of São João on Ibo Island.

Ivory and slaves were the main commodities when the Portuguese muscled their way in during the 16th century. As Ibo rose in importance under the Portuguese, they built a fort was constructed and the island's prosperity peaked in the late 18th century as it became the major supplier of slaves to the sugar plantations of France's Indian Ocean Islands. It's decline in the early 1900s was mainly due to the lack of a decent deep-sea harbour, and trading operations moved to the nearby harbour of Porto Amelia (as Pemba was then known). The local fisherfolk who remain have no use for the grand abandoned villas and administrative buildings. As part of the Quirimbas Archipelago National Park, Ibo officials are entitled to charge 250 MT entrance fee and a further 60 MT a day to stay on the island.

## En route to Ibo Island

Recently incorporated into the new **Parque National das Quirimbas**, along with a large stretch of the coastline, the archipelago offers a unique opportunity to experience the history and natural beauty of this part of the African coast. Getting there has become a lot easier now that charter flights are being offered to Ibo at 4000 MT a person (contact Kaskazini in Pemba for details and bookings), but let's rather travel the overland route. From the airport travel for 24 kilometres towards Metoro, then turn right (S13°04.354 E40°24.635) to Metuge. Carry on straight along a deeply rutted and potholed dirt road (very bad when wet). At 70 kilometres you will pass Praia de Bandar; keep left

here and follow the signs to Quissanga. Little villages rattle by and you might spot bush hunters armed with nothing more than bows and arrows. With the tripmeter on 92, you will cross a long Bailey bridge and, a couple of kilometres further, enter the little town of Mahate. There is a signboarded intersection in the middle of town (S12°31.401 E40°25.343) indicating Pemba 102 (from where you've come), Macomia 47 (to the left) and Quissanga 15 (straight on, to where you're going). Continue until you reach an incongruous traffic circle around a small monument (you will recognise the spot by a large concrete cross in the area). Turn left to Bairro de Tandanhangue. Cross a couple of dodgy little wooden bridges, drive through Tandanhangue village (ignore the 'Safe Parking' signs) and cross the tidal flats until, three hours and 116 kilometres from Pemba, you reach Baobab Beach, the jumping-off place for Ibo Island.

## Painted ladies

On Ibo, and other islands and towns along the north coast, you are likely to see young women with their faces painted white. This tradition is known as *musiro* and is used primarily to protect, soften and beautify the skin. The paste for this mask is made by grinding a branch of the msiro tree with a little water and is left on for the day. A painted white face is sometimes also an indication of the woman's marital status, or whether her husband is away for a while!

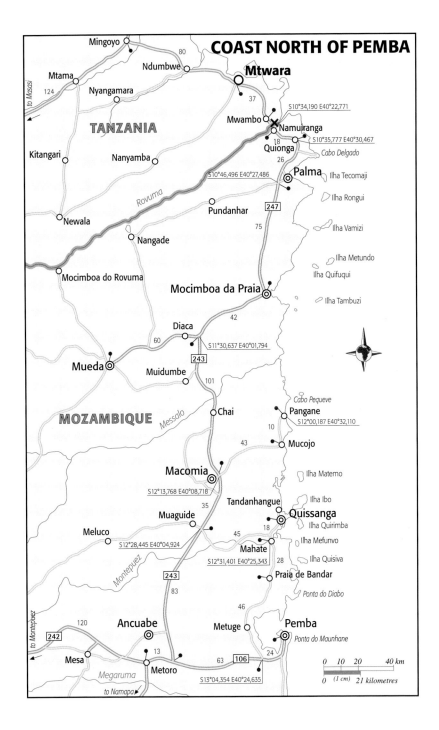

COAST NORTH OF PEMBA

Mingoyo
80
Ndumbwe
Mtama
124
Nyangamara
**Mtwara**
37
S10°34,190 E40°22,771
Mwambo
Namuiranga
18
S10°35,777 E40°30,467
Quionga
26
Cabo Delgado

TANZANIA

Kitangari
Nanyamba

S10°46,496 E40°27,486
**Palma**
Ilha Tecomaji

Ilha Rongui

Rovuma

Pundanhar
247
75
Newala

Nangade

Ilha Vamizi

Ilha Metundo
Mocimboa do Rovuma
Ilha Quifuqui

**Mocimboa da Praia**
Ilha Tambuzi

42
Diaca
60
S11°30,637 E40°01,794
243
**Mueda**
Muidumbe
101

MOZAMBIQUE
Messalo

Chai
Cabo Pequeve
Pangane
10
S12°00,187 E40°32,110

43
Mucojo

**Macomia**
Ilha Matemo
S12°13,768 E40°08,718
35
Tandanhangue
Ilha Ibo
Muaguide
**Quissanga**
18
Ilha Quirimba
Meluco
45
Ilha Mefunvo
S12°28,445 E40°04,924
**Mahate**
S12°31,401 E40°25,343
28
Ilha Quisiva
Montepuez
243
Praia de Bandar
83
Ponta do Diabo

46
120
**Ancuabe**
Metuge
**Pemba**
242
13
Ponta do Maunhane
to Montepuez
Mesa
63
106
24
Megaruma
Metoro
S13°04,354 E40°24,635
to Namapa

0   10   20        40 km

0   (1 cm)   21 kilometres

Since 1997, when I first visited this charmed place, they have improved the road and built a few mud huts on the beach, housing a small shop, bar and eating place. There is even overnight accommodation (very basic) in case you miss the last boat across to the island. But the fishermen still skilfully sail their dhows in through the mangrove trees and land their catches here, the women and children still flock around to see what has been caught and opportunistic birds still scavenge the shore – a little piece of unspoilt Africa. The huts cluster around the enclosed compound of **Ibo Island Lodge**. Here you can camp for 100 MT a person or leave your car safely enclosed and guarded for 100 MT a day. *Chapas* run between here and Pemba for about 125 MT and a dhow ride across to Ibo should cost about the same – less if you bargain well.

Boats leave from the beach at high tide and then only sporadically, so be patient and watch what the local travellers do. When it's time to go, you will have to wade out to the dhow, so take your shoes off and be prepared to get wet. Alternatively, you might be offered a ride out in a small dinghy, but this will cost you extra. Find a dry spot in the boat to stow your gear and choose a seat where you won't get too drenched by spray (but you'll still get wet). Depending on the wind, you might be poled or rowed out through the channel in the mangroves, but when you hit the open bay, a tatty old sail will be unfurled, ancient frayed ropes pulled tight and suddenly you'll be skimming over the water as efficiently as on any playboy's million-dollar yacht.

Dolphins will cavort under your bow and you might take a short cut through a mangrove swamp to suddenly come upon the little harbour of Ibo. There's more getting wet here, but when you're on dry land, put your shoes on again as there are lots of thorns about.

## Overnight on Ibo

Accommodation on Ibo Island is limited – the best, by far, is the upmarket **Ibo Island Lodge** overlooking the channel (walk straight along the sea wall from the jetty, and you'll find it on your right). Bougainvillea frames the building, large high-ceilinged rooms catch the cool ocean breeze, and Amber, the ridgeback, slumbers in the shade. Dining is on the wide front veranda – fresh pancakes for breakfast and, if you're lucky, giant lobster for dinner. This recently renovated establishment has transformed three old historical mansions into nine luxurious air-conned en-suite rooms, each with its own private veranda. There is a swimming pool and they also offer boat trips, snorkelling and a massage for those tired muscles! Daily rates are between 10 000 and 11 000 MT per person, sharing (depending on the season). Contact them on tel: +27-(0)21-702-0285, fax: +27-(0)21-702-0692, e-mail: reservations@iboisland.com, website: www.iboisland.com.

**Casa Janine** (aka Karibuni) was until recently the only accommodation on Ibo, and is situated just past Ibo Island Lodge on the Rua Basilio PO Seguro. French-speaking Janine, who has been on the island for over 15 years, offers camping for 150 MT

Fishermen pole their dhow in through the mangrove trees.

per person, dorm beds for 250 MT and rustic en-suite bungalows for 750 MT. The place is a bit run-down but serves cold beers, good home-cooked seafood meals and island-grown coffee, all at very reasonable prices. Contact Janine, tel: 27-22-0800 or 82-629-7950, e-mail: ibo_pemba@yahoo.fr.

The third option is the unmarked, TDM-owned guesthouse in town overlooking the harbour. It is hardly ever open, but the manager can usually be found in the bar/restaurant across the street. Rooms without bathrooms cost 420 MT single and 550 MT double.

The best value-for-money option is the **Cinco Portas Pensao** situated in main village. Skilfully renovated old waterfront stores have been transformed into a small guesthouse with a swimming pool, bar and restaurant. Rates start at around 1200 MT for a small single room and climb to 11000 MT for a seven-bedded apartment. E-mail: cincoportas@yahoo.com, website: www.cincoportas.com.

## Out and about on Ibo

The best way to get a feel for the island is to take a walk around the town. We start at the jetty that juts out into the little harbour. Young boys might be playing on the beach, just as they do all over the world – a bit loutish and loud

and showing off with cartwheels and somersaults in the sand. Boats waiting for the tide to rise will be loading passengers and goods before being poled out into deeper water – they'll hoist the boom, the lateen sail will billow and fill, and then they're gone. A walk along the sea wall at low tide will reward you with sightings of a good variety of waders and seabirds as the tidal flats begin to dry out.

Passing the Ibo Island Lodge on your right, you have the beach on your left (only swimmable at high tide). Once smart, but now decaying houses line this Rua Basilio PO Seguro, casuarina trees whisper in the wind, and you pass Casa Janine on your left. Carry on and you soon reach the old Portuguese **Fort of São João**. Perfectly shaped as a five-pointed star and dating back to 1791, it is in reasonable condition. Cannons protrude from the ramparts over the sea below and big spreading trees shade the courtyard. The entry fee is a bit opportunistic at 50 MT, but it does allow you to observe and photograph the silversmiths at work there. Some of their jewellery is on display and for sale at bargain prices.

Continuing around the perimeter of the island will bring you to fishermen's huts and some interesting boatbuilding activity, but we still have to explore the town, so head out of the gates of the fort and walk up the Rua de Fortaleza towards town. The old cement courts of the Discoteca Tenis will catch your eye, although it is now just a local bar. Keep left up the Rua Dona Maria Pia, past row upon row of once-quaint cottages and shops, in the direction of the

Cannons point out from the ramparts of the Fort of São João.

concrete water tower on the hill. You may come across a 'painted lady' and it could cost 10 MT to photograph her. Don't expect to find much in the way of supplies at the small municipal market (or for that matter on the rest of the island). Just past the market is another, smaller fort, which dates back to 1841. Turn right here and head down to the water's edge.

The small run-down dwelling at the harbour wall houses another silversmith where you can watch the process of jewellery-making and also purchase pieces. Swing right to stroll the promenade back into the centre of town, passing the unmarked TDM guesthouse. Keep on the street closest to the water to pass old shops and trading houses with back yards that open onto the harbour for loading and unloading. Here you will find the Cinco Portas Pensao.

The road now widens into an open square surrounded by police station, district administration and frangipani-framed governor's office. Dusty public gardens with broken benches attest to a much grander era when ladies and gents paraded in their finery, but at least the nearby post office and school are still in use. Keeping left, you pass the big old church and a beautifully ornate building covered with fine decorative cast-iron work. The final building of note on your walkabout is the ruin of the little Fort of São José, which predates the larger São João fort. A few more steps, and you're back at the jetty.

You will have noticed on your walk that there are no bars (the Muslim influence) and no restaurants (no demand), so your only options are Ibo Island Lodge and Cinco Portas Pensao. It's a good idea to bring a supply of bottled water and anything else you may require, as there is very little that you can buy on the island (sometimes fishermen will sell you the pick of their catch). And because there is no mains electricity on the island and only a few small generators, nothing much happens at night. In fact, the same is true of the day, so bring a thick book to read (and a torch).

Although the whole archipelago has been declared a national park, I hope the sealife survives the wholesale poaching that takes place. When I was last there, a large Spanish factory ship was blatantly anchored inshore off Ibo and was cleverly not fishing, but buy-ing up all the seafood it could from the local fishermen – thus encouraging and corrupting the islanders to poach their own heritage and reserves. Local politi-cians were reputed to be benefiting.

## Back to the mainland

To return to the mainland, first check when the tide will be high. Make sure you are already packed, but leave your luggage at your accommodation and go down to the jetty a couple of hours before high tide. Negotiate a price (120 MT seems fair) and then fetch your luggage just before leaving. The procedure is the same as when we came across – wade out, stow luggage, settle in, wait for last-minute stragglers and sail off. If you arrive back at Baobab Beach late in the afternoon and need to get back to Pemba by public transport, it is prob-ably wiser to stay over on the beach rather than squeeze aboard an over-loaded pick-up and tackle the rough road back in the dark.

There are other much more exclusive, upmarket and expensive options in the Quirimbas Archipelago. There are the luxurious villas on Quilalea Island that can be reached by light plane (15 500 MT per person, per night, shar-ing). You can also fly in to Matemo Island to the Rani Resort there (11 750 MT). The exclusive isolation of Medjumbe Island will set you back 13 650 MT, or the most northerly Vamizi Island, with its 10 luxury houses, is a stiff 20 000 MT a night. All these resorts offer a range of activities and pamper their guests outrageously. For more info and book-ings, contact Kaskazini in Pemba on tel: 82-309-6990, e-mail: info@kaskazini.

The old, disused warehouses that line the small harbour at Ibo attest to a more prosperous past.

com, website: www.kaskazini.com.

The alternative is to retrace your incoming route through **Tandanhangue** village (1.3 kilometres), the **Quissanga** traffic circle (6 kilometres) to the signposted intersection in Mahate (19.8 kilometres). This time, turn right onto the **Macomia** road to continue your quest northwards. The road is rough with potholes, ruts and sand, but at the main tarred road (S12°28.445 E40°04.924), turn right and head north to Macomia, another 35 kilometres on. This is the point (S12°13.768 E40°08.718) at which you can turn off east down to the coast to visit Pangane's idyllic palm-fringed beaches. Macomia has a lively market, diesel from the pumps and petrol in cans. You can also get a meal and drink in Chung's Bar at the intersection, where all the buses stop.

A rough dirt road runs for 43 kilometres from the above-mentioned inter-section down to the coast at **Mucojo**. Carry on through this village and up the coast along a very soft sandy track (engage 4×4 and deflate your tyres). Thousands of palms cover this stretch of the coast and the fronds and husks of these trees are used to cover the worst patches of the track to make it passable. Past the little village of **Nambo** and, after another 10 kilometres from Mucojo, you reach Pangane.

## Pangane

**Casa Suk** (S12°00.187 E40°32.110) seems to be the centre of the village and the most solid building – the rest of the village is made up of the reed huts of local fishermen. Casa Suk has a block of neat, clean rooms in the back yard and good vehicle security. They charge 400 MT a person in a basic room with shared ablutions. There is no bar/restaurant, but they will cook for you on order. Across the track on

Fishermen's nets litter the beach at Pangane.

the beach is a small fenced-off area, grandly called **The Pangane Beach Bar and Restaurant**, where you can sit and enjoy basic food and drinks (fish, rice and beer).

But you came down here only for one reason, and that was to stay at **Ashim's**. Ashim and his charming family run a small camp right at the end of the beach (the solid blue-and-white house stands 1 kilometre beyond Casa Suk). Out on a coral headland and almost surrounded by sea and beach, Ashim offers a choice of three tiny unfurnished coral-and-reed huts, or camping. The huts do not even have cemented floors, but are adequate if you have your own mattresses and other camping gear. They cost 400 MT each and camping is 200 MT per tent. The cold showers and flush toilets (with a bucket of seawater) are communal reed enclosures – it sounds bad, but it's attractively done.

The fishing is good around here.

Lateen-rigged sailing dhows bring in the catches, *kapenta* dries on the sand and octopus hang out on racks. If you're looking for a place to unwind, this is it.

## On to Mocimboa da Praia

Back at Macomia, you swing northward again on a road that is partly reasonable gravel, and partly bad tar. After 101 kilometres, you reach an intersection (S11°30.637 E40°01.794) where the road splits. A left turn here takes you via a tarred road through the village of Diaca and on to Mueda. The road is being rebuilt from here to Negomane where there is a new bridge across the Rovuma into Tanzania. This is now the only route for vehicles wanting to cross the river into Tanzania, but I will first take you up to the mouth of the Rovuma for those intrepid public transport travellers who want to cross there. So turn right at the intersection and let's head for Mocimboa da Praia.

# MOCIMBOA DA PRAIA

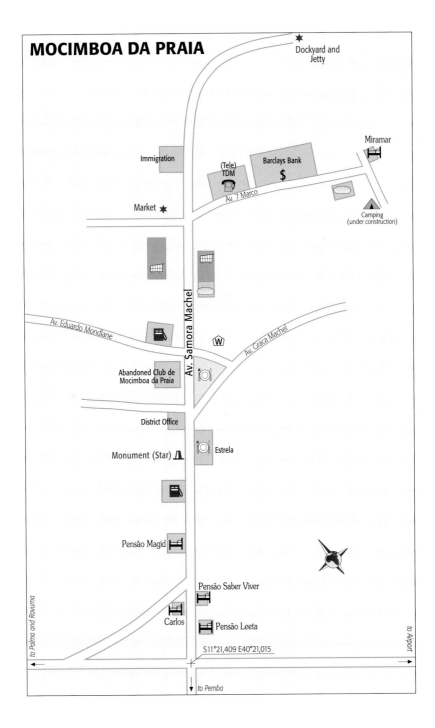

Dockyard and Jetty

Miramar

Immigration

(Tele) TDM

Barclays Bank $

Av. 7 Marco

Market ⭐

Camping (under construction)

Av. Eduardo Mondlane

Av. Samora Machel

W

Av. Graça Machel

Abandoned Club de Mocimboa da Praia

District Office

Monument (Star) 🗿

Estrela

Pensão Magid

Pensão Saber Viver

Carlos

Pensão Leeta

S11°21,409 E40°21,015

to Palma and Rovuma

to Airport

to Pemba

(If you are driving in the opposite direction, from Mocimboa da Praia south to Pemba, take care here. It is very easy to carry straight on past the turn-off and head for Mueda. You need to turn left here to get to Pemba.) It is 42 kilometres of reasonable tar to Mocimboa, which is entered via a traffic circle. The right turn leads to the aerodrome, the left to Palma, and road straight ahead on into town.

Mocimboa is entered via a long dual-carriage road (another Av Samora Machel) and within a kilometre you encounter almost all the accommodation the town has to offer. The first is **Pensão Leeta**, a scruffy double-storeyed building on the right. The ablutions are shared, the shower is cold and the toilet flushes with a bucket of water, but a double bed in a room costs only 400 MT. Contact Manuel, tel: 27-28-1147. Further down, also on the right, is the much better **Pensão Saber Viver**. Tightly run by a Muslim father and son, this is a quiet place with no bar and no drinking allowed. The rooms are even cheaper at 300 MT and have a double bed and private bathroom with a bucket shower (toilets are outside and are shared). There is a safe yard for your vehicle, but they rather cheekily charge 75 MT a night for your car. Contact Rajabo, tel: 27-28-1160. The **Carlos Resthouse and Discoteca** across the road cannot be recommended, even though their grubby double rondavels are only 200 MT a night (I think they are more often rented by the hour). The smelly toilets are a hole in the floor and the place is very noisy from the all-night bar and disco. Further

on down the road, on the left, is the long-established **Pensão Residencial Magid**. Run-down, dirty and with a noisy bar, it at least serves decent cheap food. A room with two beds and shared facilities costs 325 MT, a room with double bed and en-suite bucket bathroom is 400 MT. Parking is in a back yard. Contact Jusinto, tel: 27-28-1099.

Just past Magid is an unfinished service station that sells diesel from a road tanker, and beyond that a star monument and the district offices. Across the road is the pleasant **Estrela** bar and restaurant, and then the abandoned Club de Mocimboa da Praia on the left. There is another fuel station just down Av Eduardo Mondlane, but if we stay on Samora Machel we will find a cluster of shops selling general goods. On the right-hand side of the road is the Tekawey (take-away) Shahista, named after this newly arrived Indian couple's young daughter. There is a selection of Indian delicacies, a small stock of groceries and freshly baked bread, cake and biscuits. A small open-air market on the left is where you can buy the bare necessities, and then the road swings off to the right and heads for the beach. To carry on straight from the market would bring you to the harbour where you would be shocked to see how much timber is being shipped out. How much longer can it continue?

Rather swing right and continue on down Av 7 Marco. The TDM (telephones) is on your left, followed by the Barclays Bank. Across the road is another bakery and then you hit the beach and **The Miramar**. The Miramar is a collection of three bungalows on the beach. Grubby and run-down, with no security, it does however have a popular bar/restaurant pleasantly presided over by the hugely obese and non-moving Bebe, who rules from her bedroom-cum-kitchen. There is one more accommodation establishment. **Chez Natalie** (S11°19.901 E40°21.184) is out on the north side of town and overlooks the mangrove-circled mouth of the Mpanga River. Their en-suite bungalows sleep two persons and cost 1 800 MT a night. Camping is also available. For up-to-date info, tel: 27-28-1092, e-mail: natalie@teledata.mz.

The turn-off north opposite Pensão Saber Viver is where the *chapas* pick-ups leave from to go to Palma and on to the Tanzanian border at the Rovuma River Mouth. Enquire the night before and ask to be picked up at your hotel, as they leave very early (around 04h00).

## To the Tanzania border

You've come so far from first crossing the border into Mozambique at Ponta do Ouro that you are now close to reaching the northern tip of the country. Just 120 kilometres to go! Although the new bridge across the Rovuma at Negomane has become the preferred overland route into Tanzania for self-drivers, I will also describe the old route to the border post at the mouth of the Rovuma River. This is for those adventurous backpackers who want to take advantage of the shorter coastal route. Leaving Mocimboa da Praia, turn north to **Palma** at the aerodrome traffic circle (S11°21.409 E40°21.015). This dirt road is rough and potholed, and very bad in wet conditions. It

goes through small villages with well-known names such as Maputo and Quelimane. At 49 kilometres, there is a turn-off right to the village of **Olumbi**, but carry on straight. After about 1 hour and 40 minutes, you will reach an important intersection at 78 kilometres (S10°46.496 E40°27.486). To the right, it is 2 kilometres into Palma town – don't bother going down, I could find nothing of interest – and to the left is a very rough track that loops back around to **Mueda**. Straight across the intersection is the route to Tanzania.

Passing a big new church on your right as you leave the intersection, the track narrows to a single lane and deteriorates into deep sand. Visibility is bad, with high grass and dense bush on either side, so be careful of the speeding *chapas* pick-ups that ply this section of road. At 100.5 kilometres another track comes in from the right. This is the direct route from Palma town and one to avoid if you were coming from the north. There are reputed to be many elephants in the area and, although I didn't see any, there was plenty of fresh dung on the track. The sand becomes thicker and softer with a high 'island' in the middle and the bush crowds in closer – all 4×4 driving. The village of **Quionga** is reached at 104 kilometres. Keep right at the well (S10°35.777 E40°30.467) and go down the main street, with its old lampposts. Pass the flagpole and admin buildings and bear left at the end of the village.

The river you see now is not yet the Rovuma, but forms a tidal flat that is tricky to negotiate. The Mozambican border post of **Namiranga** is reached at

The sun sets over the Rovuma River while Tanzania beckons in the distance.

122 kilometres (S10°34.190 E40°22.771). There is a little settlement here with a shop selling basic groceries, food and beer and even rough accommodation is available at the **Selamani Moosa Border Guest House** (a room with two beds costs 200 MT). The border is a cluster of mud huts, although they are building a smart new post, and it is hassle-free, as most isolated border posts are. Ask where the latest crossing point is and head down to the banks of the river. Canoes and dugouts ply the waters, carrying passengers and their luggage across to Tanzania. Negotiate a fee before being paddled across. On the far bank you might have to walk across the marshy sand flats to where Landrover transport will drive you into the little village of **Mwambo**. Once border formalities have been completed here you can take a minibus taxi to **Mtwara** and ... bon voyage!

For those with vehicles who want to head north into Tanzania, we have to backtrack to the turn-off to Diaca and Mueda (S11°30.637 E40°01.794), 42 kilometres south of Mocimboa da Praia. From this turn-off, 72 kilometres of reasonable tar takes you to **Mueda**. Don't take the 509 road to Montepuez, but head east on the new road to **Negomane**. This road is still under construction and can be very rough in parts. After about 200 kilometres you reach the new Friendship Bridge at Negomane. The Moz border post might still be at Ngapa (130 kilometres from the new bridge) as they are still building the new one at Negomane. The Tanzanian post might also not be complete and a 10-kilometre drive will bring you to the old one, which also might not be able to issue visas and stamp carnets (this must then be done in Lindi). The road on via Masasi to **Lindi** on the coast is also under construction and can be rough.

# 23

# West through Malawi to Tete and Cahora Bassa

As you are up in the north of Mozambique, you may want to take a detour…
I suggest a route from Nampula, via Cuamba, to Blantyre in Malawi, and then
the short run to Tete. Zero the trusty speedo at the train station in Nampula and
head out east on the Av de Trabalho towards Alto Molocue.

Cahora Bassa Dam and the hydroelectric plant dominate the gorge at Songo.

After just 4.2 kilometres (S15°06.685 E39°13.661), turn right to **Ribaue** and **Cuamba**. The rocky pinnacles and domes that dot the countryside here are a challenge to any mountaineer, but the gravel road is not too demanding until you pass through **Rapale** (at 20 kilometres). Now it deteriorates and crisscrosses the railway line that runs parallel. Dusty in the dry and wet and slippery when wet, it passes through the bustling little market town of **Nomigonha**.

## On to Malema

At a higher altitude and away from the coastal humidity, **Ribaue** was once a popular refuge from lowland heat. Still a pretty town with tree-lined avenues, there is an old derelict 1930s hotel on the road out of town that must have once been the last word in luxury. A cellphone tower has been erected, so try your phone here. The road east continues through town and out past the Canam Cotton Factory. At 161 kilometres, there is an unsignposted turn-off to the left, but keep straight and, after another 4 kilometres, there is a fork (S14°58.371 E38°03.717) in the road. Keep right towards **Cuamba** (left will take you down south to Alto Molocue). This is pleasant hilly countryside with many koppies and inselbergs. **Malema** is reached at 240 kilometres, so turn left at the station (S14°56.859 E37°24.948). The town and its amenities come as a surprise out here in the dusty bush. Heading away from the station, and all on your left, you will find **Pensão Malema**, which has a limited restaurant and basic en-suite rooms, costing

100 MT single and 140 MT double. Then there's the TDM for public phones and internet, followed by a shop and the municipal market behind it. Next up is a bar, then the **Residencial Cave Negra**, a dirty, noisy place with rooms (shared facilities) for 180 MT single and 220 MT double. At the end of the road is the smart, but weirdly out-of-place **N&F Lodge** (Complexo Malaya). It is a lot more expensive than the other places in town, but is a clean, comfortable, secure, motel-like establishment with bar/restaurant and even a hairdresser on the premises. Accommodation is in four-bedroomed, self-contained bungalows where each double room is en-suite with satellite TV and 24-hour electricity. The cost is 800 MT per room. Across the road is a fuel station and shop; swing right here to leave town, passing the hospital on your right.

A jagged range of inselbergs looks like the scaly spine of a monstrous dinosaur off on the left, as the road deteriorates further. A traffic circle with a statue of the Madonna (S14°52.730 E37°00.960) is reached at 286 kilometres, where the left turn leads to Gurue (see Chapter 21). Carry on straight and pass the impressive stone gates of the Mutuali Secondary School and, a little further on, the large and incongrous old tsetse fly control building. The road now has sharp, deep potholes and is badly rutted, so slow down to 40 kph. When you cross the Lurio River into the Niassa province, the road improves and you can maintain 80 kph. The mountains keep getting bigger and better. Fortunately, there is no mountain driving, as these giants

The road to Cuamba is rugged and lonely, but boasts fantastic scenery.

rise up sheer from the flat country-side, like the giant sheer-sided monster of a mountain 20 kilometres before Cuamba. With a round cupola dome on top and waterfalls down the sides, this is the best of the bunch. Finally, 350 kilometres from Nampula and a hard day's ride, we reach Cuamba.

## Cuamba

Cuamba is an important junction town. The railway line from the coast at Nacala forks east into Malawi and north to the town of Lichinga, while roads fan out to Lichinga, Malawi, Gurue and Nampula.

As the economic hub of the Niassa province and because of its proximity to Malawi, Cuamba is a bustling town and has a lively market. Water in the taps, however, is erratic.

The town is entered along Av Eduardo Mondlane, the main street, and the first feature, just past the school, is an intersection on the left with a statue of the Madonna in the centre. Remember this spot, as this is the way out. Across the road, opposite the school, is a BP service station that doesn't always have fuel. Then there is the BIM Bank and Expresso ATM and, moving on along Eduardo Mondlane, there is a park on your right. Two blocks further on your right is a little cluster of a bar/restaurant, shop and bakery, a disused cinema and a fuel pump that almost always has diesel and sometimes petrol. Across the open square on your left is the railway station and at the end of the road is the general hospital.

Driving back along Av Eduardo Mondlane, turn down left into Rua Liberade just before the park. The **Pensão Namaacha** on your left might have closed down by the time you read this, as it was definitely on its way out when I saw it. Very shabby, with bombed-out bathrooms and dirty

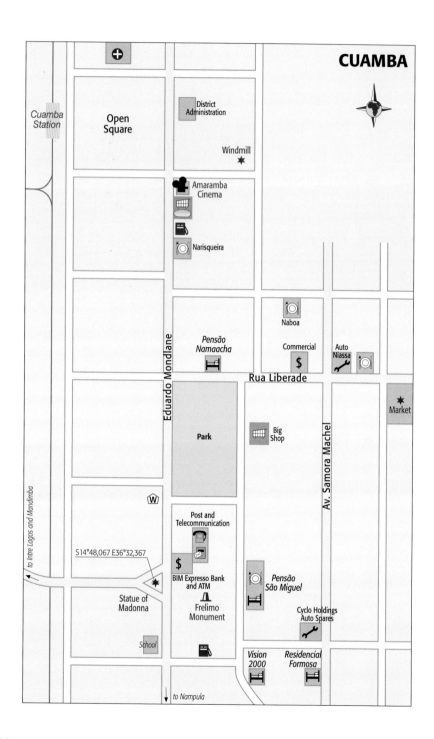

**CUAMBA**

Cuamba Station

Open Square

District Administration

Windmill

Amaramba Cinema

Narisqueira

Naboa

Pensão Namaacha

Commercial

Auto Niassa

Rua Liberade

Eduardo Mondlane

Park

Market

Big Shop

Av. Samora Machel

to Intre Lagos and Mandimba

Post and Telecommunication

S14°48,067 E36°32,367

BIM Expresso Bank and ATM

Pensão São Miguel

Statue of Madonna

Frelimo Monument

Cyclo Holdings Auto Spares

School

Vision 2000

Residencial Formosa

to Nampula

bedrooms, they charge only 250 MT a room. Whether that includes your pick of the girls that hang about there, I can't say. Facing the park on your right is a large general dealer and, if you continue down Rua Liberade, you will find another bank. One more block down, on your left is Auto Niassa for vehicle repairs, and then the market on your right. A right turn at Auto Niassa into Av Samora Machel will bring you to Cyclo Holdings Auto Spares.

Cuamba's best accommodation is at the **Hotel Vision 2000** in Av 3 de Fevereiro, down from the BP station on the main road as you come into town. First-floor double rooms with bathroom and fan cost 1200 MT. Second-floor double rooms have bathroom, air-con, fridge and satellite TV for 1600 MT, including breakfast. With a pleasant outdoor bar under thatch and a restaurant serving reasonably priced meals, this is the place to eat and drink. For details, tel: 27-16-2632, fax: 27-16-2713, e-mail: book@vision-2000.biz, website: www.vision-2000.biz. Cheaper is the **Pensão São Miguel**, just west of Vision 2000. Owned and run by a Portuguese family, it also boasts a small bar/restaurant and has secure parking in the back yard. Double rooms with shared facilities cost 400 MT, with bathroom 800 MT.

Second-class passenger trains (with restaurant cars that serve meals and drinks) run between Nampula and Cuamba every day except Mondays. One train leaves Cuamba at 05h30 and another leaves Nampula at 05h00, passing each other in the station at Mussa, and arriving at their respective destinations at around 15h00.

## On to Liwonde

To drive to **Liwonde** in Malawi from Cuamba you have two options; the obvious – and considerably easier – but longer route (325 kilometres) north via Mandimba and Mangochi, or the obscure, rough, but shorter track (190 kilometres) directly west via the border at Nayuchi. I suggest the latter, but what follows is a brief description of the northern route…

Go to the Madonna intersection in Cuamba (S14°48.067 E36°32.367), turn south and cross the railway line. Make your way through this reed-hut part of town, with its buses and trucks loading passengers and goods for the long haul ahead. A sprawling market on the outskirts of town sells mainly bright plastic ware and shiny new bicycles. Pass under the railway bridge and carry straight on (a left turn here would take you along the shorter Nayuchi route). A reasonable dirt road follows the railway line for more than 100 kilometres, and then swings west to cross the Lugenda River at about 150 kilometres. At just short of 200 kilometres, you reach **Mandimba**, where you can turn north to Lichinga. Carry on through the town and head for the border, which should be easy, but make sure you have insurance for your vehicle in Malawi, as you will be stopped and asked for it. Hold on to your Mozambican vehicle insurance (hopefully it will still be valid), because you will need it when you re-enter Mozambique at Zobue to get to Tete. Then it's just over 50 kilometres to **Mangochi**, which you will enter across the bridge over the wide Shire River. Get onto the M3 heading south (you could nip up north to Cape Maclear on Lake Malawi first) and, after approximately 75 kilometres, you will reach the intersection where the M6 from Lilongwe joins up. Turn left, cross the Shire River again and you've reached Liwonde. Continue on the M3 through Zomba to reach **Blantyre**.

The shorter route via **Entre Lagos** and **Nayuchi** also starts at Cuamba's Madonna intersection, crosses the railway line, passes the market, under the railway line again and then turns immediately left at S14°48.256 E36°31.550. A decent 80-kph dirt road runs west for 86 kilometres to a bridge at **Vila de Insaca** – but don't cross the bridge or enter the town. Turn right just before the bridge (S15°11.029 E35°52.662) onto a rapidly deteriorating narrow track. This is a 40-kph road and probably impassable when wet. You will pass through many little villages until, 23 kilometres from the bridge, you cross the railway tracks again; turn left here, and arrive in Entre Lagos. If you're doing this route in reverse – in other words, coming from Entre Lagos and heading for Cuamba – then be sure to turn right across the railway line at S14°59.501 E35°53.716.

**Entre Lagos** is a dump and the sooner you get through it the better. Customs and immigration are at the station (you can't miss them) and are fast and efficient. If you are unfortunate enough to be stuck here, ask the customs officials to help (they have a spare house), or make your way to the **Pensão Destino**, which faces the tracks a little further on. Run-down, with dirty, shared toilets, there is no food or drink, but their beds don't look too bad and cost only 70 MT each. The New Rest House around the corner is much the same.

Having completed the formalities for leaving Mozambique, follow the railway line along a sandy track for 1.5 kilometres and pass through the barrier that forms the border with Malawi. Less than 1 kilometre further is the Nayuchi border post, also in their railway station. Again, the formalities are simple and pleasant, although I think it's unfair to charge $11 for the processing of the vehicle's temporary import permit. I must mention that this border crossing has one major problem if you are crossing from Mozambique with your own car – you cannot buy Malawian vehicle insurance here, so unless you have valid insurance, perhaps from an earlier visit, you will be in trouble when you are asked for it at a roadblock. A letter from the border officials might help, but with no letter or insurance, I had to use all my negotiating skills to avoid paying a fine on my way down to Blantyre.

**Nayuchi** has the same basic non-amenities as Entre Lagos, so head out as soon as you can (it's quite easy to travel between Cuamba and Blantyre in a day).

The area is dotted with lakes that form part of Malawi's Ramsar-declared wetlands, so the birdlife is good – as is the fishing, judging by the number of boats being built and used on the small lakes alongside the road. (Entre Lagos is so named as it lies between the lakes of Chiuta in the north and

Chilwa to the south). About 43 kilometres from the Nayuchi border post, you will reach a tarred road (S14°59.881 E35°29.473). Turn left towards Liwonde. This is where you might encounter a police roadblock. They will check for two triangles, the vehicle's temporary import permit and insurance, as well as your driver's licence. Another 32 kilometres brings you to Liwonde, where you need to turn south onto the M3 and head for Blantyre via Zomba (with possibly more roadblocks).

Another option from Cuamba is to take the road north to **Lichinga**, a day's drive on a reasonable road. This pretty little town has a variety of accommodation and eating options. The best is **Hotel Girassol**, website: www.girassol-hoteis.co.mz, on Av Filipe Samuel Magaia, which also has a restaurant and can advise on heading on to Manda Wilderness or the Niassa Reserve. Lichinga is the gateway for travellers making their way to or from Malawi via Likoma Island. Travel 185 kilometres north of Lichinga to **Cóbué**, a small market town with an historic cathedral in ruins, basic food and humble accommodation in the form of **Kango Beach Lodge**, tel: 88-856-7885, and **Mira Lago** for roughly 300 MT per person per night.

A more exclusive option is to stay at the nearby, award-winning **Nkwichi Lodge**, website: www.mandawilderness.org. They are the driving force behind the Manda Wilderness Project, and also offer silky white beaches and high-quality accommodation. Local lake transport is possible from Likoma Island on the famous old Malawian

## The Zomba Plateau

If you are not in a hurry to reach Blantyre, you might want to explore the Zomba Plateau. Situated high above Zomba town, it is one of Malawi's most popular walking and hiking areas – the indigenous forests and interesting birdlife are the main attractions. Turn off right in the town and go up past the golf club. There are guest lodges and two campsites: the forestry camp and another at the Kuchawe trout farm.

ferry, the *Illala*, or from Cóbué on a Mozambican vessel called *The Dangalila*, which travels a route heading north from Metangula, via Cóbué to the Tanzanian border on a Thursday and south back to Metangula on a Saturday. An alternative form of transport is to take local minibuses (*chappas*) leaving for Lichinga daily from both Cóbué and Metangula. Accommodation in Metangula is limited, with the cheaper, more basic option at Chuamba Beach or a higher level facility called **Mbuna Bay**, website: www.mbunabay.com.

In addition to the Manda Wilderness area, there is also the vast Niassa Reserve to the east, which is home to **Lugenda Wilderness Camp**, website: www.lugenda.com, which provides a luxurious base for exploring this stunning, untouched region.

## Blantyre

Approaching Blantyre, you will first encounter its large suburb, or sister city, **Limbe**. Keep right at the first major traffic intersection and make your way onto the Kamuzu Highway, through the Independence Arch and across the intersection with Makata Road. The sprawling Chichiri Mall on your left has a huge, well-stocked Shoprite supermarket as its main tenant and also boasts fashion shops, banks, a pharmacy, takeaways, a branch of Soche Tours, and a PostNet agency for phone, internet, copying and DHL.

Carry on down Kamuzu Highway through the industrial area (for motor spares and workshops, as well as gas refills) to the circle at the bottom – you will recognise it by the clock tower (S15°47.275 E35°00.817). Carry on straight into the city centre or turn right at the clock tower for the recommended accommodation.

Turn right into Chileke Road at the clock-tower circle and pass under the railway bridge. Take the first left turn, drive through the busy Wenela bus station, and you will end up in front of **Doogle's Backpacker Lodge** (S15°47.031 E35°00.898). A favourite stopover for travellers crossing Africa, the facilities include a swimming pool, TV lounge, good internet connection, reasonably priced meals and one of the most popular bars in Blantyre. Camping is $5 a person, dorm beds $7 and double rooms are $25 a night – all share the same bathrooms. For enquiries, tel: +265-(0)1-62-1128, e-mail: doogles@ africa-online.net.

The top hotel in Blantyre is the centrally situated **Mount Soche Hotel** on Glyn Jones Road. With a swimming pool, satellite TV, 24-hour room service, a business centre and two very good restaurants, its rooms range from standard at $190/220 single/ double to superior suites at $330 double. For details, tel: +265-(0)1-62-0588, fax: +265-(0)1-62-0154, e-mail: info@ sunbirdmalawi.com, website: www.sunbirdmalawi.com. **Ryalls Hotel**, down the road, is new, but a little cheaper. For information, tel: +265-(0)1-62-0955. Another recommended place to stay is **Kabula Lodge**, in the quiet suburb of the same name (follow the signs past Mount Soche Hotel). Family run and popular with volunteer workers on extended stays, it offers a range of accommodation from $10 for basic singles to $30 for self-contained doubles and use of the well-equipped kitchen. For information, tel: +265-(0)1-62-1216. For takeaways, visit Nando's (or maybe you've had enough piri-piri chicken) on the corner of Henderson Street and Haile Selassie Road, and for a good vibey pub try Cactus, down Slater Road.

There is a Mozambican Consulate on Kamuzu Highway, near to the Masalima post office. Transit visas (for passage through the Tete Corridor) are issued on the same day for $11, or overnight for $7. Proper tourist visas cost $20 and take three days to process. Any one of the many banks in town will change money for you, or better still, use one of the private forex bureaux in the city centre, close to the Mount Soche Hotel.

The new **Mwaiwathu Hospital** in Chileka Road just above the bus station (as well as Doogle's) offers a comprehensive medical service and is open all hours. Contact the hospital, tel: +265-(0)1-62-2999. Many travellers go on the free tour offered by **Carlsberg Brewery** (tel: +265-(0)1-67-0222) on Wednesdays at 14h30, more for the free beer swilling than an interest in the brewing process, I'm sure…

Malawi has a good bus network, and buses run in all directions from the bus station near Doogle's. Different levels of luxury and speed determine the price and departure times – ask at Doogle's or the bus station. Blantyre is also internationally very well connected by luxury coach to Zimbawe and South Africa. Fuel is freely available all over town (watch out for the ethanol blend, which has a very low octane rating).

## On to Tete

To get out of Blantyre and on your way to Tete, make your way up Glyn Jones Road from the clock-tower traffic circle and turn right at the next intersection (Oilcom service station is on your right). Travel for 8 kilometres to a traffic circle and go straight across. Another 50-odd kilometres of excellent tar brings you to the bridge across the Shire River, and on the other side is a right turn to Lilongwe. Carry on straight to **Mwanza** (another 46 kilometres of good road) and refuel before crossing the border back into Mozambique (fuel is cheaper in Malawi). The crossing should be trouble free and not too expensive if you still have valid Mozambican vehicle insurance. Immigration will cost you 40 MT per person and there is another 45 MT for your vehicle's temporary import permit.

**Moatize** is about 100 kilometres from the border and has most amenities, but

with Tete less than 20 kilometres down the road, it's not worth stopping here. Cross the Revubue River, pass the airport on the right and just past the mCel tower is the turn-off north to eastern Zambia. Carry on to the impressive 540-metre concrete suspension bridge across the Zambezi that carries you into Tete. Please note that this bridge is currently being repaired and only one lane is open, causing some delays.

**Tete**, like so many old towns of Mozambique, predates the arrival of the Portuguese. If you want to camp here, turn off left just before the bridge and drive downstream for less than a kilometre to **Jesus e Bom Campsite** (S16°09.318 E33°36.018). Laid out on the banks of the mighty Zambezi, with a great view of the bridge and town, this grassy spot offers the only camping in Tete. There is electricity, and flush toilets, but the showers are cold (there is no need for hot water in this temperate, often stuffy, climate). The charge is 100 MT a person, plus 150 MT a vehicle a night. Contact Riaan Terblanche, tel: 25-22-0195.

Be careful when rejoining the main road at the bridge. If you want to head away from Tete towards Malawi, drive under the bridge and right, to come up pointing away from the town. If you're going to cross the Zambezi into Tete, don't go under the bridge, but turn right just before it and swing up to face the town. The *transitos* on duty at the bridge love catching and fining motorists who take the wrong option, or cross the solid white line in the road. There is a 20-MT toll to cross the bridge. To carry on towards the Zimbabwean border

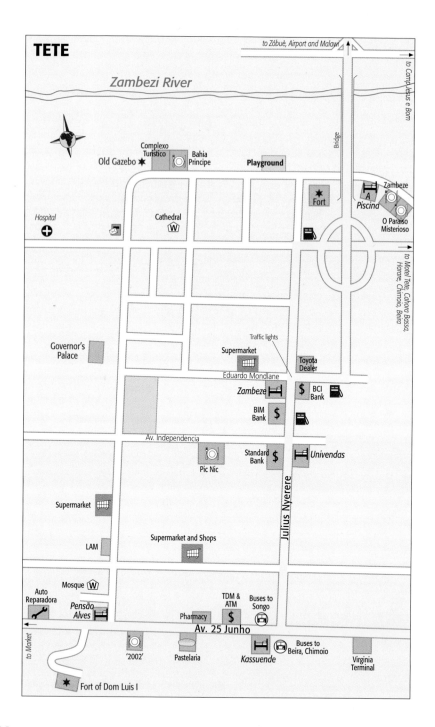

# TETE

Zambezi River

to Zóbuè, Airport and Malawi

to Complexos e Bom

Bridge

Old Gazebo ★

Complexo
Turístico

Bahia
Principe

Playground

Zambeze

Hospital

Cathedral
Ⓦ

Fort ★

A
Piscina

O Paraíso
Misterioso

to Motel Tete, Cahora Bassa,
Harare, Chimoio, Beira

Governor's
Palace

Traffic lights

Supermarket

Toyota
Dealer

Eduardo Mondlane

Zambeze

$ BCI
Bank

BIM
Bank $

Av. Independencia

Pic Nic

Standard
Bank $

Univendas

Supermarket

Julius Nyerere

Supermarket and Shops

LAM

Mosque Ⓦ

Auto
Reparadora

Pensão
Alves

Pharmacy

TDM &
ATM

Buses to
Songo

$

Av. 25 Junho

to Market

'2002'

Pastelaria

Kassuende

Buses to
Beira, Chimoio

Virginia
Terminal

Fort of Dom Luís I

The suspension bridge at Tete crosses the mighty Zambezi River.

without driving into the centre of Tete, take the first turn left across the bridge to get out of town. You will pass the **Motel Tete** (S16°09.889 E33°35.933) on the banks of the Zambezi as you leave. This motel has 20 rooms, a restaurant, safe parking and no noisy bar. A double en-suite room with TV, air-con and fridge costs 1800 MT a night. For info, tel: 25-22-3467 or 25-22-3498.

To enter the centre of Tete and explore, carry on straight over the bridge and turn right – but watch out for one-way streets. Make your way down Av Eduardo Mondlane to the traffic lights, passing the BP garage on your left. On the corners of this intersection with Av Julius Nyerere is a bank, the Hotel Zambeze and the main **Toyota** dealer, tel: 25-22-2847, fax: 25-22-2391, e-mail: toyota.tete@tele-data.mz. Turn left into Julius Nyerere

to pass more banks and, on the next corner (with Av Independencia), is the Univendas Store for hardware, tools and spares – upstairs, above the shop, are rooms to let. Down the side streets is an assortment of shops, but keep going till you run into the T-junction of Av 25 Junho. Turn right into this street, which is abuzz with buses, *chapas*, bars, restaurants and the Kassuende Hotel on your left. There's the TDM (for public telephones) and a pharmacy on your right and a bakery on your left. Further down, on the right-hand corner, is the Pensão Alves and, on your left, the road up to the Fort of Dom Luis. Further on is the covered market and an auto-repair works.

Now head down to the road along the banks of the Zambezi. Starting upstream, you will come across an iso-lated old gazebo perched in the middle of the mud – a favourite spot for the Portuguese colonials to enjoy their sundowners. Lower down, you pass the Complexo Turistico Bahia Principe, then a children's playground and another fort. This riverside drive passes under the bridge to the A Piscina and Zambeze O Paraiso Misterioso bar/restaurants.

## Overnight in Tete

The best accommodation in town is the **Hotel Zambeze** on the corner of Av Eduardo Mondlane and Julius Nyerere. It's newly renovated and very central, and at five storeys (fortunately the lift works), there are great views, especially from the excellent rooftop restaurant. The rooms are all en-suite and range in price from 2 200 MT double to 2 700 MT with air-con, TV and fridge (breakfast included in all). For information, tel: 25-22-3100. The next best place to stay is **Predio Univendas**, a neat, low-key collection of rooms and apartments above the Univendas Store on Av Julius Nyerere. All rooms have air-con and are large and airy, with very good security – there is a private yard for your car. Rates are 1 000/1 200 MT single/double with shared facilities, 1 400/1 600 MT with en-suite facilities, while the larger two-roomed suites cost 1 500/1 800 MT. For details, tel: 25-22-3198.

The **A Piscina**, tel: 25-22-3084, offers accommodation in a pleasant garden setting below the bridge on the banks of the Zambezi. A little dilapidated and almost always full, plain double rooms using shared ablutions cost 900 MT a night, en-suite single/double 700/900 MT. But most people rather visit A Piscina for the popular bar and restaurant. Moving down the accommodation scale, there is the **Pensão Alves**, tel: 25-22-2523, at the end of Av 25 Junho. It's a bit of a dump with a noisy but reasonably priced bar and restaurant. Plain single rooms cost 700 MT and doubles 850 MT, but the nightly disco will probably keep you awake. Back along Av 25 Junho, around where the buses rev and hoot, is the **Hotel Kassuende**, cheap at 600 MT single and 700 MT double, en-suite air-conned doubles cost 800 MT. For bookings and info, tel: 25-22-2531. All intercity buses congregate in this area on Av 25 Junho and you will find transport to Beira, Malawi and Zimbabwe.

## Eating out in Tete

Other than the bars and restaurants attached to hotels already mentioned, there are two comfortable eateries on the banks of the river, where it is pleasant to sit and sip and sup while the mighty Zambezi drifts by. The **Complexo Turistico Bahia Principe** is upstream near the gazebo and the **Zambeze O Paraiso Misterioso** is just below the bridge.

A good place in town for light meals and refreshments is the **Pic Nic Bar and Restaurant** on Av Independencia. Their prego rolls are 50 MT and hamburgers 75 MT, and can be enjoyed indoors or out on the patio.

The best place to eat, however, is the **Why Not Bar**, near the GPZ Building. It's a little hard to find, but persevere and you will find yourself in a welcoming bar and esplanade restaurant that serves

The Fort of Dom Luis I, which overlooks Tete, used to house slaves but is now derelict.

excellent local and regional cuisine. The Portuguese-style bakery just below the bridge, opposite the Petromoc fuel station, is also definitely worth a visit.

## In and around Tete

You should also check out the two forts in town. A really far-flung outpost during the early colonial days, Tete relied on the defences of the fort that stands on the water's edge. The other one, the **Fort of Dom Luis I**, was where they housed the slaves that were in transit down to the coast. Situated up the hill from Pensão Alves in Av 25 Junho, you will have to tread carefully when exploring, as it is now used as the neighbourhood toilet.

## Cahora Bassa

An interesting excursion from Tete is a visit to the **Cahora Bassa** dam. Taking your distance from the bridge in town,

drive out past Motel Tete on good tar for 20 kilometres until you reach the turn-off right at S16°18.399 E33°31.054 (signposted to Songo). The road north to Cahora Bassa is also good tar, and 136 kilometres from Tete, you will pass the left turn (S15°38.898 E32°47.708) to Ugezi Tiger Lodge, the best accommodation in the area. Songo town is just 5.5 kilometres straight ahead, up a winding road through the hills.

Songo is a typical company town and exists mainly for the construction and electricity companies – everything and everyone belongs to them. Pretty and well laid out, it has good schools and a hospital. The main intersection in town is at S15°36.727 E32°46.352, where you turn left to enter the small town centre. Here you will find a decent supermarket, banks, service station, pharmacy, TDM and post office.

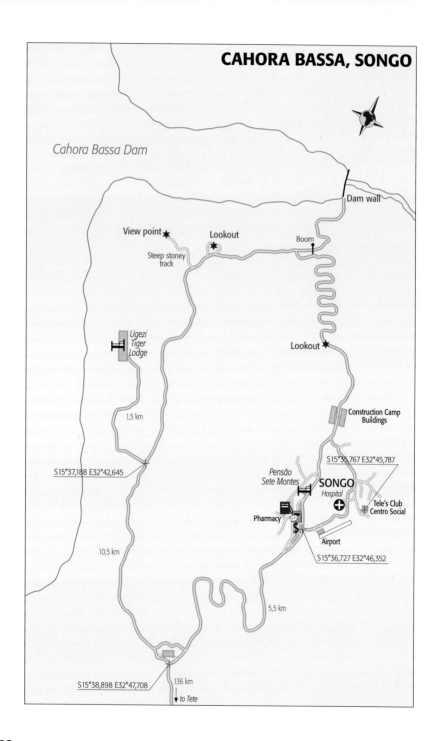

# CAHORA BASSA, SONGO

Cahora Bassa Dam

Dam wall

View point ★   Lookout

Boom

Steep stoney track

Ugezi Tiger Lodge

Lookout ★

Construction Camp Buildings

1,5 km

S15°35,767 E32°45,787

S15°37,188 E32°42,645

Pensão Sete Montes   SONGO

Hospital

Tele's Club Centro Social

Pharmacy

Airport

10,5 km

S15°36,727 E32°46,352

5,5 km

S15°38,898 E32°47,708   136 km

▼ to Tete

A drive across a bougainvillea-covered traffic circle will bring you to the unmarked **Pensão Sete Montes**, a neat, tidy and quiet place with secure parking, but no bar or restaurant. They have 16 en-suite double rooms with fridges for 800 MT a night and one larger suite with TV and air-con for 1 100 MT. For information, tel: 82-865-0070, fax: 25-28-2341.

If you turn right at the town's main intersection, you'll pass the airport and hospital, and heading up right you will find the **Club Centro Social** (S15°35.767 E32°45.787). Still beautifully maintained among lush gardens, this was once the hub of the construction company's social life. Now privatised and known as Tele's Club, it offers a well-stocked bar, elegant restaurant, large swimming pool and comfortable accommodation. Single rooms cost 850 MT a night and double suites 1 400 MT – all have air-con, and some have TV. Contact the club, tel: 25-28-2497.

Continuing out of town, you pass through the old construction camp and suddenly the dam wall is below you. The road winds down a switch-back series of hairpin bends with many opportunities and spots to stop and enjoy the view of the narrow gorge. At the bottom is a boom that blocks your way to the wall, so turn left here and continue along this tarred road around to even more excellent lookout points. The best is up a steep, stony 4×4 track to a hilltop that rewards you with a great view of the expanse of the lake. Carry on around the lake shore until, at S15°37.188 E32°42.645, you come to the turn-off to **Ugezi Tiger Lodge**. It's

a short, rough dirt road down past the *kapenta* fish-drying plants to the lodge. Nestled in the hills and bays above the dam, the stone and thatch buildings blend in perfectly. Grassed, shaded and with stunning views, the campsites and chalets are most welcoming and the small swimming pool (there are too many hippos and crocs in the dam) offers relief from the heat. This is a fisherman's paradise, and the bar and restaurant are decorated with mounted and stuffed, record-breaking fish and trophies. Groups fly in, rent boats and tackle, and go back home with broad smiles on their faces.

Camping in your own tent costs 300 MT a person and attractive double en-suite stone chalets are 1 100 MT per person. Set-menu suppers are a reasonable 320 MT. For further information, contact Emelio or Annetjie in Mozambique, tel: 25-28-2049 or 82-599-8410, or in South Africa, +27-(0)82-539-6411, e-mail: info@ugezitigerlodge.com, website: www.ugezitigerlodge.com.

From Cahora Bassa, head back to the Tete road and turn right (south). From this intersection, it is 71 kilometres to the unsignposted traffic circle at Luenha (S16°50.182 E33°16.464). Turn right and it's another 48 kilometres to the Zimbabwean border at Nyamapanda and then another 235 kilometres to Harare. Carry on straight at the circle for 258 kilometres of reasonable (but narrow) tar, through Guro and Catandica, to connect with the EN6 highway. Once you reach the EN6, you can, of course, head west into Zimbabwe, east down to Beira or south on the EN1 to Maputo.

# 24

# Portuguese words and phrases

Fancy phrase books list dozens of rules and even more exceptions, but you'll be just fine if you remember that 's' is usually pronounced *sh*, 'c' is pronounced *s*, and 'm' as *n*. To get a feel for the language, listen to people speaking around you – and then give it a try. Don't be afraid to make mistakes, Mozambicans are very understanding.

While Mozambique's national language is Portuguese, in areas frequented by tourists, many residents are well able to speak English.

## Counting

1 *um/uma* (one beer = *uma cerveja*)
2 *dois/duas*
3 *tres*
4 *quatro*
5 *cinco*
6 *seis*
7 *sete*
8 *oito*
9 *nove*
10 *dez*
11 *onze*
12 *doze*
13 *treze*
14 *catorze*
15 *quinze*
16 *dezasseis*
17 *dezassete*
18 *dezoito*
19 *dezanove*
20 *vinte*
21 *vinte e um*
30 *trinta*
40 *quarenta*
50 *cinquenta*
60 *sessenta*
70 *setenta*
80 *oitenta*
90 *noventa*
100 *cem*
500 *quinhentos*
1 000 *mil*
2 000 *dois mil*
10 000 *dez mil*

## Greetings and pleasantries

Hello *Ola*
Goodbye *Ciao*
Friend *Amigo*
Good morning *Bom dia*
Good afternoon *Boa tarde*
Good evening/night *Boa noite*

How are you? *Como esta?*
I am well *Estou bem*
Yes *Sim*
No *Nao*
Please *Por favor*
Thank you *Obrigado*
You're welcome *De nada*
Sorry *Desculpe*
I am a poor traveller *Eu sou viajante*
   *pobre*
My name is… *Me chamou…*
I don't speak Portuguese *Nao falo*
   *Portugues*
I don't know *Nao sei*
I don't understand *Nao compreendo*
No problem! *Nao faz mal!*
Okay *Tudo bem*

## Questions

What is your name? *Como se chama?*
How much (cost)? *Quanto custa?*
What? *Que?*
When? *Quando?*
When does that bus leave? *Quando sai*
   *esta machimbombo?*
Right now? *Agora mesmo?*
Where? *Onde?*
Here? *Aqui?*
There? *Ali, la?*
How far? *Quantos kilometros?*
Have you got…? *Tem…?*
Where from? *Donde?*
Where is…? *Onde fica esta…?*
Who? *Quem?*
Do you know? *Voce sabe?*
May I (take a photo)? *Da licenca…?*

## Time

Yesterday *Ontem*
Today *Hoje*
Tomorrow *Amanha*
Day *Dia*

Morning *Manha*
Night *Noite*
Now *Agora*
Before *Antes*
After *Depois*
Never *Nunca*
Sunday *Domingo*
Monday *Segunda-feira*
Tuesday *Terca-feira*
Wednesday *Quarta-feira*
Thursday *Quinta-feira*
Friday *Sexta-feira*
Saturday *Sabado*

## Descriptions
Good *Bom/Boa* (m/f)
Large *Grande*
Small *Pequeno/a* (m/f)
A lot *Muito/a* (m/f)
A little *Pouco/a* (m/f)
Nothing *Nada*
Enough *Bastante*
That's enough! *Basta!*

## Eating and drinking
Restaurant *Restaurante*
Roadside *Restaurante quiosque*
To eat *Comer*
Menu printed/hand-written *Cardapio/ementa*
Set menu *Menu*
Breakfast *Matabicho*
Lunch *Almoco*
Dinner *Jantar*
Meat *Carne*
Beef *Carne de vaca*
Steak *Filete de bife*
Well done/medium/rare *Bem passado/medio/mal passado*
Kebab *Espetada*
Steak roll *Prego no pao*
Pork *Carne de porco*

Eggs *Ovos*
Chicken *Frango*
Peri-peri fried chicken *Galinha frita com piri-piri*
Fish *Peixe*
Crab *Caranguejo*
Crayfish *Lagostim*
Lobster *Lagosta*
Prawns *Camarao*
Calamari *Lulas*
Fresh *Fresco*
Fruit *Fruta*
Rice *Arroz*
Pasta *Massa*
Chips *Batatas fritas*
Maize porridge *Nsima*
Vegetables *Legumes*
Bread *Pao*
Coffee *Café*
Tea *Cha*
Milk *Leita*
Water *Agua*
Mineral water *Agua mineral*
Beer *Cerveja*
Spirits *Aguardente*
The bill *Conta*
Cheap *Barato*
Fair price *Bom preco*
Too expensive *Muito caro*

## In town...
City/town *Cidade*
Road *Estrada*
Left *A esquerda*
Right *A direita*
House *Casa*
Shop *Loja*
Supermarket *Supermercado*
Market *Mercado*
For sale *Vende-se*
Bank *Banco*
Money *Dinheiro*

Change *Cambio*
Traveller's cheques *Cheques de viagem*
Black market *Candonga*
Hotel *Hotel*
Small hotel *Pensão*
Room *Quarto*
Single/twin *Simples/duplo*
Double (room for married couple) *Casal*
Bed *Cama*
Bathroom/toilet *Casa de banho*
Ladies *Senhoras*
Gents *Senhores*
Shower *Chuveiro*
Wash *Lavar*
Nightclub *Boite/discoteca*
Doctor *Medico*
Bus *Machimbombo*
Truck *Camiao*
Train *Comboio*
Ticket *Bilhete*

## And for the desperate...

I feel sick *Estao enjoado*
Take me to the hospital *Levar-me para a hospital*
My car has broken down *Meu carro esta quebrado*
I need a mechanic *Preciso de um mecanico*

*Adeus, boa viagem!*

# Index